# Excel Data Analysis

*Your visual blueprint™ for creating and analyzing data, charts, and PivotTables*

## 2nd Edition

*by Jinjer Simon*

WILEY

Wiley Publishing, Inc.

**Excel Data Analysis: Your visual blueprint™ for creating and analyzing data, charts, and PivotTables**

Published by
**Wiley Publishing, Inc.**
111 River Street
Hoboken, NJ 07030-5774

Published simultaneously in Canada

*Library of Congress Control Number:* 2005924603

ISBN-13: 978-0-7645-9780-0

ISBN-10: 0-7645-9780-9

Manufactured in the United States of America

10 9 8 7 6 5 4 3 2

2K/RR/QV/QV/IN

## Trademark Acknowledgments

## Contact Us

For general information on our other products and services please contact our Customer Care Department within the U.S. at 800-762-2974, outside the U.S. at 317-572-3993 or fax 317-572-4002.

For technical support please visit www.wiley.com/techsupport.

## Permissions

**Microsoft**

Microsoft Excel screen shots reprinted with permission from Microsoft Corporation.

### Dublin Castle

The easily defensible site of Dublin Castle made it the perfect location for a tenth-century Viking fortress. Between 1208 and 1220, King John built a heavily fortified castle there, and for the next three hundred years it housed royalty, prisoners, colonial governments, and state functions. In 1684, fire destroyed much of the medieval structure. The subsequent rebuilding created a lavish location for society functions until the late 1800s, starkly contrasting with the poverty, starvation, and rebellion raging outside its gates. With a single tower still standing from the thirteenth century, Dublin Castle stands a silent witness to eight centuries of Irish history.

Learn more about Ireland's historic sites in *Frommer's Ireland,* available wherever books are sold or online at www.frommers.com.

WILEY

# PRAISE FOR VISUAL BOOKS...

"This is absolutely the best computer-related book I have ever bought. Thank you so much for this fantastic text. Simply the best computer book series I have ever seen. I will look for, recommend, and purchase more of the same."

—David E. Prince (NeoNome.com)

"I have several of your Visual books and they are the best I have ever used."

—Stanley Clark (Crawfordville, FL)

"I just want to let you know that I really enjoy all your books. I'm a strong visual learner. You really know how to get people addicted to learning! I'm a very satisfied Visual customer. Keep up the excellent work!"

—Helen Lee (Calgary, Alberta, Canada)

"I have several books from the Visual series and have always found them to be valuable resources."

—Stephen P. Miller (Ballston Spa, NY)

"This book is PERFECT for me - it's highly visual and gets right to the point. What I like most about it is that each page presents a new task that you can try verbatim or, alternatively, take the ideas and build your own examples. Also, this book isn't bogged down with trying to 'tell all' – it gets right to the point. This is an EXCELLENT, EXCELLENT, EXCELLENT book and I look forward purchasing other books in the series."

—Tom Dierickx (Malta, IL)

"I have quite a few of your Visual books and have been very pleased with all of them. I love the way the lessons are presented!"

—Mary Jane Newman (Yorba Linda, CA)

"I am an avid fan of your Visual books. If I need to learn anything, I just buy one of your books and learn the topic in no time. Wonders! I have even trained my friends to give me Visual books as gifts."

—Illona Bergstrom (Aventura, FL)

"I just had to let you and your company know how great I think your books are. I just purchased my third Visual book (my first two are dog-eared now!) and, once again, your product has surpassed my expectations. The expertise, thought, and effort that go into each book are obvious, and I sincerely appreciate your efforts."

—Tracey Moore (Memphis, TN)

"Compliments to the chef!! Your books are extraordinary! Or, simply put, extra-ordinary, meaning way above the rest! THANK YOU THANK YOU THANK YOU! I buy them for friends, family, and colleagues."

—Christine J. Manfrin (Castle Rock, CO)

"I write to extend my thanks and appreciation for your books. They are clear, easy to follow, and straight to the point. Keep up the good work! I bought several of your books and they are just right! No regrets! I will always buy your books because they are the best."

—Seward Kollie (Dakar, Senegal)

"I am an avid purchaser and reader of the Visual series, and they are the greatest computer books I've seen. Thank you very much for the hard work, effort, and dedication that you put into this series."

—Alex Diaz (Las Vegas, NV)

## Credits

**Project Editor**
Maureen Spears

**Acquisitions Editor**
Jody Lefevere

**Product Development Manager**
Lindsay Sandman

**Copy Editor**
Jill Mazurczyk

**Technical Editors**
Kerwin McKenzie
Barbara A. Prillaman
Allen Wyatt

**Editorial Manager**
Robyn Siesky

**Permissions Editor**
Laura Moss

**Media Development Specialist**
Laura Moss

**Manufacturing**
Allan Conley
Linda Cook
Paul Gilchrist
Jennifer Guynn

**Screen Artists**
Elizabeth Cardenas-Nelson
Jill A. Proll

**Book Design**
Kathryn S. Rickard

**Production Coordinator**
Maridee Ennis

**Layout**
Sean Decker
Jennifer Heleine
Amanda Spagnuolo

**Cover Illustration**
Shelley Norris

**Proofreader**
Vicki Broyles

**Quality Control**
Brian H. Walls

**Indexer**
TECHBOOKS Production Services

**Special Help**
Cara Buitron

**Vice President and Executive
Group Publisher**
Richard Swadley

**Vice President and Publisher**
Barry Pruett

**Composition Director**
Debbie Stailey

## About the Author

**Jinjer Simon** has been actively involved in the computer industry for the past 18 years. Her involvement includes programming, providing software technical support, training end-users, developing written and online user documentation, creating software tutorials, and developing Web sites. She is the author of several computer books, including *Excel Programming: Your visual blueprint for creating interactive spreadsheets*, and *Windows CE 2 For Dummies*.

## Author's Acknowledgments

As an author, it is my responsibility to recognize each of the individuals that contributed to the completion of this book. Although my responsibility is to produce the content for the book, many others are responsible for getting the book pulled together.

I would like to recognize the efforts of everyone at Wiley Publishing for all the hard work on this project.

I would also like to thank my technical editors, Allen Wyatt and Kerwin McKenzie. They provided some great input on the content of this book. With her statistical knowledge, Barbara Prillaman also helped with Chapter 11.

I want to thank my agent, Neil Salkind at Studio B, for working out the kinks in the project. Finally, I want to thank my husband, Richard, and children, Alex and Ashley, for their patience while I completed this project.

# TABLE OF CONTENTS

# TABLE OF CONTENTS

## How to Use This Visual Blueprint Book

*Excel Data Analysis: Your visual blueprint for creating and analyzing data, charts, and PivotTables* uses clear, descriptive examples to show you how to do something with Excel. If you are already familiar with analyzing data using Excel, you can use this book as a quick reference for many data analysis tasks.

## Who Needs This Book

This book is for the experienced computer user who wants to find out more about Excel data analysis. It is also for more experienced users who want to expand their knowledge of the different features that Excel has to offer.

## Book Organization

*Excel Data Analysis: Your visual blueprint for creating and analyzing data, charts, and PivotTables* has 11 chapters and five appendixes.

The first chapter, "Getting Started with Excel," introduces you to various data analysis options. You learn how to select a range of cells, how to use named ranges, label ranges, and styles, as well as how to create a custom template.

Chapter 2, "Organize Worksheet Data," shows you how to create Excel lists. In this chapter, you learn how to create, add, sort, customize and consolidate your data.

Chapter 3, "Evaluate Worksheet Data," helps you learn how to apply conditional formatting and filters. It also includes tasks on validating data and creating scenarios.

The fourth chapter, "Creating Formulas," builds simple and complex formulas with the insert funtion dialog box. It also shows you how to use the Solver, and create a conditional formula.

In Chapter 5, you learn all about external data, including how to properly copy and import it, as well as how to work with database queries and the DAVERAGE feature.

Chapters 6 to 8 show you how to optimize the presentation of you data with charts, PivotTables, and PivotCharts.

In Chapter 9, you learn how to use VBA to create macros.

In Chapter 10, you find out all about forms and form controls, and in Chapter 11, you learn all of the many useful Add-ins that Excel provides.

The five appendixes include Keyboard Shortcuts, an Excel Function reference, a VBA Quick Reference, and a section on formulas for those not familiar with Excel.

## What You Need to Use This Book

To perform the tasks in this book, you need a computer with Microsoft Windows 98, ME, NT 4.0, 1000, or XP installed, as well as Microsoft Excel 2000 or 2002. You do not require any special development tools, because all the tools are part of Excel.

## The Conventions in This Book

A number of styles have been used throughout *Excel Data Analysis: Your visual blueprint for creating and analyzing data, charts, and PivotTables* to designate different types of information.

### Courier Font

Indicates the use of Visual Basic for Applications (VBA) code such as tags or attributes, scripting language code such as statements, operators, or functions, and code such as objects, methods, or properties.

### Bold

Indicates information that you must type.

### Italics

Indicates a new term.

## Apply It

An Apply It section takes the code from the preceding task one step further. Apply It sections allow you to take full advantage of the code.

## Extra

An Extra section provides additional information about the preceding task. Extra sections contain the inside information to make working with Excel and VBA code easier and more efficient.

### What's on the CD-ROM

The CD-ROM included in this book contains the sample files for the book as well as trial versions of software that you can use to work with *Excel Data Analysis: Your visual blueprint for creating and analyzing data, charts, and PivotTables*. An e-version of the book is also available on the disc.

# Excel Data Analysis Options

**E**xcel's functionality falls into three different categories: entering data, analyzing data, and displaying the results. Understanding and accurately performing these functions help the analyst organize data, recognize trends, and generally gain insight into whatever situation started the data gathering process. Although the main focus of this book is on the tools Excel provides for data analysis, it also explores the available methods for entering data and displaying the analyzed results.

When you group related data values in your worksheet, you can use Excel's built-in tools to perform simple functions such as summing or averaging related numeric values, or to create charts to visually display data. Excel also lets you create formulas to automatically calculate results after a user inputs data into your worksheet, and create custom macros, which perform repetitive tasks for you. You can use PivotTables to cross-tabulate data that you have stored in lists, and a PivotChart to graphically display a PivotTable. Exel has advanced analysis tools to perform more sophisticated data analysis.

## Data Entry

The foundation of data analysis is data entry accuracy, which directly impacts your results, and ultimately, your interpretation of those results. Although manually typing data in a worksheet to create a data list is the simplest method, you may find it the most cumbersome when you must analyze a large amount of

data. Fortunately, you can gather data from other sources, such as already created external databases, and import the data it directly into your worksheet. You can also create data forms to simplify the process of inputting data into specific columns.

### Data Lists

In its simplest form, a *data list* is merely a group of common values, such as items you want to purchase from the grocery store. When you place this type of information in Excel, you typically group related data values. For example, you place grocery items in one column and the quantity of each item to purchase in the next column. See Chapter 2 for more information on working with data lists.

### Data from External Sources

Excel interfaces with many different Microsoft Office programs, making it possible to acquire data from external sources. One simple way to do this is to copy and paste data; you can also import text files directly into Excel. Typically, organizations store large quantities of data in database files. You can perform a database query to access an external database and import the desired data values. See Chapter 5 for more information on working with external data sources.

### Data Forms

If you need to manually input data into Excel, you can simplify the process by creating a *data form*, which consists of a worksheet or a dialog box with fields into which a user can input data. With a data form, you can request the specific data

values. You can also use VBA to verify that you have appropriate data before entering it in the worksheet column. See Chapter 10 for more information about the creation of data forms and use of form controls.

## Data Analysis

When you analyze data, you perform a function to compare different values. Data analysis occurs when you do something as simple as totaling the numeric values in a column or sorting a list alphabetically. You can perform more complex comparisons by creating formulas or by writing macros with the VBA editor. Excel also provides a set of analysis tools that perform complex analysis, such as calculating descriptive statistics.

### Formula Creation

You can use *formulas* to create a custom calculation that analyzes data values in a cell or series of cells. You create formulas using any combination of cell references, mathematical operators, and the built-in functions available in Excel. See Chapter 4 for more information about creating formulas, and Appendix D for formula basics in Excel.

You can also create custom functions that you can call from any workbook using the VBA editor. See Chapter 9 for information on creating custom VBA functions.

### Macro Creation

Because they combine a series of calculations that you want to perform into one step, *macros* help you save time by automating any tasks that you perform in Excel. You can create a macro by recording a series of keystrokes or by manually coding the macro using the VBA editor in Excel. See Chapter 9 for more information on creating custom macros.

### PivotTables

You use PivotTables to perform a *cross-tabulation* of data, which is summarizing data into one or more classifications. *PivotTables* analyze data from both an Excel worksheet and an external database all within the same table. Everything in a PivotTable is *dynamic*, meaning that each time you change a value, any corresponding cells update immediately. See Chapter 7 for more information on working with PivotTables.

### Analysis Tools

Excel provides several other analysis tools that you can use with your data values, including conditional formatting, which formats data based on specific criteria, filtering, and even data validation. See Chapter 3 for built-in Excel data analysis tools.

Excel's Add-in data analysis tools provide more complex analysis of your data values. You can use these tools to find moving averages, run an ANOVA analysis on your data, or determine rank and percentile values. See Chapter 11 for more information about Add-ins.

## Result Presentation

While Excel's analysis tools can provide detailed numeric summaries of your data values, you can also use them to create graphical representations of your data. After you analyze your data, you have different options for displaying your results.

### Chart Creation

In Excel, you can create *charts*, which provide a visual representation of your data values. You can embed a chart directly into a worksheet or create a separate chart sheet. Excel provides fourteen different chart types, each of which has at least two different subtypes or variations. After you determine the desired chart type, you can customize it further by changing such options as text fonts and font colors. See Chapter 6 for more information on creating and customizing charts.

### PivotCharts

*PivotCharts* combine all of the same functionality of standard Excel charts with the dynamic characteristics of PivotTables. The result is a graphic representation of a PivotTable that updates whenever you change your data. See Chapter 8 for more information on working with PivotCharts.

# Excel Data Types

In Excel, a *data type* refers to the type of value stored in a cell. When you input data, Excel automatically parses it and determines its data type. Excel recognizes three different data types: text, numeric, and formula.

The default data type that Excel assigns to a cell determines the type of data analysis you can apply to it. For example, most data analysis tools require numeric values; if you try to use a text value, the tools return error messages.

## Text

*Text data types* contain letters for use as text or labels within a worksheet. You typically place *labels* in a worksheet to identify columns and rows that contain numeric values. However, not all values that contain a letter are text. For example, although 1.45E+05 contains a letter, Excel recognizes it as a number expressed in scientific notation.

You can use any combination of letters and numbers in a cell as long as the total number of characters in the cell does not exceed 32,000 characters. By default, when Excel determines that a cell contains text, it left-justifies the entire contents of the cell.

You cannot perform any mathematical operations on a number as long as the cell also contains text. For this reason, you may want to consider separating text and numeric values into two separate cells. If you want Excel to treat a numeric value, such as Zip Code or Social Security Number, as text, you place an apostrophe (') before the numeric value in the cell.

## Numeric

A *numeric value* is any number, percentage, currency, time, or date value. By default, Excel formats all numeric values by right-justifying them in the cell. Because Excel has a specific method for storing date and time values, they are considered numeric values. You can customize the look of numeric values using the Number tab on the Format Cells dialog box.

### Number

Excel allows nearly any number you can possibly type in a cell within the range 2.250748585072E-308 to 1.797693486231E308. You can input numbers in a wide variety of formats or use the six different built-in number formats to customize how a number displays in a cell.

### NUMERIC CHARACTERS

You can use any of the following characters to express a numeric value: 0 1 2 3 4 5 6 7 8 9 + , - ( ) / $ % . E e. The placement of the characters within the number is important. For example, the letters E and e allow you to express large numbers, such as 1,256,000.000,000 in a format that is easier to display, 1.256E+07, called scientific notation. If you use an E in any other location, such as preceding a number E54, Excel treats the cell contents as text.

### FRACTIONS

If you type a fraction in a cell without preceding it with a number, Excel automatically converts it to a date. To avoid this conversion, place an apostrophe (') or zero (0) in front of it. No matter what number precedes a fraction, you must leave a space between the number and the fraction.

### NUMBER PRECISION

Excel only guarantees precision up to 15 digits and converts any digits beyond 15 to zeros without rounding values up to the nearest place. For example, Excel converts both 35,555,545,365,875,988 and 35,555,545,365,875,922 to 35,555,545,875,900. Obviously this limitation makes storing large numbers, such as a 16-digit credit card number, in their entirety difficult. To avoid truncating credit card numbers, you can format cells as text or create a special number format. See the section "Create a Custom Number Format" for more information.

## Numeric *(continued)*

### Dates and Time

Excel uses the *Western*, formally called *Gregorian*, calendar as a basis for all dates and times, and stores them as a combined number. Dates are all sequential, whole numbers from 1 to 2958465. Excel stores times, which are all portions of the dates, as decimal values. For example, if you type the value **12/05/02 4:00 PM** in a cell, Excel stores it as the numeric value 37595.66667, where 37595 represents the date portion, and .66667 represents the time.

You can apply any mathematical calculations to compare and manipulate dates and time. For example, you can add, subtract, or determine the elapsed time between two dates and times. The cell's formatting determines how the date or time value displays.

#### DATES

Although a date displays in a cell on your worksheet, Excel actually stores its numeric equivalent. Using the Western calendar, Excel determines the number of days in each month. For example, January always has 31 days, and February has 28 days with the exception of leap year.

Excel for Windows bases all dates on what is commonly referred to as the 1900 date system, which recognizes 1/1/1900 as the first date with a stored value of 1. The last date that Excel recognizes is December 31, 9999 or 12/31/9999, which it stores as 2958465. If you use Excel on a Macintosh computer, dates are based on a 1904 date system, which means 1/1/1904 has a value of 1 and 12/31/9999 has a value of 2957003.

Although the two operating systems use different date systems, you can convert them when moving worksheets between a Windows and a Macintosh computer. If you open a Macintosh-created Excel (version 2.0 or later) worksheet in Windows, the dates automatically convert to the 1900 date format. Likewise, opening a Windows-created worksheet on a Macintosh converts dates to the 1904 system. You can also manually force the date conversion in Excel for Windows by selecting the 1904 date system option on the Calculation tab of the Options dialog box.

If you decide to use two-digit dates in Excel, you must exercise caution when entering them. Excel interprets two-digit years between 00 and 29 as the years 2000 though 2029. Excel interprets two-digit years between 30 and 99 as 1930 to 1999. To avoid errors, consider always using a four-digit year.

#### TIME

Excel stores all time values as decimal values between 0 and 0.99999999, with 12:00 midnight being 0, and 11:59:59 PM being 0.99999999. So a time that displays as 12:00 P.M. (noon) has a value of 0.5.

By default, Excel bases all times on a 24-hour clock, commonly known as military time. This means that if you enter 10:30 without an A.M. or P.M., Excel assumes you mean 10:30 A.M. If you want 10:30 P.M., enter P.M. after the time, or use the corresponding 24-hour clock value of 22:30.

## Formula

You can create formulas within any cell of a worksheet to evaluate data values in other cells within your worksheet. For example, the following formula adds the numeric values in cells A1 through A10 and displays the total in the cell containing the formula.

```
=SUM($A$1:$A$10)
```

You must always precede formulas with an equal sign, which signals that what follows is a formula that Excel needs to evaluate. You can use any of the built-in functions, mathematical operators, constant values, and cell references to create a formula. Although you can use any combination of elements in a formula, the total number of characters in the formula cannot exceed 1,024 characters.

Excel formats a cell based upon the resulting *value* of the formula. For example, most formulas return a numeric value; therefore, by default, Excel right-justifies the returned value of numeric formula cells like other numeric cells. See Chapter 4 for more information about creating formulas in your worksheets. For more on formula basics, see Appendix D.

# Locate a Value in a Worksheet

To locate values that match specific criteria without manually scrolling through a large list of data values, you can use Excel's Find option. A data analyst can quickly use this feature to find any number or word, such as a region's sales forecast for the year or a salesman's name. You simply enter what you want to search for in the Find what field in the Find and Replace dialog box.

If you do not know the exact value you want to locate, you can use one of two wildcard characters as part of the search. You use either an asterisk (*) or a question mark (?) to denote a missing character from a value. The question mark represents one value. For example, if you enter a search value of 1?4, Excel finds the values 104, 114, and any other three digit number that matches the pattern. An asterisk represents any number of missing characters. For example, 1*4 finds not only the value 114, but also 1234, and 199854.

When you search, Excel finds the first match for the specified pattern after the active cell. If the located cell is not correct, you can repeat the search to find the next cell.

## Locate a Value in a Worksheet

**1** Click Edit⇨Find.

Excel displays the Find and Replace dialog box.

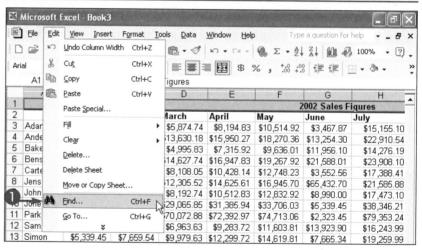

**2** Type the value you want to locate in the Find what field.

Use * to replace a series of characters or ? to replace a single character.

**3** Click Find Next.

- Excel locates the cell containing a matching value.

Repeat step 3 to continue searching.

When you find the correct value, click Close to close the dialog box.

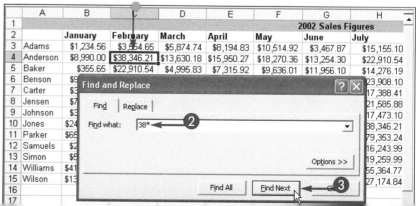

# Select a Range of Cells

**Y**ou can make modifications to several cells in a worksheet simultaneously, a process referred to as *selecting a range of cells*, by choosing all the related cells together before implementing the changes. Typically, you select a range of cells to apply different formatting options, to copy cells, or to change the Excel value type. The range of cells does not need to be contiguous; you can select cells from different locations in a worksheet. See the section "Copy and Paste a Range of Cells" for information on copying a range of cells. See the section "Create a Custom Number Format" for more information on formatting cells.

You can select anywhere from a single cell to the entire worksheet. Excel highlights the group of cells to remind you of your selection. If you select multiple ranges of cells simultaneously, Excel highlights each selected range.

## Extra

To select an entire row or column, you simply click the corresponding identifier. For example, to select all cells in column C, you click the C identifier for the column. To select multiple columns, you click the first column and then continue holding down the mouse button as you drag to the other columns you want to select. To select entire rows, you click the row identifiers on the left side of each row.

You can select a smaller group of cells by clicking a cell in one corner of the desired selection range, holding down the mouse button, and dragging until you select the desired range.

To select a noncontiguous range of cells, select the first block of cells, and then press the Ctrl key and select the next block. If you do not hold down the Ctrl key, Excel unselects the first range of cells when you select a new range of cells.

## Select a Range of Cells

**1** Click the corner of the first block of cells.

**2** Drag the mouse to highlight the desired cells.

**3** Press Ctrl.

**4** Select the next block of cells.

Repeat steps 3 and 4 to select all cell blocks.

● Excel highlights each of the selected cell blocks.

Any changes you make affect only the highlighted cells.

# Name a Range

I f you need to reference a specific range of cells in multiple locations, it can become tedious to remember the cell locations. You can create range names to easily locate specific information, to avoid having to remember the cell locations, and for use in any formulas that you create. For example, if you create a range name in Sheet1 named Sales_Amounts, in Sheet2 you can create a formula that sums the range by typing the following:

`=SUM(Sales_Amounts)`

Using the named range eliminates the need to specify a worksheet or cell reference. Although the example shows how to access a range from any worksheet in the same workbook, you can also reference a named range of cells from another workbook. For example, `=SUM(Sales2002!Sales_Amount)` references a named range in the workbook Sales2002.xls. See Chapter 4 for more information on creating formulas.

You create the range name in the Define Range dialog box. Your range names can consist of up to 255 characters, but you only see about the first 16 characters of the name in the Name box. Therefore, you may want to use names that you can easily distinguish after viewing the first few characters.

Excel only allows you to use a range name once in a workbook; therefore, if you have a duplicate name in another worksheet, you must use a different name. If you create a range name that already exists, Excel replaces the previously specified range with the new range. To avoid potential errors, verify that you have a unique range name before using it.

If you duplicate a worksheet containing a named range, Excel only recognizes the range name in the original worksheet for other worksheets in the workbook. You can only access the copied range name on the copied worksheet.

## Name a Range

① Select the range of cells that you want to name.

**Note:** See the section "Select a Range of Cells" for more information on selecting a range.

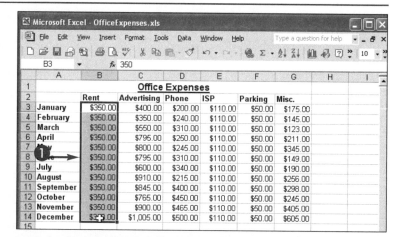

② Click Insert⇨Name⇨Define.

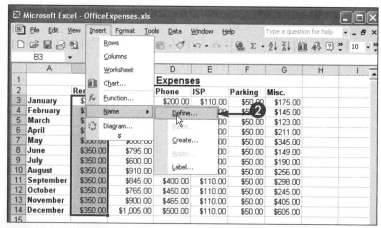

The Define Name dialog box displays.

**3** Type the name of the range.

- You can click the Collapse Dialog button to make a previously assigned range appear in the Refers to box.

**4** Click OK.

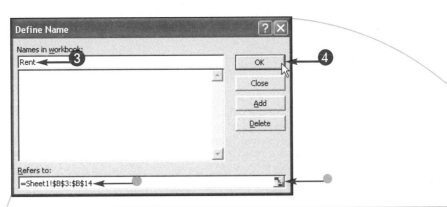

Excel creates the new range name.

- You can click next to the Name field to see the current range names.

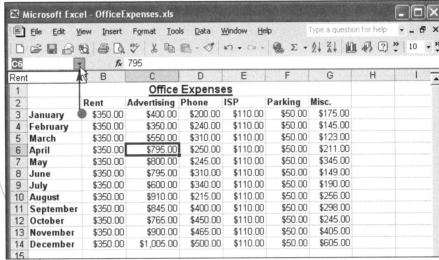

---

## Extra

If you no longer want to use a named range, you can delete it by clicking Insert⇨Name⇨ Define. In the Define Names dialog box, select the range name and click Delete.

When you delete a named range, you only remove the name. The cells referenced by the name remain unchanged. If you have a formula that references the deleted range name, the error #NAME ? displays in the cell containing the reference. You must update each formula that references the deleted range name.

If you have a worksheet that includes formulas that reference cells from a named range, you can convert the cell references to the range name. To do so, select the cells containing the formula and click Insert⇨ Name⇨Apply to display the Apply Names dialog box. The dialog box displays the names that exist within the workbook. Click OK to update the formula in the selected cell to include the named ranges.

Keep in mind that Excel only updates the range names within the existing worksheet and not those in other worksheets.

# Create Label Ranges

You can automatically have Excel use the column or row labels as the range names for your worksheet. This eliminates time required to manually create a range for each column or row of data in your worksheet. Excel creates names based upon the labels in the top row, bottom row, left column, or right column within the range of cells. For example, if your worksheet contains various office expenses for an entire year, you can create named ranges of monthly expenses. If the month names are in the left column, Excel creates the range name from the left column labels.

In the Create Names dialog box you must first select the range of cells containing both the labels and the cells for the named ranges. For example, if your top row contains the column names for the worksheet, and the remaining

rows contain the corresponding data values, you must select both the labels and the data values. When you activate this option, Excel creates a separate range name for each label within the range of selected cells.

If you have labels in the top row and the left column, and you select the top row option, Excel only creates range names for the top row. If you want to create range names for both the top row and left column, you must select both options in the Create Names dialog box.

Although Excel uses your worksheet labels to create the range names, only the selected cells become a part of the corresponding range. For example, if column C contains telephone expenses, but you only selected a range of cells that contained rows 1 through 12, Excel does not create a range for the any values beyond row 12.

## Create Label Ranges

① Select the range of cells containing labels.

**Note:** See the section "Select a Range of Cells" for more information on selecting a range.

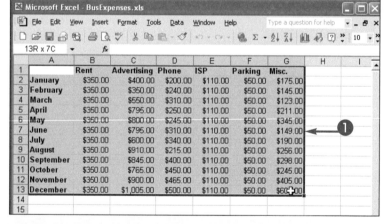

② Click Insert➪Name➪Create.

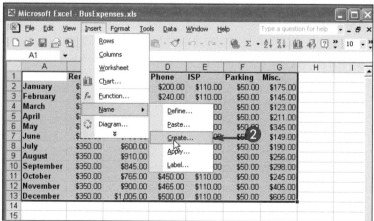

The Create Names dialog box displays.

**3** Click the option corresponding to the location of the labels.

**4** Click OK.

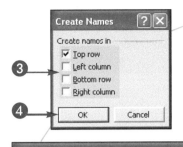

**Create Names**

Create names in
☑ Top row
☐ Left column
☐ Bottom row
☐ Right column

OK    Cancel

Excel creates the range names.

● Click next to the Name field to see the current range names.

Microsoft Excel - BusExpenses.xls

File  Edit  View  Insert  Format  Tools  Data  Window  Help    Type a question for help

A1

| | B | C | D | E | F | G | H | I |
|---|---|---|---|---|---|---|---|---|
| Advertising | | | | | | | | |
| ISP | Rent | Advertising | Phone | ISP | Parking | Misc. | | |
| Misc. | $350.00 | $400.00 | $200.00 | $110.00 | $50.00 | $175.00 | | |
| Parking | $350.00 | $350.00 | $240.00 | $110.00 | $50.00 | $145.00 | | |
| Phone | $350.00 | $550.00 | $310.00 | $110.00 | $50.00 | $123.00 | | |
| Rent | $350.00 | $795.00 | $250.00 | $110.00 | $50.00 | $211.00 | | |
| 6 May | $350.00 | $800.00 | $245.00 | $110.00 | $50.00 | $345.00 | | |
| 7 June | $350.00 | $795.00 | $310.00 | $110.00 | $50.00 | $149.00 | | |
| 8 July | $350.00 | $600.00 | $340.00 | $110.00 | $50.00 | $190.00 | | |
| 9 August | $350.00 | $910.00 | $215.00 | $110.00 | $50.00 | $256.00 | | |
| 10 September | $350.00 | $845.00 | $400.00 | $110.00 | $50.00 | $298.00 | | |
| 11 October | $350.00 | $765.00 | $450.00 | $110.00 | $50.00 | $245.00 | | |
| 12 November | $350.00 | $900.00 | $465.00 | $110.00 | $50.00 | $405.00 | | |
| 13 December | $350.00 | $1,005.00 | $500.00 | $110.00 | $50.00 | $605.00 | | |
| 14 | | | | | | | | |
| 15 | | | | | | | | |

## Extra

You can quickly eliminate any unwanted named ranges using the Define Name dialog box, which you display by clicking Insert⇨Name⇨Define. The Define Name dialog box lists all of the names defined within the current workbook. To delete a named range, click it and then click Delete. Excel only deletes the range name. It does not delete any data.

You can change a range from the Define Name dialog box by selecting the desired range, specifying the range of cells in the Refers To field, and clicking Add. To create a new range of cells, type the new range name in the Names in workbook field, specify the desired range in the Refers To field, and click Add. You can use dates as the names for your ranges. However, if your labels are numeric dates, Excel must reformat the label to match the name rules. For example, 1/31/2002 begins with a number and contains a slash character, which you cannot use in range names. If this date exists in a label column that you use to create names, Excel changes the range name to _1_31_2002. See the section "Name a Range" for more on naming ranges. See Excel Help for specific range naming rules.

# Modify Named Ranges

After you create a named range, Excel continues to use the stored named range whenever you refer to it with the assigned range name. If you change the worksheet by adding or removing corresponding data values, you must update the corresponding named ranges so that Excel references the appropriate cells when you use that range name. To create named ranges, and for more on the benefits of using them, see the section "Create Label Ranges."

When you modify a named range, the changes affect every location that refers to the corresponding range. For example, if you create a formula that uses a specific named range, and then change the cells that the range name references by deleting a column of data, the formula continues to reference the new version of the named range. See Chapter 4 for more information on creating formulas.

You use the Define Names dialog box to modify a named range. In this dialog box, you select the desired range name and make the appropriate modifications either by entering them in the Refers to field or by using the Collapse Dialog button to select a new range of cells. If you have multiple ranges to modify, you can use the Add button to save the changes to the first named range and then modify the next range name.

If you change the actual range name in the Define Names dialog box, Excel actually creates a new range name and keeps the old range name. You can delete the old range name using the Delete button. See "Create Label Ranges" for information on deleting a range name.

## Modify Named Ranges

① Click Insert⇨Name⇨Define.

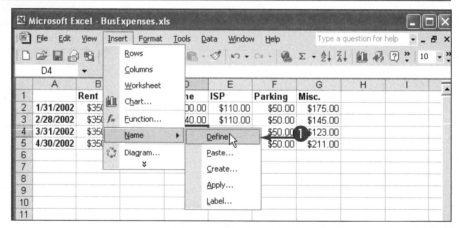

The Define Name dialog box displays.

② Click the name of the range you want to modify.

③ Click the Collapse Content button.

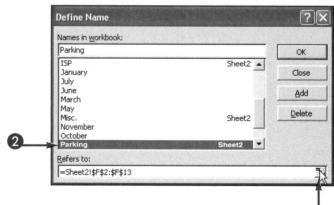

The corresponding cells in the selected range display.

④ Change the range selection.

**Note:** See the section "Select a Range of Cells" for more information.

⑤ Click the Restore dialog button.

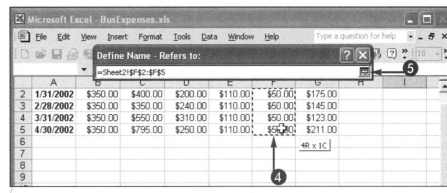

- The revised range selection displays in the Refers to field.

⑥ Click Add to update the saved range.

⑦ Click OK.

Excel saves the revised range.

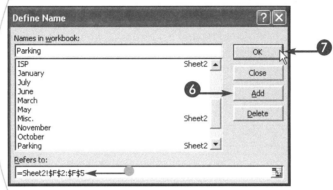

---

## Extra

When you have several different named ranges in a workbook, you may find it difficult to keep track of them all. Excel provides a feature that quickly creates a list of all names and the corresponding cell ranges. To create the list of named ranges, click Insert⇨Name⇨Paste. In the Paste Name dialog box, click the Paste List button. Excel creates a list with the first column containing the range names, and the second column identifying the corresponding cell ranges. For example, if cells B2 through B10 contain your advertising expenses, Excel pastes values similar to the following:

```
Advertising    =Sheet1!$B$2:$B$12
```

The range reference simply identifies the cells within the named range. Excel first lists the name of the worksheet containing the range and then the cells within the range. See Appendix D for more information on cell references.

Excel places the list in your active worksheet starting in the cell containing your cursor. Therefore, it is a good idea to place your cursor in a blank cell with plenty of blank cells below it. Excel places no links in the list, so to keep it up-to-date, you must re-create it whenever you change the named ranges.

# Copy and Paste a Range of Cells

If you want to use the same values in multiple locations, instead of retyping, you can copy and paste. For example, you may want to copy a data list for use in another report, or duplicate a formula in multiple cells. You can repeat information within Excel using the Copy and Paste options. When you copy a cell or range of cells, Excel duplicates everything in the cell — including the cell values, formulas, formatting, comments, and data validation — and leaves the original cell values unchanged. You can multiple cells so long as they are adjacent. You cannot copy multiple cell ranges.

When you apply the Copy command to a range of cells, Excel surrounds the cells with a dotted line. The selected cells remain marked until you perform a task that deselects them. You can quickly press the Esc key to deselect cells. You can also apply menu options that change the worksheet, including copying another range of cells, inserting cells, or hiding rows.

After you copy a range of cells, you can paste the cell contents at any location within your current workbook, another Excel workbook, or any other Microsoft Windows program. Excel replaces the content of the cells where you paste with the copied values. You can paste the copied cells as long as you have not copied another range of cells or until you close Excel.

Be careful when you paste the copied cells. The best method is to select the first cell where you want to paste the contents of the cells and then apply the Paste command. If you attempt to select the entire range of cells where you want Excel to paste the contents and do not select the exact number of cells, you receive an error message.

## Copy a Range of Cells

① Select the cells you want to copy.

**Note:** See the section "Select a Range of Cells" for more information.

② Click Edit⇨Copy.

You can also copy by clicking the Copy button (🖻).

Excel displays a dotted line around the copied cells.

## Paste a Range of Cells

① Place the cursor where you want to paste the cells.

② Click Edit⇨Paste.

You can also click the Paste button.

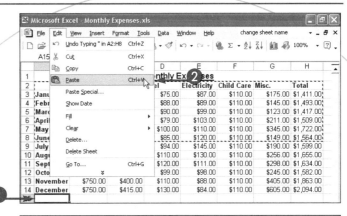

● Excel places a copy of the copied cells in the new location.

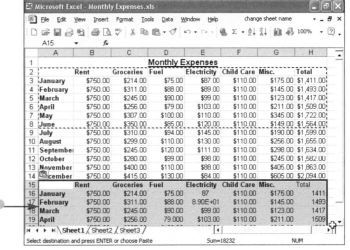

# Create a Custom Number Format

I f you want the numbers in your worksheet to have a specific format, for example, three decimal places, you can create a custom number format. With one definition, you can control how Excel formats a positive value, negative value, zero value, and text value. You can use any combination of the four format types, but you must place them in order and separate them with semicolons:

```
Positive Number Format; Negative Number
Format; Zero Value Format; Text Format
```

Excel applies one specified format for all four conditions. If you specify two different formats, Excel applies the first one to both positive and zero values, and the second to negative values. The following example formats positive numbers with two decimal places and a dollar sign, negative numbers in red and parentheses, zero values as 0, and text in cyan:

```
$#,330.00;[Red]($#,##0.00);0;[Cyan]
```

You create custom number formats using any combination of the format codes with 0 and # being the most useful numeric codes. You use 0 to define digit placement. For example, if you type **000.000**, Excel displays the value 670.45 as 670.450. The # tells Excel not to display insignificant zeros in the value. You can use color names in square brackets to define color formatting. For example, for red text, a popular color for negative values, you type **[Red]** before the format.

You can place characters, such as parentheses, within your format. For example, the following custom format displays positive numbers with two decimal places and a dollar sign, negative numbers in red and parentheses, zero values as 0, and text in cyan. The format uses the $ , . and parentheses symbols.

```
$#,##0.00;[Red]($#,##0.00);0;[Cyan]
```

## Create a Custom Number Format

① Select the cells you want to format.

**Note:** See the section "Select a Range of Cells" for more information.

② Click Format⇨Cells.

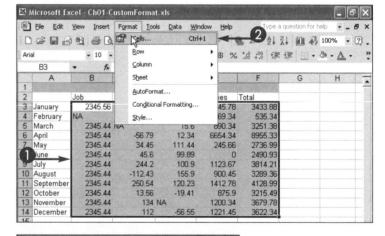

The Format Cells dialog box displays.

③ If it is not displayed, click the Number tab.

④ Click Custom in the Category list box.

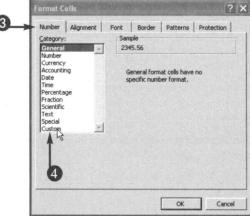

● A list of current custom formats displays in the Type box.

⑤ Type the desired custom format in the Type field.

⑥ Click OK.

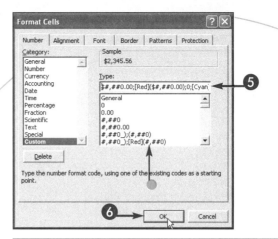

Excel applies the custom format to your cell selection.

---

## Apply It

If you cannot find a default format you want for dates and times, you can create custom date and time formats. To do so, you combine the codes, presented in the tables, for the day, year, month, hour, minute, and seconds. You can use these codes with any of the custom number codes, such as the color codes. For example, to display the date and time as 3:45 PM March 14, 2002 in green, you type:

**Example:**
`[Green]h:mm AM/PM mmmm dd, yyyy`

| DATE SYMBOLS | DESCRIPTION |
|---|---|
| d | Use **d** to display days as 1–31 or **dd** to display days as 01–31. Use **ddd** for a three-letter day name abbreviation, Mon–Sun. If you want the entire day name, use **dddd**. |
| m | Use **m** to display months as 1–12 or **mm** to display months as 01–12. Use **mmm** for a three-letter month name abbreviation, Jan.–Dec. If you want the entire month name, use **mmmm**. |
| y | Use **yy** to display a two-digit year, such as 01 or **yyyy** to display the entire year. |

| TIME SYMBOLS | DESCRIPTION |
|---|---|
| h | Use **h** to display hours as 0–23 or **hh** to display single-digit hours with leading zeros, such as 09. |
| M | Use **M** to display minutes as 0–59 or **MM** to display single digit minutes with leading zeros, such as 08. Make sure to use a capital **M**, or Excel will view it as months. |
| s | Use **s** to display seconds as 0–59 or **ss** to display single-digit seconds with leading zeros, such as 05. |
| AM/PM | Displays either AM or PM with the specified time. |

# Apply AutoFormat to a Worksheet

I f you want to quickly change the appearance of your worksheet, you can apply a predefined format. Excel provides 15 different formats that create a table-like layout for your data. The formats work best when your worksheet contains row and column headings and totals for rows and columns.

You select a predefined format from the AutoFormat dialog box. At the bottom of the dialog box, you find six different format options: Number, Borders, Font, Alignment, Patterns, and Column Width/Height. By default, Excel selects all six options for you. You can adapt any one of the predefined tables by deselecting options to achieve the effect that you want. For example, if you deselect the Font category, Excel does not make any font changes. As you select or deselect different formats, the AutoFormat dialog box reflects the changes letting you view how the various options affect a particular table format before you select it.

Excel replaces any previously applied custom formatting with those that you select in the AutoFormat dialog box. For example, if you have previously selected Arial Black as the font for the entire worksheet, and you apply the Accounting 1 format, Excel changes the font to Arial, the default font for the Accounting 1 style.

The cells that you select before applying a format greatly affect how Excel applies that format to your worksheet. If you select only one cell in a range of cells, Excel examines the worksheet and applies the selected format to all surrounding cells that contain values. As soon as Excel encounters a row or column of blank cells, it no longer applies the formatting. If you type values in the adjoining cells after you apply the format, those cells automatically receive the selected format. If you select a range of cells, Excel only applies the selected format to those cells.

## Apply AutoFormat to a Worksheet

**①** Select the range of cells you want to format.

**Note:** See the section "Select a Range of Cells" for more information.

**②** Click Format⇨AutoFormat.

The AutoFormat dialog box displays.

**③** Click Options.

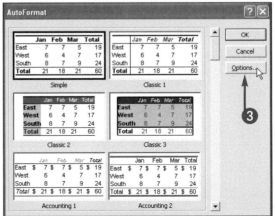

Excel lists the format categories at the bottom of the dialog box.

④ Click the desired table format.

● You can easily remove AutoFormatting by selecting the None format option.

⑤ Click to remove check marks from any unwanted format categories.

⑥ Click OK.

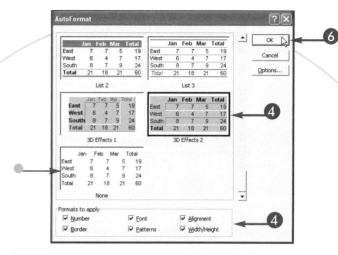

Excel applies the selected predefined format settings to the worksheet.

## Extra

Clicking Options in the AutoFormat dialog box displays a list of the format categories. You can select or deselect these options before applying a format to gauge the effect they have on your worksheet. The following table lists each format option and what it does:

| CATEGORY | DESCRIPTION |
|---|---|
| Number | Specifies the formats for numeric values, such as which values receive currency symbols. Selecting this category overrides any number formats applied using the Number tab in the Format Cells dialog box. |
| Font | Defines all font settings including font type, size, bold, italic, underline, font color, and font effects. |
| Alignment | Controls the alignment of the values within each cell. |
| Border | Controls which cells have borders and specifies properties, including line thickness and line color. |
| Patterns | Defines the background design and color of the table. |
| Width/Height | Adjusts the width of each column and height of each row to accommodate the cell contents. In most formats, Excel makes all columns the same width so that the values within each cell are visible. |

# Create a
# Named Style

I f you consistently apply specific formatting options within a worksheet, you can use a named style to simplify the formatting process. When you have a style that contains the formatting you want, you simply apply that style to selected cells within a worksheet. For example, you can create a Stocks style the changes numbers to fractional values and displays them in Arial 10 point font and bold. The advantage of creating and applying style is that you can update them to suit your needs. For example, if you want your Stocks style to apply italics to your worksheet, you simply modify the style, and Excel automatically updates the formatting in all cells using that style.

You create styles from the Style dialog box by modifying an existing style. Excel provides six default styles, which you can select in the Style name field. Normal is the default

style Excel applies to all cells of your worksheet. The other styles provide default Number formats for formatting numbers with commas, currency, or percent.

You modify default style format options using the six tabs in the Format Cells dialog box: Number, Alignment, Font, Border, Patterns, and Protection. You can modify the various properties of your style by selecting options in any one of these tabs. For example, if you specify that you want to center the text within the cell, the Alignment option displays the value: Horizontal Center.

When you create a new style, it becomes a part of only the existing workbook. To make the style available to other workbooks, you need to create a template. See the section "Create a Custom Template" for more information about creating templates.

## Create a Named Style

① Select the cells where you want to apply the style.

**Note:** See the section "Select a Range of Cells" for more information.

② Click Format➪Style.

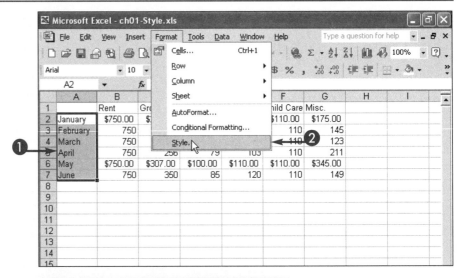

The Style dialog box displays.

③ Type a name for your style.

④ Click Modify.

The Format Cells dialog box displays.

⑤ Make the desired formatting selections.

⑥ Click OK.

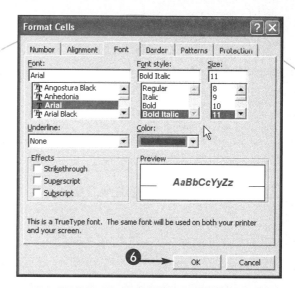

The Style dialog box displays the format settings for the style.

A check mark displays next to each type of formatting with settings listed next to them.

⑦ Click Add.

Excel creates the new style.

## Apply It

Styles are most useful when you can easily apply them to your worksheet, and using the Style dialog box is the quickest way to do so. Unlike Microsoft Word, Microsoft Excel does not have the Style dialog box as a default option on any of its toolbars. To add the feature, click Tools⇨Customize. In the Customize dialog box, click the Commands tab. In the Categories box, click Format. A list of the available format commands displays in the Commands box. Click the Style dialog box and drag it to one of the toolbars displayed at the top of your Excel window. You can now click the down arrow on the toolbar and view a list of available styles.

After creating a new style, you can apply it at any location. To do so, select the cells you want to change and click Insert⇨Style. In the Style dialog box, click the down arrow next to the Style name field and then the desired style. The check boxes under Style Includes correspond to tabs from the Format Cells dialog box with the corresponding setting displayed next to the tab.

# Create a
# Custom Template

If you frequently create worksheets with the same layout, such as a weekly stock analysis report, you can make a template to eliminate repetitive tasks. *Templates* provide a desired layout complete with specific styles, border settings, headers, footers, and even default text and images, such as a company logo.

You create a template by designing a generic workbook that contains the worksheet layouts you want and then change any aspect of it to suit your needs. You can create custom styles, number formats, customized macros, and formulas. You can also specify custom column and row headings in a template. For example, if you generate a budget worksheet each month, you can create a Budget template that contains the column headings for all expenses and includes formulas for summing the totals. See the sections "Create a Custom Number Format" and "Create a Named Style" for information on creating custom styles and number formats. See Chapter 4 for information on creating formulas and Chapter 9 for more

about macros. Your custom template can contain settings for the entire workbook. For example, if you only want the workbook to contain one worksheet, you simply remove the other worksheets before saving your template.

You can now save your generic workbook as a template. On the Save As dialog box, you select the Template (*.xlt) option in the Save as Type field. The option may also appear as Template. When you do so, Excel specifies a default storage location similar to the following:

```
C:\Documents and Settings\user_name\
Application Data\Microsoft\Templates
```

Your drive letter may differ, and you must replace user_name with the username you use to log in to Windows. You should allow Excel to store your workbook in the default location. This ensures that the template appears in the General tab of the Templates dialog box when you create a new workbook.

## Create a Custom Template

① Create your default workbook with the features you want in the template.

② Click File ➪ Save As.

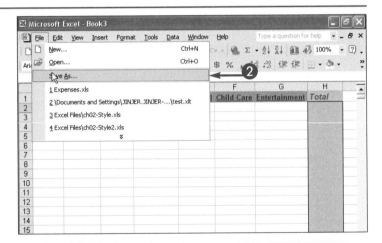

The Save As dialog box displays.

③ Click the Template (*.xlt) option.

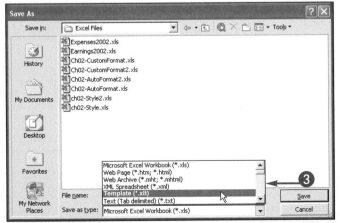

- The Templates folder displays as the storage location in the Save In field.

**4** Type a name for your template.

**5** Click Save.

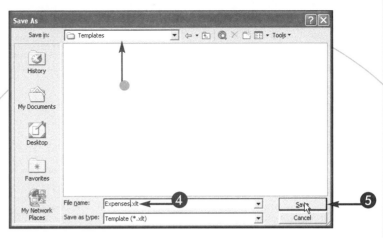

- Excel creates the specified template.

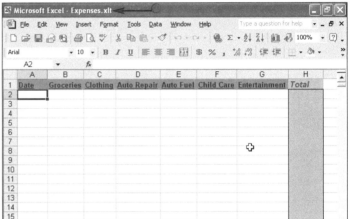

## Apply It

When you create a new blank workbook, Excel uses the default system settings to create it — the default font settings and three blank worksheets. Excel uses the system default settings as long as a default workbook template does not exist. If you consistently make changes to every new, blank workbook, you can make a default workbook template that always loads.

To do so, you first create a workbook that contains all your desired format settings, custom macros, formulas, and a default number of worksheets. When you save the workbook as a template, name it Book.xlt and save it in the XLStart folder, which is typically located in the following location:

```
C:\\Program Files\Microsoft Office\Office10\XLStart
```

Each time you create a new workbook, Excel uses the default Workbook template you modified.

You can also create a default worksheet template by clicking Insert⇨Worksheet. You must save the worksheet template in the same location as the workbook template, but name it Sheet.xls. Excel copies the contents of the Sheet.xls worksheet into your workbook each time you add a new worksheet.

# Protect Worksheets

I f you intend to share your worksheet with other users, you may want to password protect it to ensure that users cannot alter values in individual cells. By protecting the worksheet, you ensure that the integrity of the data remains intact, no matter who views the worksheet contents.

To protect a worksheet, you use the Protect Sheet dialog box. Excel requires you to specify a password to protect and unprotect the worksheet. Use a password that you can easily remember; after you apply a password to a worksheet, no one, including you, can alter the worksheet without specifying the appropriate password. After you unprotect a worksheet, it remains that way until you protect it again.

The Protect Sheet dialog box gives you further control over others' actions by allowing you to specify the functions that users can perform while the worksheet is protected. There

are fifteen different options from which to choose, including locking and unlocking cells, formatting, and inserting or deleting cells. If a user attempts to perform a task that is not allowed, Excel displays a message box indicating that the worksheet is protected. In order for users to make any modifications to a protected worksheet, they must unprotect the worksheet with the appropriate password.

By default, Excel applies allow the user to select both locked and unlocked cells. When users select a protected cell, they can view the contents of the cell in the Formula bar. If you have created formulas that you do not want others to view, you should make sure both of these options are not selected. If users select an unprotected cell, they can modify the cell in the Formula bar.

## Protect Worksheets

① Click Tools⇨Protection⇨Protect Sheet.

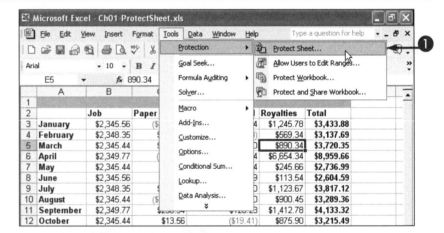

The Protect Sheet dialog box displays.

② Make sure you select the Protect worksheet and contents of locked cells option.

③ Type the password to protect the worksheet.

④ Select the options you want to allow the user to perform while the worksheet is protected.

⑤ Click OK.

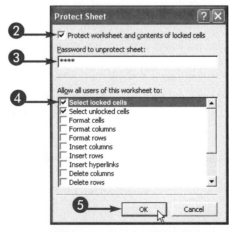

The Confirm Password dialog box displays.

⑥ Re-type the password in the field.

⑦ Click OK.

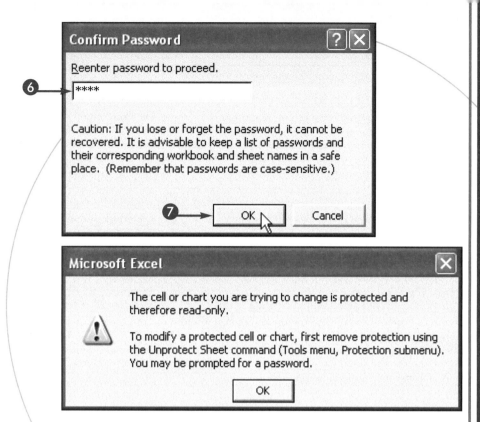

**Confirm Password**

Reenter password to proceed.

****

Caution: If you lose or forget the password, it cannot be recovered. It is advisable to keep a list of passwords and their corresponding workbook and sheet names in a safe place. (Remember that passwords are case-sensitive.)

OK        Cancel

Excel displays a message box if the user attempts to alter a protected portion of the worksheet.

**Microsoft Excel**

The cell or chart you are trying to change is protected and therefore read-only.

To modify a protected cell or chart, first remove protection using the Unprotect Sheet command (Tools menu, Protection submenu). You may be prompted for a password.

OK

## Apply It

If you want to modify a protected worksheet, you must click Tools⇨Protection⇨Unprotect Sheet. In the Unprotect Sheet dialog box, type the password that locks the worksheet in the Password field and click OK.

By default, Excel allows you to lock all cells of the worksheet, so that users can view the cells' contents without altering it. You can unlock certain cells in the worksheet so that users can input values, such as sales total, so that formulas in other cells can perform calculations.

You specify the lock status of a cell in the Protection tab of the Format Cells dialog box. Select the range of cells to unlock, click Format⇨Cells to display the Format Cells dialog box, and then click the Protection tab. Click the Locked option to unlock the selected range of cells (☑ changes to ☐ ).

You can also select the Hidden options, which hides the contents of a cell in the Formula bar if a user selects the cell. This ensures that a user cannot view special formulas. Just like the Locked option, the Hidden option only takes effect if you protect the worksheet.

# Create a List

**E**xcel provides a great location for creating and maintaining a list of data values for data analysis. A *list* refers to a series of rows in a worksheet that contain related values. To make the list of values easier to interpret, the first row typically contains labels for each column. For example, you can create a list of stock quotes with each row representing a different stock symbol and each column identifying separate dates for each stock quote.

Of course, the most obvious method for creating a list is to simply type the appropriate values in each row or column. Another method involves creating a list from the Form dialog box. The Form dialog box takes the column headings in the range of cells you select and uses them to label the data fields. A separate data field displays for each heading.

For example, if you have the column headings Name, Address, City, and Phone, the Form dialog box displays text boxes for each of the selected headings.

To create a list of data in the Form dialog box, you must first specify your column headings in the top row of the area in your worksheet where you want to create a list. You can only do this if you have at least one blank row following your headings. It is not necessary to use the first row, Row 1, for column headings; you can place headings in any row of the worksheet.

When the Form dialog box displays, it requests the values for the first row in your list. Each row of data is typically referred to as a *data record*. You enter the values in the corresponding text fields.

## Create a List

**1** Type the column headings for your list.

**2** Select one of the cells in the row.

**Note:** See Chapter 1 for information on selecting a range of cells.

**3** Click Data➪Form.

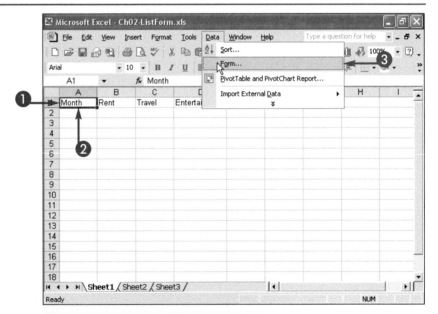

**4** Click OK.

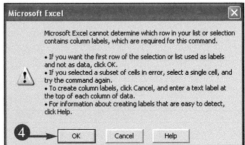

26

A dialog box displays with text boxes for each column.

**⑤** Type the desired data value in each text box.

- You can click New to add another row of data.

- You can click Restore to clear any values typed in the text boxes.

**⑥** Click Close.

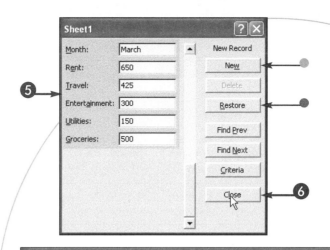

The data values specified in the Form dialog box display in the worksheet.

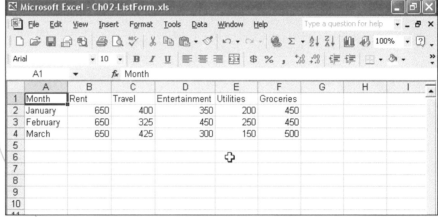

## Apply It

To remove an item, scroll through the list by clicking either the Find Next or Find Prev buttons until the record you want to remove displays. Click Delete, and Excel removes the record from the list in the worksheet.

The Form dialog box allows you to find the rows or data records that meet specific criteria. For example, you can identify the months when your sales losses exceeded $1000.00. You search for values using the Criteria option. When you click Criteria, Excel clears the data values from the cells. Type the criteria you want to match and click the Find Next or Find Prev button. You can search for records matching specific criteria by typing values into any of the text fields. For example, to find the months where customer returns of purchased merchandise equaled $2000.00, you type **$2000.00** in that text field, whereas, to find months where returns exceeded $2000.00, you type **>$2000.00**. Or you can type **<$2000.00** to find those months where returns were less than $2000.00. Use the Find Next and Find Prev buttons to scroll through the records that match the criteria.

# Add a Series to a List

You can quickly create a series in a list and avoid repetitive entries by using the Fill Handle. A *series* is simply a list of values that are either the same value or are incremented by the same value. For example, you can have a series of dates as either 1/1/2003, 2/1/2003, or January 1, 2003, February 1, 2003. A series of numbers can increment by adding, subtracting, multiplying, or even dividing by the same value. For example, 2, 4, 6, 8 is a list of numbers that increment by adding 2 to each value. For more information on lists, see the section "Create a List."

Although Excel creates a series when you present it one value, to ensure that your series properly increments, you must provide both the first and second values in the series. Excel examines these values, assesses the pattern, and creates the remaining series. If the cell contains a numeric value — also known as a *label* — Excel simply repeats it in the specified cells. If you provide a date, Excel increments the date based on its format. For example, for a date that contains a day, such as 2/14/2002, Excel increments the dates by one day. If the cell only contains the month, Excel increments the dates by one month.

Excel calls the black square at the bottom-right corner of the selected range of cells the *Fill Handle*. When you drag this handle either down or to the right, Excel uses the values in the originally selected cells to create the series in the expanded range of cells. As you drag across each cell, Excel displays the value that it will place in the cell.

## Add a Series to a List

① Type the first and second data values for the series.

② Select the cells in the series, or multiple series.

**Note:** See Chapter 1 for information on selecting a range of cells.

● Excel highlights the cells to show they are selected.

③ Click and drag the Fill Handle to specify a range of cells for the series.

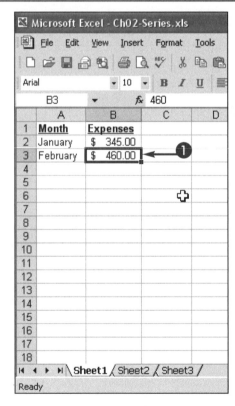

- As you drag, Excel outlines the range of cells that will contain the series.

- Excel displays the value that it will place in last cell.

④ Release the mouse button.

Excel creates the series in the specified cells.

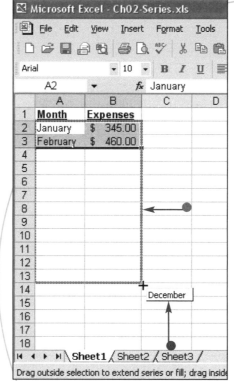

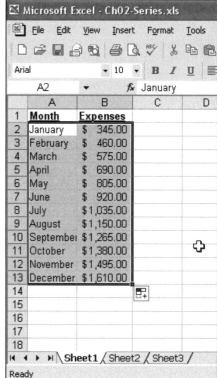

LEARNING
RESOURCES
CENTRE

HAVERING
COLLEGE

## Extra

You may want to choose the amount to increment a series of data values. To do so, click Edit⇔Fill⇔Series. In the Series dialog box that displays, you can enter exactly how you want values to increment, the type of increment, and even a stop value. For example, if you have the date 5/15 in a cell, the Fill Handle automatically increments by days, making the next value 5/16. If you want to display dates that are 15 days apart, you simply type **15** in the Step Value field and click the Day option ( ○ changes to ⊙ ) in the Date Unit section. If you want dates that are exactly one month apart, you click the Month option and type **1** in the Step Value field. If you want all dates from May 15 to the end of the year, you type **12/31** in the Stop value field.

When you use the Series dialog box with dates, you must select the Date Unit options ( ○ change to ⊙ ) corresponding to the part of the date you want to increment. In other words, if you want the date to increase by one month, you click the Month option.

# Sort
# a List

With Excel, you can quickly sort rows or columns in ascending or descending order based upon the criteria you specify. For example, you can sort a range of rows based upon the names listed in the first column. If you want to sort by a different order, you need a custom sort order as described in the section "Create a Custom Sort."

When you sort your list of records in ascending order, the list sorts so that the smallest numbers are at the top of the list. If you sort text labels, Excel sorts alphabetically from A to Z. In descending order, Excel produces the opposite results, placing the largest numbers at the top of the list and sorting alphabetically from Z to A. For more on lists, see the section "Create a List."

You specify your sort criteria in the Sort dialog box. Excel first sorts your data by the column you select in the Sort By field, and then by the column you select in the Then By field. You have the option of specifying a third sort criterion to further sort the list.

If you select a list of data with a row of column headings, you must select the Header Row option so that Excel does not sort that row. Also, when you select a column in the Sort By and Then By fields, Excel displays the column names from the header row. If you do not have a header row, Excel displays Column A, Column B, and so on, as the selections.

By default, the Sort dialog box sorts by columns in your worksheet. If you want to sort by rows, you must change the sort options via the Options button in the Sort dialog box. Changing this option allows you to select a specific row instead of a column.

## Sort a List

### SORT BY COLUMNS

1. Select the range of cells containing the list to sort.

**Note:** See Chapter 1 for information on selecting a range of cells.

2. Click Data⇨Sort.

   The Sort dialog box displays.

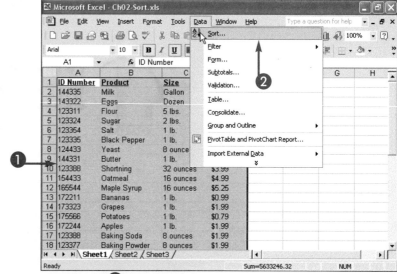

3. To change sort columns, click here and select the desired column.

4. If desired, click Descending to change the sort to descending order.

5. Repeat steps 3 and 4 in the Then By field for additional sort criteria.

6. Click OK.

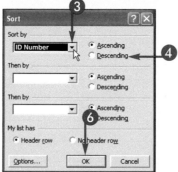

Excel sorts your columns by your criteria.

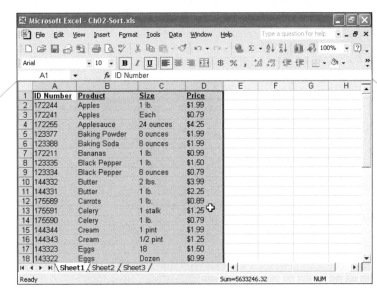

## SORT BY ROWS

1. Follow steps 1 and 2 in the previous section to access the Sort dialog box.

2. Click Options.

   The Sort Options dialog box opens.

3. Click the Sort left to right option.

4. Follow steps 3 to 6 of the previous section to sort by rows.

   Excel sorts your rows by your criteria.

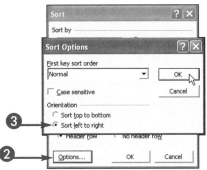

---

### Extra

Excel sorts data based upon your sort criteria and its own built-in sort rules. For an ascending order sort, Excel uses the following rules. If you sort in descending order, Excel reverses these rules.

1. Custom sort orders have first precedence. See "Create a Custom Sort" for more information.

2. Excel places numbers at the top of the sort, and then sorts from smallest to largest number with the smallest negative number at the top of the list, and the largest positive number at the bottom.

3. Excel sorts alphanumeric values alphabetically based upon the following order of characters:
   0 1 2 3 4 5 6 7 8 9 (space) ! " # $ % & ( ) * , . / : ; ? @ [ \ ] ^ _ ` { | } ~ + < = > A B C D E F G H I J K L M N O P Q R S T U V W X Y Z.

4. Excel places a False logical value before a True one.

5. Error values remain in the order they appear in the worksheet.

6. Excel places blank values at the bottom of the list.

# Create a
# Custom Sort

Y ou can create custom sort orders to sort your lists in Excel. This is a great feature when you want to sort your list by something other than alphabetically or numerically. See the section "Sort a List" for more information. A custom sort provides a great data analysis tool, as you can sort a large list of data in a specific order, such as by department or month. For example, if your list contains a column of month names, you probably want to sort based upon the order of the months in the year, not alphabetically by month name. For more on lists, see the section "Create a List."

Excel provides four default custom sort lists for sorting days of the week and month names. You can use these sort orders or create your own unique lists, such as employee names, department locations, seasons, and so on. When you select a custom sort order, Excel sorts your list based upon the order

you specify. For example, if you define the following custom sort order, Excel sorts the list using the order of the words in the list. Therefore, Excel sorts all records that contain First to the top, followed by those containing Second:

`First, Second, Third, Fourth, Fifth, Sixth`

Although you perform your custom sort order using the Sort dialog box, before you can perform the sort, you must first create a custom sort order list to make it available for all workbooks that you edit.

You can create your own custom sort orders using your own custom lists. You create sort order lists in the Custom Lists tab of the Options dialog box. After you create a custom list of words, you can select it at any point in the Sort Options dialog box.

## Create a Custom Sort

### CREATE A SORT ORDER

**1** Click Tools➪Options.

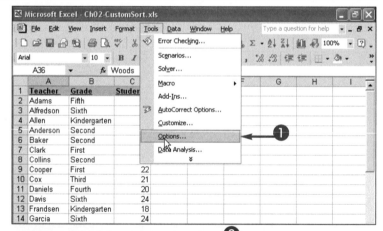

The Options dialog box displays.

**2** Click the Custom Lists tab.

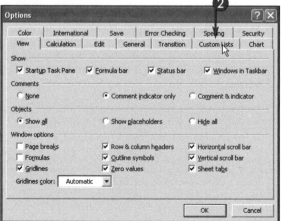

③ Click NEW LIST in the Custom lists box.

④ Type the order in which you want to sort your list, pressing Enter after each list item.

⑤ When you complete the list, click Add.

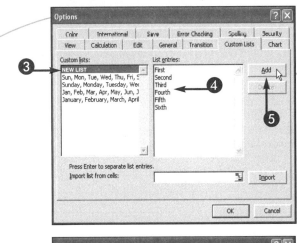

● Excel adds the sort order list to the Custom lists box.

⑥ Click OK to close the Options dialog box.

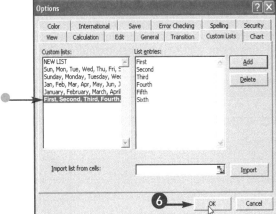

## Apply It

Instead of manually typing a list to use for your sort, you can import a list of data values from any open worksheet. You can do so by using the Import List From Cells field in the Custom Lists tab. You can either manually type the range of cells containing your list, or select the range of cells containing the list within a worksheet.

To select the range of cells, click the Collapse Dialog button ( 🔳 ) to reduce the size of the Options dialog box. Locate the worksheet containing the sort order values and select the corresponding cells. The selected range of cells displays in the field. Next, click the Restore Dialog button ( 🔳 ) to restore the Options dialog box back to the original size. See Chapter 1 for more information on selecting a range of cells.

Click the Import button in the Custom Lists tab, and Excel adds the values from the selected range of cells to the List entries box. The values appear in the list in the order they appear in the selected cells. You can make any desired modifications to the list by typing or deleting values. Finally, click Add to create the sort order. For a clearer picture of how to work the Collapse Dialog and the Restore Dialog buttons, see the section "Consolidate Data."

continued ➔

A fter you create your custom sort order in the Options dialog box, you can use it to sort data in rows or columns of any worksheet. You perform a custom sort in basically the same fashion as any other sort in Excel using the Sort dialog box, but the custom sort takes precedence over built-in sort rules in Excel. See the section "Sort a List" for information on sort order precedence.

To apply a custom sort, you first select the data that you want to sort in the Sort dialog box's Sort By field. When you use a custom sort, Excel only applies it as the first sort that occurs. In other words, Excel applies your custom sort order to a row or column that you specify in the Sort By field in the Sort dialog box and ignores the Ascending and

Descending options for that field. See the section "Sort a List" for information on sorting by rows or columns. No matter what custom sort order you intend to use, Excel always uses the custom sort order as the first sort and then the sorts specified in the Then By fields.

You can specify a custom sort order in the Sort Options dialog box. See the section "Sort a List" for more information about the Sort dialog box. The First key sort order field provides a list of the available sort orders. Excel has four default custom sorts for dealing with days of the week and month names. It also provides sorts for both the full month and day names and the three-letter abbreviations. If you create your own custom sort order lists, Excel places them in the First Key Sort Order list below the default lists.

### Create a Custom Sort *(continued)*

#### APPLY A CUSTOM SORT

① Display the Sort dialog box.

**Note:** See the section "Sort a List" for more information.

② In the Sort by field, select the row or column to sort by.

③ Click Options.

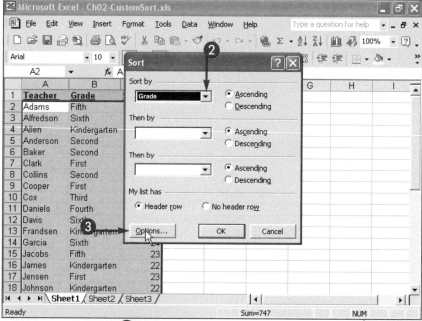

The Sort Options dialog box displays.

④ Click ▾ next to the First key sort order field.

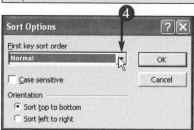

A list of current custom sort orders displays.

⑤ Click the desired sort order.

⑥ Click OK to close the Sort Options dialog box.

⑦ Click OK to close the Sort dialog box.

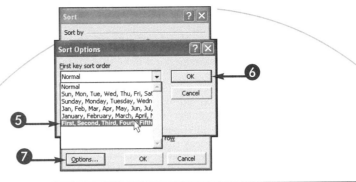

Excel sorts the selected list using the custom sort order.

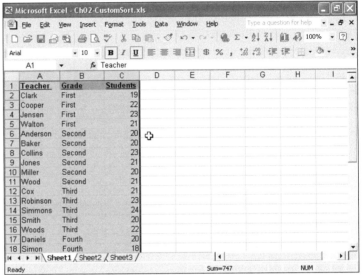

---

## Extra

With custom sorts, Excel uses the order of the values in the list to determine how to sort your data. Excel sorts the records that match the list first and then sorts the remaining items in ascending order at the list's bottom. For example, if your custom list contains the values High, Medium, and Low, Excel places the records with the value High first, followed by the Medium values, and finally those with a value of Low. If the column or row contains other values, such as Very Low or Extremely High, Excel places those values at the bottom of the list so that the order becomes High, Medium, Low, Extremely High, and Very Low.

By default, sorts in Excel are not case-sensitive. For example, if the data you are sorting includes the values milk and Milk, Excel treats them as identical values, even through the M is capitalized on the second word. If you want to perform a case-sensitive sort, click the Options button in the Sort dialog box to display the Sort Options dialog box. When you click the Case sensitive option (☐ changes to ☑ ), Excel makes all three sorts specified in the Sort dialog box case sensitive.

# Consolidate
# Data

I f you have related data values in multiple worksheets, or even workbooks that you want to combine into one location, you can do this using the Consolidate option. When you use this option, Excel merges the data from the specified locations into one central location, combining any common data values by whatever method you specify. A good use of this feature is to combine different workbooks containing sales data for the year into one consolidated worksheet so that you can analyze all the data.

Before you merge your data values, you must first decide where you want to place everything. You can make the location either a separate worksheet in an existing workbook, or a worksheet in a separate workbook. You then select the first cell where you want Excel to place the consolidated values. In the Consolidate dialog box, you specify the ranges of the workbooks or worksheets that you want to consolidate and the type of consolidation to perform.

The options in the Function field in the Consolidate dialog box determine how Excel combines the data values when you perform the consolidation. By default, Excel selects Sum, the most common consolidation function, to consolidate values. The Sum function adds the values in each of the merged ranges. For example, if each worksheet contained monthly sales figures for a salesperson named Simon, Excel totals the sales amounts for each month and places these totals in the consolidation worksheet.

After you determine how Excel will merge your data, you can decide what range of cells you want to merge. You can manually enter the range in the Reference field, select a range from an open worksheet, or open another workbook and select the range of cells.

## Consolidate Data

### SELECT A CONSOLIDATION FUNCTION

1 Select the top-left cell of the worksheet on which you want to consolidate data.

2 Click Data⇨Consolidate.

The Consolidate dialog box displays.

3 Click the function you want to perform.

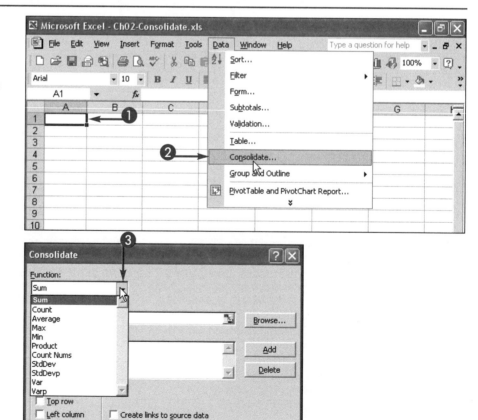

## SELECT THE RANGE TO CONSOLIDATE

- If you do not have the worksheet containing your range open, you can click Browse to open it.

④ Click the Collapse Dialog button.

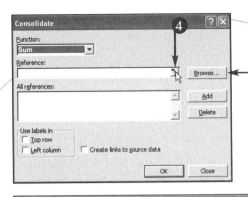

The Consolidate dialog box collapses to display only the Reference field.

⑤ Click the tab of the worksheet containing the data to merge.

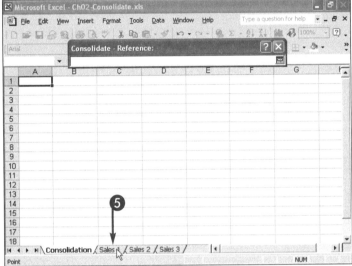

## Extra

You use the Function field to specify the method by which Excel combines your data into one worksheet. Excel provides several different consolidation functions for merging data:

| FUNCTION | DESCRIPTION |
| --- | --- |
| Sum | Adds values between the merged ranges. |
| Count | Counts the number of values in the merged ranges. |
| Average | Averages the values in the merged ranges. |
| Max | Finds the maximum value in the merged ranges. |
| Min | Finds the minimum value in the merged ranges. |
| Product | Multiplies values and returns the result. |
| Count Nums | Counts the number of numeric values in the merged ranges. |
| StdDev | Estimates the standard deviation of the values in the merged ranges. |
| StdDevp | Calculates the standard deviation of the values in the merged ranges. |
| Var | Estimates the variance of the values in the merged ranges based upon a sampling of the values in the range. |
| Varp | Calculates the variance of the values in the merged ranges using all values in the range. |

continued →

If you manually enter a range of data, you must include the worksheet name and the cells to merge. For example, if you want to merge cells A1 through A15 from Sheet1, you type: 'Sheet1'!$A$1:$A$15

When you manually specify a worksheet name, you must type the name of the worksheet between single quotes. Also, you use an exclamation mark to separate the worksheet name reference from the range of cells. Therefore, in the sample range, 'Sheet1'! indicates the worksheet containing the range of cells to consolidate. You define the range of cells by selecting first and last cells in the range, separating the cell references with a colon. See Chapter 1 for more information on specifying a range of cells.

To specify a range in an open workbook, you select the appropriate range of cells until they correctly appear in the

Reference field of the Consolidation dialog box. When you accept the range of cells, Excel adds them to the All References box. You must define the range for each of the worksheets that you want to combine.

If you do not have the worksheet containing the data values open, you can locate the appropriate workbook via the Browse button. Excel opens the workbook so you can select the desired range of cells.

Excel needs to know what labels to use for the combined data values. Excel matches the data in the specified worksheets based upon matching labels in the top row, left column, or both. You need to select at least one of the location options.

Keep in mind that consolidating data does not affect the values contained in the original worksheets.

## Consolidate Data *(continued)*

⑥ Select the range of cells containing the data to consolidate.

- Alternatively, you can type the range in the Reference field.

The range of the selected cells displays in the Reference field.

⑦ Click the Restore Dialog button.

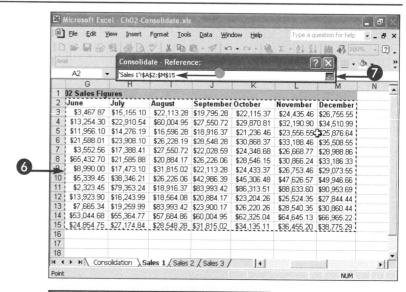

⑧ Click Add to add the range to the All references list box.

⑨ Repeat steps 5 to 8 to select the other ranges.

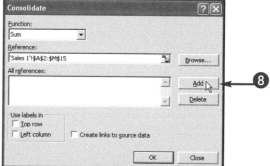

The All references box displays the ranges to consolidate.

**⑩** Click the location of your label.

**⑪** Click OK.

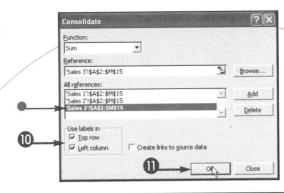

Excel consolidates the data values in the specified ranges.

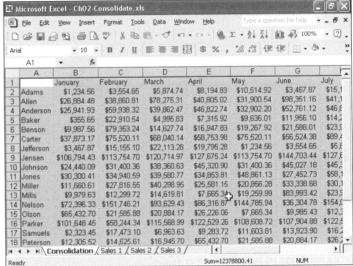

---

## Extra

When you consolidate, Excel simply copies or combines the data in the specified ranges into the consolidation location. If you modify the data after you perform the consolidation, Excel does not automatically update to reflect your changes. To have it do so, you must click the Create links to source data option (☐ changes to ☑ ) in the Consolidate dialog box. This option places formulas in each cell of the consolidation worksheet. These formulas link directly back to the consolidated data, allowing Excel to automatically update after you make modifications to the original data.

If you choose to use this option, you must ensure that Excel can always find the worksheets containing the consolidation data. You do this by placing the original worksheets in the same locations. Each time you open the worksheet, Excel attempts to locate the consolidation data so that it can update the worksheet. Excel opens the original worksheets and updates the data in the consolidation worksheet. If Excel cannot locate a consolidation range, the worksheet will not reflect all the data you modified.

# Outline
# Your Data

You can create an outline of your data in Excel to group common information together in sections. The feature allows you to expand and collapse individual sections, which is handy to an analyst who has long worksheets of data and must find certain parts of the worksheet quickly. For example, if you have sales by region one worksheet with each month totaled, you can collapse the regional records and view only the total sales amounts for each month.

You can either create a manual outline by identifying each group of related data records, or you can have Excel create an automatic outline. You manually outline by first selecting the rows or columns you want to group. When you activate the Group command, Excel places all the rows or columns you select in a section. If you have a specific row or column that you want visible when you collapse the group, you simply do not make it part of the selection range.

The automatic outline feature typically works best when you have total and subtotal rows and columns. See Chapter 3 for information on subtotaling. You select at least one cell in the range you want to outline and activate the Auto Outline command. Excel examines the contents of the worksheet and creates an outline based on the formulas that you have applied to the worksheet. For example, if your worksheet has a total row, Excel treats that as the summary data, or top level. If you have subtotals, Excel groups them with the corresponding data records.

You can use the outline symbols to hide and show the detail records in your worksheet. The minus sign hides the corresponding rows or columns, while the plus sign expands your records. Excel uses numbers to identify the different summary levels. The first level collapses everything and shows only the summary records.

## Outline Your Data

### MANUAL OUTLINE

① Select the rows containing the records to group.

② Click Data⇨Group and Outline⇨Group.

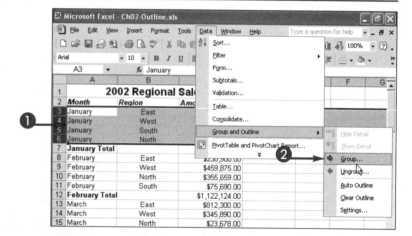

● Excel groups the selected data records.

● You can click the minus button to hide the grouped records.

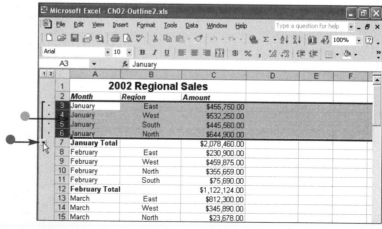

## AUTOMATIC OUTLINE

1 Select a cell in the range to outline.

2 Click Data⇨Group and Outline⇨Auto
Outline.

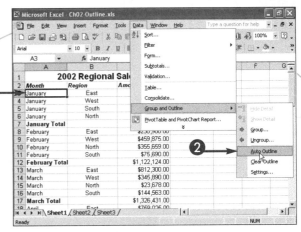

Excel automatically creates an outline.

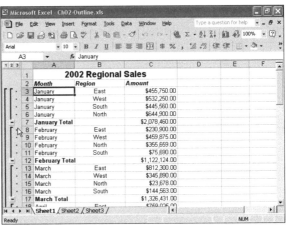

---

### Apply It

You can have Excel apply special formatting
to your worksheet as it creates the outline.
This can quickly help you identify different
outline levels. To apply special formatting,
you must first create format styles for your
outline in the Style dialog box. See Chapter 1
for more information on creating styles. You
must create your styles using specific names:

To apply custom formatting, click Data⇨
Group and Outline⇨Settings to display the
Settings dialog box. Click the Automatic
Styles option (☐ changes to ☑ ) and then
click Create. Excel creates your outline using
the styles you created.

| STYLE NAME | DESCRIPTION |
| --- | --- |
| RowLevel_1 | Defines the formatting for the first row level in your outline. |
| RowLevel_2 | Defines the formatting for the second row level in your outline. |
| RowLevel_x | Where x equals another number to define a format level. |
| ColLevel_1 | Defines the formatting for the first column level in your outline. |
| ColLevel_2 | Defines the formatting for the second column level in your outline. |
| ColLevel_x | Where x equals another number to define a format level. |

# Apply Conditional Formatting

You can have Excel analyze the data values for specific criteria, and apply conditional formatting when the criteria are met. This comes in handy for the analyst who wants to emphasize data that has reached a critical value. For example, you can highlight net sales losses of over $2,000.00 so that they are readily apparent to users who view your worksheet.

The Conditional Formatting dialog box allows you to create up to three different conditional formatting statements for each range selection. For example, you can create a formatting to apply to cell values between 0 and 1,000, another format for values between 1,001 and 5,000; and then a third for values over 5,000. The Conditional Formatting dialog box allows you to specify formatting for the cells based upon either the value of a cell or a formula. You can only specify conditional formatting using formulas that return a logical value of either True or False. You

specify whether you want conditional formatting for the cell value or a formula in the first list box in the Conditional Formatting dialog box.

To create conditional formatting for the value of a cell, you must select the conditional operator you want to use to check the cell contents. Following the previous example, to change the cell formatting if the cell's value is greater than $2,000.00, you select the greater than conditional operator.

In the value fields, you must specify the value for the condition. You have three options for these fields. You can enter a constant in the field — any number, alphanumeric value, or logical value. Alternatively, you can enter a formula to return the desired value. You can also select a range that contains the values by collapsing the dialog box. See Chapter 1 for more on selecting ranges. See Chapter 4 for more information on formulas.

## Apply Conditional Formatting

① Select the range of cells for the conditional formatting.

**Note:** See Chapter 1 for information on selecting a range.

② Click Format⇨Conditional Formatting.

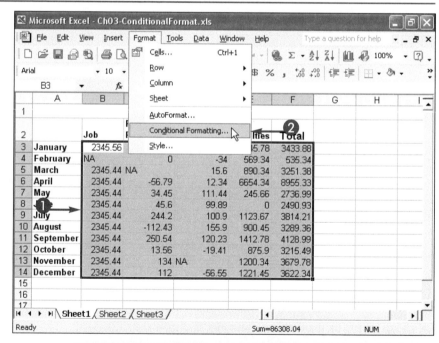

The Conditional Formatting dialog box displays.

③ Click Cell Value Is from the list of options.

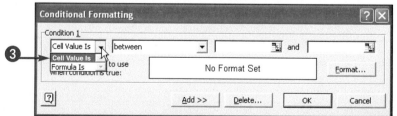

④ Click the desired operator from the list of options.

**Note:** If you select Formula Value Is in step 3, the second list box does not display.

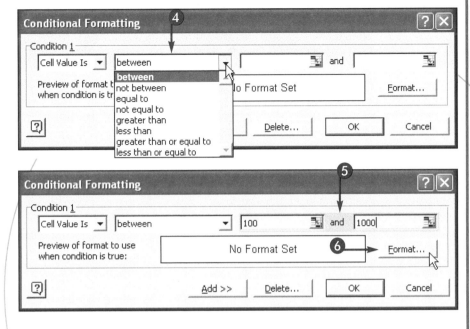

Either one or two fields display for values.

⑤ Type the values for the condition in the fields.

⑥ Click Format.

## Extra

You can hide any error messages that may display in a cell by creating a conditional format definition. To do this, you use the ISERROR function to create a formula that checks for an error in the cell. For example, if a formula in a cell divides by zero, Excel returns the #DIV/0! error message. To hide any such error messages, select the range of cells and then click Format⟡Conditional Formatting. In the Conditional Formatting dialog box, click the Formula Is option in the Condition 1 field. In the next field, type the following definition, replacing *A1* with the first cell in the selected range of cells.

`=ISERROR(A1)`

By specifying the cell reference of the first cell, Excel applies the conditional formatting to every cell in the selected range.

Click the Format button to display the Format Cells dialog box. In the Font tab, select White as the color and click OK. The text in any cells containing error messages displays in white and hides the error messages.

continued ➔

**A**fter you select conditions, you must specify the formatting you want to apply via the Format button in the Conditional Formatting dialog box. The Format Cells dialog box has three tabs for setting the formatting you want: Font, Border, and Patterns. When you close the dialog box, you can view selected formatting in the Preview window of the Conditional Formatting dialog box and decide if it is what you want. See Chapter 1 for more information about formatting cells.

You can create up to two further definitions, making a total of three conditional formatting definitions for the selected range. Remember that if Excel encounters cells that meet more than one of the conditional formatting definitions, it only applies to the first one. If you are not careful about how you lay out your conditional formatting statements, you may not achieve the results you desire. For example,

assume you want all values over 1,000 to appear in blue font, and the values between 1,500 and 2,000 to appear in green font, and you create two conditional format statements and apply them. If the conditional formatting definitions are in that order, all values such as 1,555 or 1,900 will appear in blue because they meet the condition of the first definition, greater than 1,000 in blue, and Excel ignores the second conditional formatting definition.

To make the conditional formatting work correctly, you must place the formatting for values between 1,500 and 2,000 first, followed by the conditional formatting for values over 1,000. Therefore, it is extremely important to ensure that the conditional formatting definition that covers the broadest range of values appears last, such as the greater than 1,000 definition.

## Apply Conditional Formatting *(continued)*

The Format Cells dialog box displays.

**7** Specify the format for the condition.

**8** Click OK.

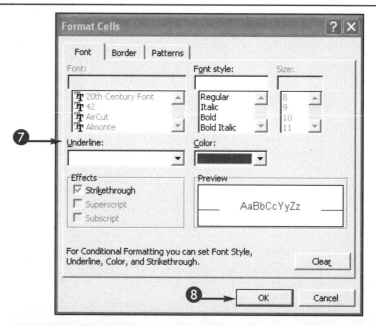

- The Preview field displays a sample of the formatting selections.

**9** Click Add.

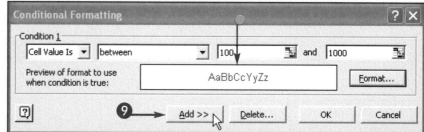

- Excel displays the fields to create a second conditional formatting definition.

**⑩** Repeat steps 3 to 8 to create the second definition.

- If desired, click Add and repeat steps 3 to 8 to create a third definition.

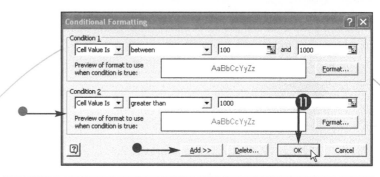

**⑪** Click OK.

Excel applies the conditional formatting definition to the selected cells.

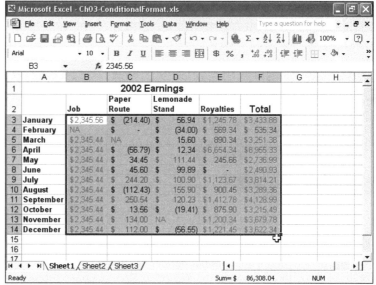

---

## Extra

After you apply conditional formatting to a worksheet, the only way to recognize cells that contain conditional formatting is to select the cell and then view the Conditional Formatting dialog box. A quick way to locate cells containing conditional formatting is to use the Go To Special dialog box. You can display the Go To Special dialog box by clicking Edit⇨Go To and then clicking Special in the Go To dialog box. In the Go To Special dialog box, click the Conditional formats option (○ changes to ◉). Excel provides two additional options: All and Same. Click All to find the cells that contain any conditional formatting. If you only want to find cells with the same conditional formatting as the currently selected cell, click Same. Click OK and Excel locates the cells that contain the specified formatting.

You can remove any of the conditional formatting by selecting the range of cells and clicking Format⇨Conditional Formatting to display the Conditional Formatting dialog box. Click Delete, and the Delete Conditional Formatting dialog box displays. Click the options (□ changes to ☑) that correspond to the conditional formats you want to remove.

# Summarize Data with Subtotals

I f you want to summarize a data list based upon common values, you can use the Subtotal option to automatically insert subtotals for common records and a final total for the entire data list. For example, if your data list contains monthly calls made by the sales department, Excel can subtotals the number of calls for each month and then create a total for the number of calls that year at the end of the data list. Excel does this by monitoring the value in the Month column and inserting a subtotal whenever the value changes, for example, when January changes to February. If each record in your data is unique, such as a separate amount for each month, a subtotal amount displays under each record.

To create subtotal amounts, first sort your list grouping all common records together based upon the column you want to use to group the data. You must label each column

because Excel uses the labels to identify your cells in the Subtotal dialog box. For more on sorting your data, see Chapter 2. For more on labeling columns or rows, see Chapter 1.

Located in the Subtotal dialog box, the At each change in field defines the column label you want Excel to monitor for changes, and when it notes a change, it inserts a subtotal. You control the location of the subtotal in the Add subtotal to box. The Use function field defines the function that Excel uses to summarize the data. Although the default function is Sum, you can select other functions to count records or determine average values.

The checkboxes at the bottom of the dialog box control the placement of the subtotal row within the worksheet. By default, Excel replaces any subtotals in the data list and places subtotals above each group.

## Summarize Data with Subtotals

① Select the range of cells to subtotal.

**Note:** See Chapter 1 for information on selecting a range.

② Click Data⇨Subtotals.

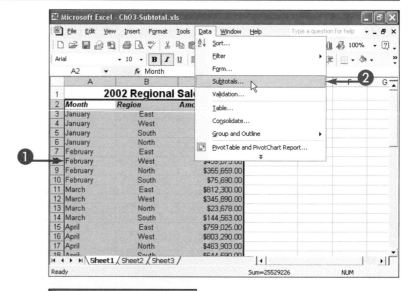

The Subtotal dialog box displays.

③ Select an appropriate column name from the At each change in field.

④ Select the function that you want to insert.

⑤ Click the column or columns to which you want to apply the function.

● Click an option to replace current subtotal rows, place a page break between groups, or to place subtotals below each group.

⑥ Click OK.

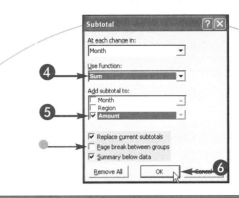

Excel summarizes the data using the selected function.

This example sums each group and creates subtotal and final total amounts.

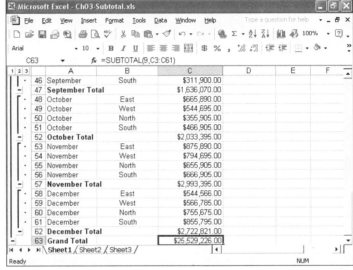

---

## Extra

The Subtotal option actually inserts the SUBTOTAL function in each summary row in the form of a formula, which updates automatically whenever you modify a value in the corresponding data records. You can make modifications to each formula to alter the summary range or function. See Chapter 4 for information on formulas.

The first argument of the SUBTOTAL function defines the function that summarizes the data records. Excel uses numbers between 1 and 11 to identify the functions in the following order: Average, Count, Count Nums, Max, Min, Product, StDev, StDevP, Sum, Var, and VarP. The second argument specifies the range of cells to subtotal. For example, the following formula sums the subtotal range, and uses a 9 in the first argument to correspond to the Sum function, the ninth function in the list:

=SUBTOTAL(9,B3:B10)

If you want to remove all subtotals from your worksheet, click Data➪Subtotals to display the Subtotals dialog box. Click the Remove All button. Excel removes the subtotal and final total rows from the worksheet.

# Filter
# a List

When analyzing large data lists, limiting exactly what information displays in your worksheet is often necessary. In Excel, this limiting process is referred to as *filtering*. You can filter your list of data records with the AutoFilter command so that only the records that match specific criteria display in the worksheet. Each worksheet row is treated as a separate record. For example, if you have a list of monthly sales from different regions, you can filter the list to display only the sales within the Western region. When you apply a filter, Excel simply hides the records that do not match the specified filter criteria.

When you select the AutoFilter option, Excel examines the values in each column, applies your filter criteria, and places arrow buttons at the top of each column of data. Excel identifies the columns with filters by changing the

color of the arrow on the button from black to blue. The arrow reveals a menu of all the unique values within that column. If you select one of the values, Excel displays all the records that contain that value and hides the other records. To filter by multiple column values, you filter the first column and then select a different value in a second column.

Excel places three filter options at the top of each menu. The (All) option allows you to undo a filter and redisplay the records that are currently hidden by the filter. You use the other two options, (Top 10) and (Custom), to further customize the filter. The (Top 10) option filter lets you view the ten highest or ten lowest records. The customize filter lets you view specific rows within one column using custom filter definitions. See the section "Create a Custom Filter" for more information about the (Custom) option.

## Filter a List

### APPLY THE FILTER

① Select the list of records that you want to filter.

**Note:** See Chapter 1 for information on selecting a range of values.

② Click Data⟶Filter⟶AutoFilter.

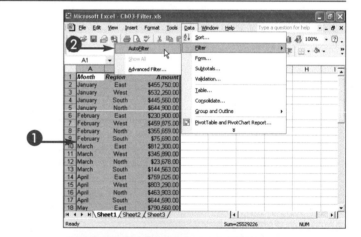

● Excel places arrow buttons at the top of each column.

③ Click an arrow above the column you want to filter and select the desired filter value.

You can apply filters to multiple columns by selecting filters for the other columns.

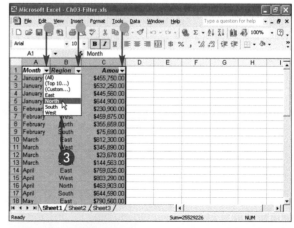

Excel hides the records that do not contain the selected filter value.

## REMOVE THE FILTER

1 Click Data➪Filter➪AutoFilter again.

Excel displays a check mark next to the AutoFilter option indicating filters exist in the worksheet.

Excel removes any filters and redisplays any hidden records.

---

### Apply It

If the column contains only numeric values, you can find the highest or lowest records in your list by selecting the (Top 10) option in the filter menu. In the Top 10 AutoFilter dialog box that displays, you can select the largest or smallest values in the list and view the values either as a percentage or by criteria entered in the three fields. For example, if you have a list of currency amounts, you can filter it to display only the records containing the ten highest values by selecting Top in the first list box, 10 in the second field, and Items in the final field. To see the smallest numbers, you select Bottom in the first field. If you only want the five highest values, you must select 5 in the second field.

If you want to filter by a percentage, such as the Top 50%, you type the percentage in the second field and then select Percent in the final list box.

If you attempt to select the (Top 10) option in a column that does not contain all numbers, Excel does not display the Top 10 AutoFilter dialog box.

# Create a Custom Filter

f you want to filter a list so that you can view specific rows within one column of data, you can create a Custom AutoFilter definition. The Custom AutoFilter allows you to specify two different filter definitions to control the records that display and helps you narrow data to a specific category in a column. For example, using the equals operator, you can create a filter that displays only the records from two specific departments, months, or sales areas. Excel hides all other records with the exception of those that you specifically request.

Like the section "Filter a List," you apply an AutoFilter to your data, but you use the Custom AutoFilter dialog box to build the criteria for your two filters. You decide whether the values must meet both definitions, or just one by selecting either the And or Or options. If you click And, a

value must meet both the first and second criteria, or the record does not display. If you click Or, the value only needs to meet one of the two criteria definitions.

Once you select an operator, you can define what values you want to include in your filter. You can use the ? and * wildcard values to specify characters. For example, if you want all data values that start with A and end with L, you type **A*L**. Excel displays records that contain the words that match the pattern, such as April and anvil. See Chapter 1 for more information on using wildcard characters.

If you want to filter the data records based upon a combination of values in multiple columns, such as sales in the West region for January and sales in the East region for March, see the section "Create an Advanced Filter."

## Create a Custom Filter

① Apply an AutoFilter to a list.

**Note:** See the section "Filter a List" for more information on AutoFilters.

② Click the (Custom) option on the filter menu.

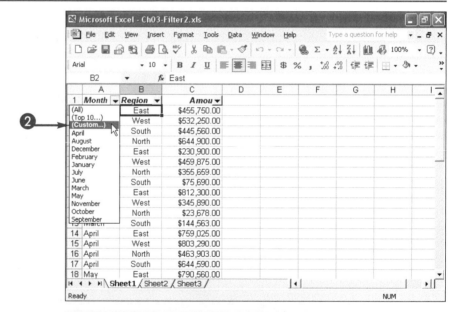

The Custom AutoFilter dialog box displays.

③ Click the desired filter operator.

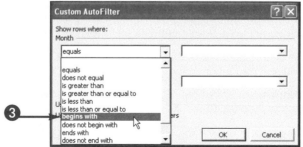

④ Type or select the value to match in the second field.

⑤ Click either the And or the Or option to have the filter find values that match both or either of the criterion.

⑥ Repeat steps 3 and 4 for the second filter definition.

⑦ Click OK.

Excel filters the list based upon the custom filter definition.

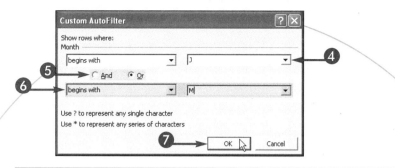

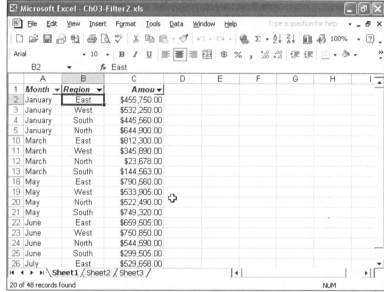

## Extra

Excel has a variety of operators to define your filter. The following table gives their functions:

| OPERATOR | DESCRIPTION |
|---|---|
| equals | Searches for data that matches the specified value. |
| does not equal | Searches for data that does not match the specified value. |
| is greater than | Searches for data that is larger than the specified value. |
| is greater than or equal to | Searches for data that matches or is larger than the specified value. |
| is less than | Searches for data that is less than the specified value. |
| is less than or equal to | Searches for data that matches or is smaller than the specified value. |
| begins with | Searches for data that starts with the specified string, such as A. |
| does not begin with | Searches for data that does not start with the specified string. |
| ends with | Searches for data that ends with the specified string. |
| does not end with | Searches for data that does not end with the specified string. |
| contains | Searches for data that contains the specified string. For example, West and East both contain the string st. |
| does not contain | Searches for data that does not contain the specified string. |

# Create an
# Advanced Filter

You can filter your data to include a combination of values from multiple columns using the Advanced Filter. This filter is more complex than the Custom AutoFilter, illustrated in the section "Create a Custom Filter," because your filter is no longer limited to one column of data. Although you can create larger filter definitions with this feature, you may find the definitions more confusing to use because you create them manually.

Before you apply the Advanced Filter, you must enter a filter definition in your worksheet. The definition consists of a row of headings for the filter definition, as well as the criteria for the filter. You can place the filter definition in either the same worksheet as the records you want to filter, or in another worksheet altogether. Wherever you place it, you want to enter it in a cell that is not readily visible on the worksheet.

In the Advanced Filter dialog box, you specify a range of cells containing the filter definition in the Criteria range field, and the cell containing your comparison operator. You also have the option of placing the filtered records either back in the original location or in another location within the same worksheet. If you select the former option, Excel hides the records that do not meet the specified filter criteria. If you opt for a new location, Excel copies the data that matches the filter criteria and places it in the new worksheet location.

When you apply the advanced filter definition, Excel displays all records that match the criteria — even duplicated records. You can select the Unique Records Only option to eliminate the duplicate records, but if you do so, Excel does not tell you which records are duplicated. If you want a total of the number of records that match the criteria, avoid selecting this option.

## Create an Advanced Filter

① Type column headings for filter definition in a worksheet.

② Type filter definition.

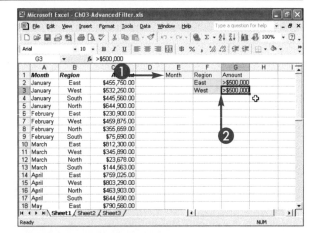

③ Select a range of cells to filter.

④ Click Data➪Filter➪Advanced Filter.

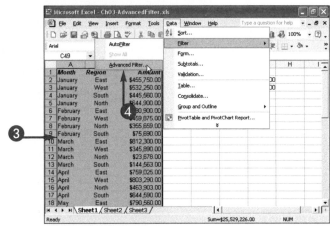

- The Advanced Filter dialog box displays with the selected range in the List range field.

**5** Type the filter criteria range in the Criteria range field.

- You can also click the Collapse Dialog buttons to select the range of cells.

**6** Click OK.

Excel filters the list by hiding the records that do not match the criteria.

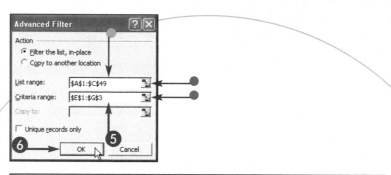

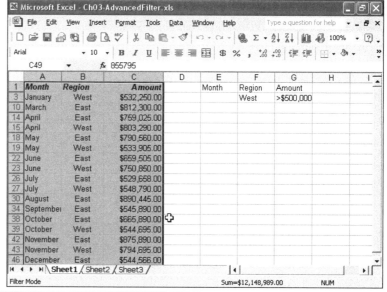

---

## Extra

You type all advanced filter definitions into the worksheet before you select the Advanced Filter option. How you do so is critical to how Excel interprets the definition. Each filter definition consists of at least two rows. The first row contains the column headings of the columns you want to filter. Each successive row defines the filter criteria. For example, to find the sales for January in the East region type:

**Example**

| Month | Region |
| --- | --- |
| January | East |

The placement of the criteria determines how Excel compares them. Excel uses the AND operator to join filter criteria in the same row, and the OR operator for criteria in separate rows. For example, Excel interprets the following filter definition as "Month equals January and Region equals East OR Month equals February and Region equals West."

**Example**

| Month | Region |
| --- | --- |
| January | East |
| February | West |

You can also use the comparison operators in your filter definitions: =, >, <, >=, <=, or <>. For example, to find all sales for January greater than $50,000, you type:

**Example**

| Month | Amount |
| --- | --- |
| January | >$50,000 |

# Create
# Scenarios

One major benefit of analyzing data is forecasting future events with today's information. By asking "what-if" and constructing various scenarios with your data and the Excel Scenario Manager, you can direct your current activities to reach long-term company goals. For example, you can create several scenarios to determine the cost of a business loan at various interest rates. Comparing these scenarios can help you decide which rate is financially feasible. By viewing individual scenarios, you can quickly see how an increase or decrease in an interest rate can impact your monthly budget. You can also construct scenarios that involve changing multiple cell values. For example, you may not only want to change the interest rate, but also the loan amount with each scenario.

Constructing scenarios will change your worksheet's data. For that reason, you may want to create one scenario that contains your original data, or copy your worksheet before applying the scenario feature.

You create each scenario in the Add Scenario dialog box. First, you specify the cells in which you want to see predicted changes. See Chapter 1 for information on selecting a range of cells. You specify multiple cells by separating each cell reference with a comma, for example: **A3:D4**. Next, you assign new values to each cell in the Scenario Values dialog box. Excel uses these values whenever you select the corresponding scenario. For example, if you specify a value of 45 for A3, Excel changes the cell value of A3 to 45 every time you select the scenario.

From your input, Excel generates a scenario. You can apply a specific scenario at any time and change the specified values of the worksheet by simply selecting it from the Scenario Manager dialog box. When you select a different scenario, Excel changes the values of the cells as specified in the scenario.

## Create Scenarios

① Click Tools⇨Scenarios.

The Scenario Manager dialog box opens.

② Click Add.

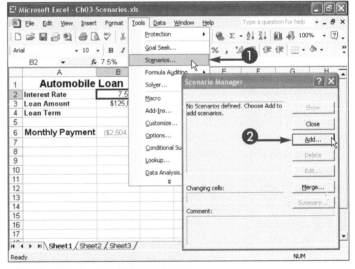

The Add Scenario dialog box displays.

③ Type the scenario name.

④ Specify the cells to change.

- You can type comments about the scenario in the Comment box.

⑤ Click OK.

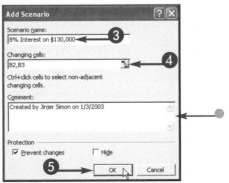

The Scenario Values dialog box displays.

**6** Type the value for each cell.

**7** Click OK.

● You can click Add to display the Add Scenario dialog box and create another scenario.

You can repeat steps 2 to 7 for each scenario you want to create.

The Scenario Manager dialog box opens.

**8** Click Show to apply the scenario.

The values designated for the scenario change in the corresponding cells.

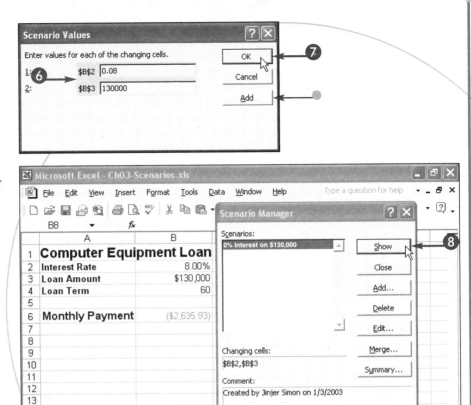

You can use the options at the bottom of the Add Scenario dialog box to protect your scenario. The Prevent changes option prevents users from modifying the scenario. If you select Hide, users can no longer view the scenario when they open the worksheet. These options only work when you protection your worksheet. See Chapter 1 for information on worksheet protection.

If you want to compare the results of all scenarios at once, you can create a summary report by clicking the Summary button in the Scenario Manager dialog box. When you do so, the Scenario Summary dialog box opens and gives you access to two summary options. The Scenario summary lets you create a worksheet table that compares your individual scenarios. The option generally works best when you change the same cells in each scenario. The Scenario PivotTable option creates a PivotTable report, which is highly recommended when different cells are involved in the scenario calculation. See Chapter 7 for more information on working with PivotTables.

# Validate
# Data

To increase the accuracy of your data, you can limit what a user can and cannot enter into a specific cell. By default Excel does not compare values against expected criteria. Entering the wrong type of data values can produce inaccurate results when you apply any data analysis tool. To ensure users can only enter specific values in a cell or a range of cells, you can use the data validation options to prevent unacceptable entries. This is especially helpful in situations where you have multiple users entering data in the same worksheet. With data validation, you specify a range of allowable values, and if the user types something other than these values, Excel displays an error message and does not place the value in the cell.

You create the validation definition for the selected cells in the Settings tab of the Data Validation dialog box. Any value, the default in the Allow field, allows all entries. You

can change this to a specific data type. For example, if you want to allow currency values, such as $10.50, you select Decimal in the Allow field.

The Data field has operators that define the valid range of data. For example, if you select greater than, you type the minimum value allowed in the Minimum field. If you select the between or not between operators, both Minimum and Maximum fields display in the dialog box so you can define the range of the values to validate.

In the value fields, you must specify the valid values for the selected cells. Excel displays either one or two value fields based upon the selected operator in the Data field. You have two options for these fields. You can enter a constant in the field — any number or alphanumeric value, or you can select a range.

## Validate Data

① Select the range of cells for the validation definition.

**Note:** See Chapter 1 for information on selecting a range of cells.

② Click Data➪Validation.

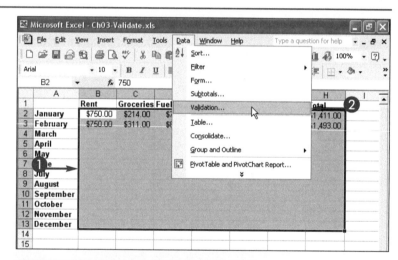

The Data Validation dialog box displays.

③ Select the desired data type from the Allow field.

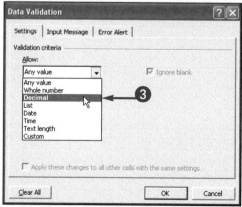

④ Select the appropriate operator from the Data field.

⑤ Type the appropriate validation value in the field or fields that appear.

Depending upon the operator selected, the Minimum, Maximum, or both fields display.

⑥ Click OK.

Excel displays an error message if a user types an invalid value.

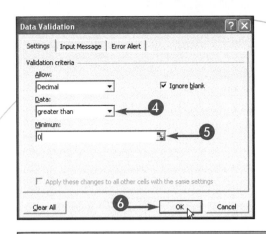

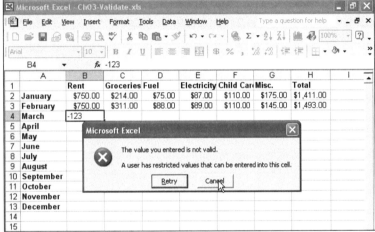

## Apply It

You can customize the error message that displays when a user types the wrong value in a cell. In the Error Alert tab of the Data Validation dialog box, you select the type of error that you want to display, specify a title for the message box, and type an error message.

Excel offers three types of error messages: Stop, Warning, and Information. The only difference between the three is the icon that appears on the message box. The title you type in the Title field appears at the top of the message box. If you do not enter a title, "Microsoft Excel" appears on the box. If you type a message in the Error message field, remember to include information about the valid values for the cell.

You can have a message display when a user selects a validation cell. You do so by typing the message in the Input Message tab of the Data Validation dialog box. Type a title for the message in the Title field and the text of the message in the Input Message field. For example, if you want a user to type a value between 1 and 10 in the cell, you create a message that reads: "Type a number between 1 and 10."

# Sum Cells with the AutoSum Button

You can apply the AutoSum button on the Standard toolbar to quickly sum adjoining cells in a worksheet. The AutoSum button helps an analyst automatically create a SUM function in the active cell. The range of cells in the formula always includes a cell that is adjoining the active cell.

When you activate the AutoSum button, Excel examines the cells' values and determines whether to sum the cells located to the left of the active cell or those above the active cell. For example, if cells D1 through D10 contain a list of numbers and the active cell is D11, when you select the AutoSum button, Excel creates a formula to sum the values in cells D1 through D10, and places the formula in D11.

In the worksheet, Excel draws a blue colored border around the cells that it will sum together. You can change the range to include more or fewer cells. If you modify the selected range of cells, an adjoining cell to the formula cell must remain part of the selected range. For example, if the formula is in cell D11, the range of cells must include either cell D10 or C11 because both of these cells adjoin D11. You can also modify the range of cells by manually typing a new range in the formula. See Chapter 1 for more on selecting a range of cells.

After you specify the range of cells to sum, you can accept or reject your entries using the Enter or Cancel buttons on the Formula bar. The result of the formula appears in the selected cell, and Excel moves to the next cell. If you are not familiar with building formulas in Excel, see Appendix D.

## Sum Cells with the AutoSum Button

### CREATE THE FORMULA

① Click the cell where you want to place the sum.

② Click the AutoSum button.

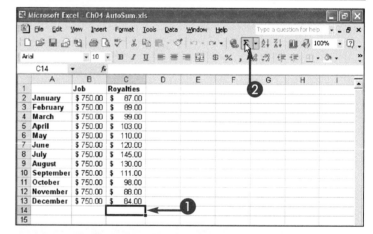

- Excel outlines the range of cells to sum.

- The formula contains the range of cells to sum.

③ Press Enter or click the Enter button to accept your entries.

- You can click the Cancel button to clear the Formula bar.

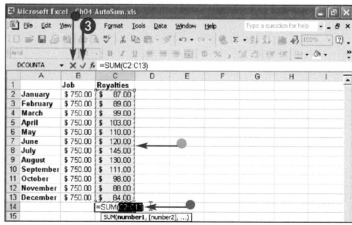

- A sum for the range of cells displays in the active cell.

## VIEW FORMULA

④ Click the cell in step 1.

- Excel displays the formula in the Formula bar.

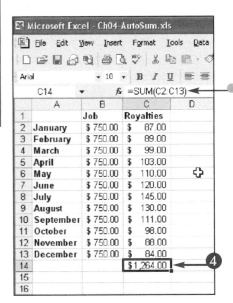

## Extra

Excel actually has four other common functions accessible via the AutoSum button ($\Sigma$) other than the Sum function, which you can apply using the steps in this section. Just like the SUM function, Excel applies the selected function to the adjacent cells when you select the cells in the adjoining row or column. The following table describes the available functions.

| FUNCTION | PURPOSE |
|---|---|
| Sum | Adds the adjoining cells and places the total in the selected cell. |
| Average | Determines the average value in the adjoining range of cells. |
| Count | Counts the number of numeric values in the adjoining range of cells. If any of the cells contain a non-numeric value, Excel ignores that cell. |
| Max | Finds the maximum value in the adjoining range of cells. |
| Min | Finds the minimum value in the adjoining range of cells. |
| More Functions | Displays the Insert Function dialog box. See the section "Add a Function via the Insert Function Dialog Box" for information on using the Insert Function dialog box to add a function. |

# Add a Function via the Insert Function Dialog Box

*F*unctions, which are pre-built formulas, help you analyze data because you can quickly insert calculations without manually entering them. Using the Insert Function dialog box is the easiest method for inserting functions because it alphabetically lists all of the functions available in Excel along with their arguments. *Arguments* are the values you must provide for the function to return the result. All you have to do is select a function, provide the appropriate arguments, and Excel does the rest.

You can search for a specific function using the Search field or select from one of Excel's pre-set categories. When you select a function, its description appears at the bottom of the dialog box along with any arguments. See Appendix D for more information about arguments and functions.

You use the Function Arguments dialog box to define the values you want to use for arguments. Excel displays each required argument in bold, as well as an argument description at the bottom of the dialog box. If the cells surrounding the active cell contain values, Excel places default cell references in the first argument field. You must provide a value for each required argument. You can either enter a constant value in the cell or specify a cell reference for the argument.

Excel also calculates the results of the formula based upon the specified arguments, and indicates that result at the bottom of the dialog box. When you see the appropriate result, you can close the Function Arguments dialog box and the Excel pastes the function in the selected cell.

## Add a Function via the Insert Function Dialog Box

① Click the cell where you want to place the function.

② Click Insert⇨Function (𝑓𝑥).

You can also click the Insert Function button insert button.

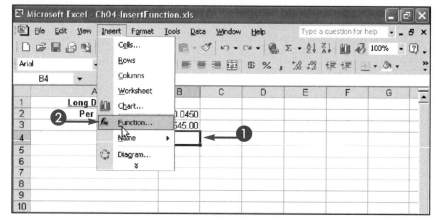

The Insert Function dialog box displays.

● You can search for a specific function using the search function.

You can select a category.

③ Click a function.

● Excel displays a description of the function.

● Excel provides arguments for the function.

④ Click OK.

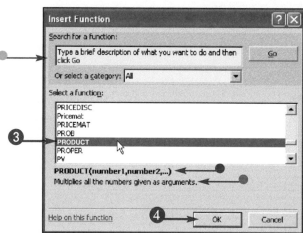

The Function Arguments dialog box displays with a list of required arguments and their descriptions.

⑤ Type the arguments in each argument field.

○ You can click the Collapse Dialog button and select the cells containing the arguments.

⑥ Click OK.

○ Excel places the formula in the selected cell.

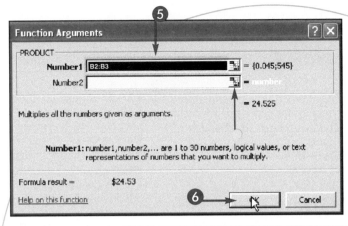

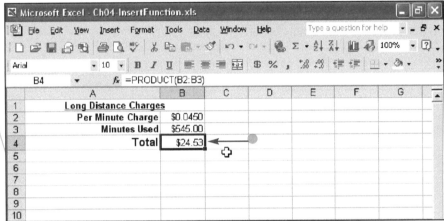

## Extra

Selecting almost any of the available Excel functions requires that you provide values for each argument. When you look at a formula that contains a function, you see the different arguments of the function enclosed in parentheses with a comma separating each individual argument. For example, the POWER function requires two arguments, the number to raise to the power, and the power. If you want to raise the value in cell A1 to the power of 3, you create a formula similar to the following:

**Example:**
=POWER(A2,3)

Some functions have a specific number of arguments, while other functions, such as SUM, allow you to specify up to 30 different argument values. In some instances, the function requires a variable number of arguments; as you type an argument in a field, Excel adds a new argument field.

You can specify the value for each argument either by typing the value directly in the argument field or by specifying a cell reference. See Chapter 1 for more on selecting ranges. If you have questions concerning a specific function or argument, you can utilize the Help on this function link to access Excel's help.

# Edit
# Formulas

After creating a formula in a cell, the data analyst can update it to accommodate new data. You can modify the cells a formula references, change its arguments, or move the formula to an entirely new cell within the worksheet. For more on working with functions and arguments in Excel, see Appendix D.

You can modify a formula and the arguments either by editing it directly within the worksheet, or if your formula includes a function, by using the Function Arguments dialog box. To modify a formula, you select the cell containing the formula. Alternatively you can select the cell and edit the formula in the Formula bar on the toolbar. This places the cursor in the cell, and highlights the cells that the formula references. Each argument of the formula displays in a different color in the formula, and the referenced cells are outlined in the same color, making it easy to identify each argument value.

You can change an argument of the formula in the Function Argument dialog box, which allows you to select new cell ranges for each argument. When you accept the changes, Excel updates the cell references. You access the Function Argument via the Insert Function button.

When you move data to a new cell on your worksheet, Excel copies the data and pastes it to the new location. All cell references in the formula, whether absolute or relative, remain the same. For example, if you move the formula =SUM(A1:A5), which has relative reference, in cell A6 into cell B6, the cell references in the formula remain unchanged. You move a formula simply by dragging it to a new cell. Excel moves any formatting with the data. For example, if the original cell containing the formula was Bold Arial 10pt, the new cell also displays the formula result in Bold Arial 10pt.

## Edit Formulas

### MODIFY A FORMULA

① Double-click the cell containing the formula.

Excel color-codes the referenced cells.

② Highlight the cell reference, and select a new one.

Excel changes the cell reference in the formula.

③ Press Enter to update the formula.

### CHANGE ARGUMENTS

① Click the cell containing the formula.

② Click the Insert Function button (ƒₓ) to display a dialog box.

**Note:** See "Add a Function via the Insert Function Dialog Box" for more information.

③ Type the desired range changes to the formula arguments.

④ Click OK to update the formula.

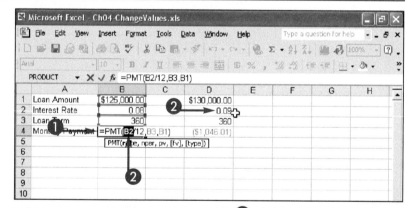

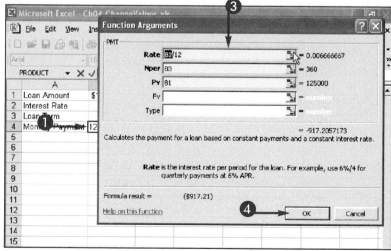

## MOVE A FORMULA

**1** Click the cell containing the formula you want to move.

**2** Click the edge of the border and drag to a new cell.

Excel outlines the new location in a dotted line.

**3** Release the mouse button.

● Excel pastes the formula in the new cell.

All cell references remain the same.

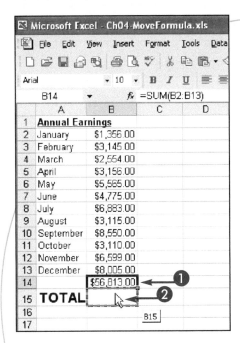

---

## Extra

To use the same formula in multiple cells, you can use the Fill Handle to quickly copy the formula to adjoining cells in the same row or column. This changes all relative cell references within the formula. For example, copying =SUM(A2:E2) from cell F2 to cell F3, results in: =SUM(A3:E3). The Fill Handle is the black box on the bottom-right corner of a selected cell. You simply drag it to an adjacent range of cells. Excel outlines the cells where the formula will copy with a dotted line. Excel copies the formula and any cell formatting to the new cells.

You can use named ranges instead of cell ranges in your formulas. You can type the name directly into a cell or into the Formula bar. You can also use named ranges in arguments by typing them into the Function Argument dialog box. See Chapter 1 for more information on creating named ranges.

If you create named ranges after creating a formula, you can convert the cell ranges to named ranges by selecting the cell and then clicking Insert⇨Name⇨Apply. The Apply Names dialog box displays the names within the workbook. Click OK to update the formula.

# Evaluate a Formula

I f the formula you create does not seem to return appropriate results, you can use the Evaluate Formula dialog box. This option allows you to step through the execution of the formula, letting you view how Excel applies each argument.

The Evaluate Formula dialog box displays the formula and the values you supply as arguments. For example, if you have a formula that sums the values in cells A1, B1, and C1, Excel displays the following in the dialog box:

=A1+B1+C1

You step through the calculation of the formula in the same order Excel uses to solve it. When your formula includes a function, Excels solves for each argument of the function, and then solves the rest of the formula. For example, when you apply the Evaluate button to the above example, Excel changes the formula to display the value of the first argument:

=4+B1+C1

When all arguments have values, Excel inputs the arguments into the function, solves the formula, and displays the result. You can repeat the process using the Restart button.

The Step In button allows you to the view the actual contents of the referenced cell before applying it to the formula by displaying it in a separate box. The Step Out button applies the argument to the function and continues the process.

The Evaluate Formula dialog box only allows you to view the execution of a formula; it does not allow you to modify the formula. If you want to change any portion of the formula, you must exit the Evaluate Formula dialog box to make modifications. See the section "Edit Formulas" for more on modifying the formulas in your worksheet.

## Evaluate a Formula

① Click the cell containing the formula to evaluate.

② Click Tools➪Formula Auditing➪Evaluate Formula.

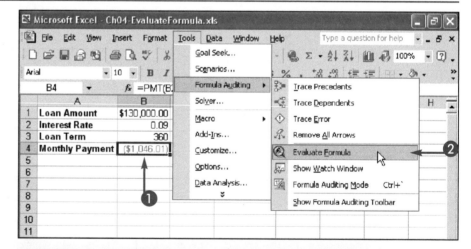

The Evaluate Formula dialog box displays.

③ Click Evaluate.

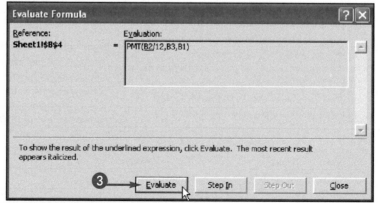

- Excel evaluates the first argument.

④ Continue clicking Evaluate to view the result of each argument.

- You can click Step In to view the contents of a referenced cell.

- You can click Step Out to continue the evaluation process after you have clicked Step In.

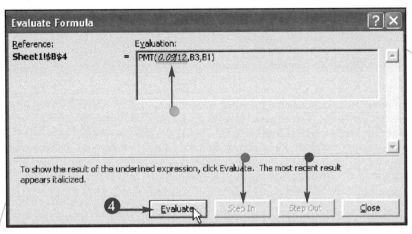

- When all arguments are calculated, Excel calculates the associated function and displays the result of the formula.

- You can click Restart to step through the formula again.

- Click Close to close the Evaluate Formula dialog box.

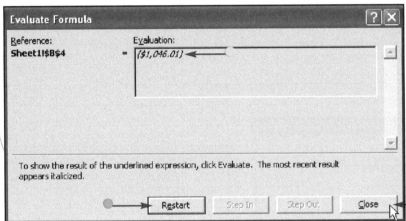

## Extra

You can view a graphical representation of your formula by clicking Tools➪Formula Auditing➪Trace Precedents. This option draws blue arrow from each cell containing an argument to the formula cell. By selecting this option, you can visually identify the exact cells required to make your formula execute properly. You can use this option only on one cell at a time.

If you want to find out which formulas use a specific cell as an argument, you can view a graphical representation of the cells by clicking Tools➪Formula Auditing➪Trace Dependents. This option draws blue arrows to each cell that contains a formula that uses the active cell as an argument. By displaying the dependent cells for a cell, you visually identify the formulas that require the cell. If you perform this option before deleting a value from a cell, you can quickly determine if your deletion affects any formulas on your worksheet. You can remove arrows that are drawn for dependents or precedents on a worksheet by clicking Tools➪Formula Auditing➪Remove All Arrows.

# Using Solver to Produce Specific Values

If you want to create a formula in your worksheet that produces a specific result, you can use the Solver option to determine the necessary argument values. This is a handy tool for the analyst who wants to determine how much of a product a division must sell to make a specific profit, or, using the PMT function, how much money to borrow and make a monthly payment of $1500 on a business loan.

In the Solver Parameters dialog box, you specify what cell, always the cell containing the formula, must produce the expected result. You must also define what results your formula must produce. You can have Excel solve the formula until it matches, is larger than, or is less than the specific end result value. For example, you can select the Value of option to find the values that return –1550 from the PMT function, which returns a negative value to indicate a payment amount.

To produce the desired results for your function, Excel changes the values of the cells referenced by your arguments; therefore, you must specify which cells Excel can modify. In the business loan example, if you want to change both the mortgage amount and the interest rates, you specify these cell references, and Excel calculates a solution by modifying them. When the Solver finds a solution, you can either apply the new cell values or return to the original values. Note that after you apply the Keep Solver Solution option, you cannot undo the changes to the cells.

The Solver option is an Excel Add-in, which means that by default, the option is not loaded. If you do not find it in the Tools menu, you can load it in the Add-ins dialog box. See Chapter 11 for more information on loading Add-ins in Excel.

## Using Solver to Produce Specific Values

① Click the cell containing the formula.

② Click Tools➪Solver.

The Solver Parameters dialog box displays.

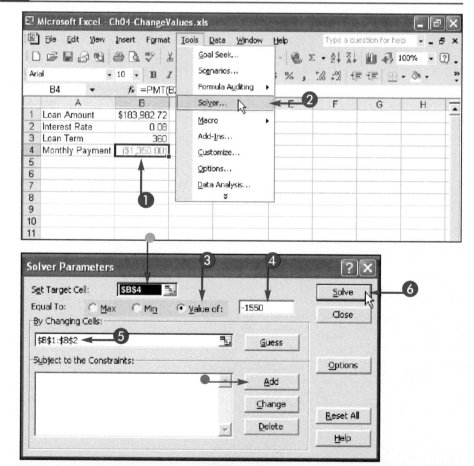

● The Set Target Cell field contains the formula cell reference.

③ Click an end result option.

④ Type the desired formula value in this field.

⑤ Type the range of cells to change.

● You can add constraints by clicking Add.

⑥ Click Solve.

The Solver Results dialog box displays.

⑦ Click the Keep Solver Solution option to apply the changes to the worksheet.

- To restore the original values, you can click this option.

⑧ Click OK.

- Excel permanently changes the values in the worksheet cells.

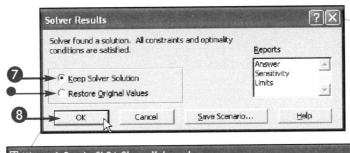

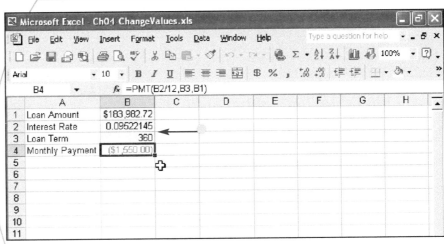

## Apply It

If you want to limit the changes that Excel can make to cell values or target cells, you can create *constraints*. For example, you can tell Excel that you want a decimal value in a cell to be less than .08.

You define constraints by clicking the Add button in the Solver Parameters dialog box. This displays the Add Constraint dialog box. In the Cell Reference field, specify the reference of the cell. Remember you only need to create constraints for the cells that Excel may change to solve your formula.

In the second field, you can select one of five operators.

In the Constraint field, specify the comparison value. For example, for the maximum decimal value you type .08 in the Constraint field. Click OK to close the Add Constraint field and apply your constraints.

| OPERATOR | PURPOSE |
|----------|---------|
| <= | The cell must be equal to or greater than the constraint. |
| = | The cell must be equal to the constraint. |
| >= | The cell must be equal to or less than the constraint. |
| Int | The cell must be an integer. |
| Bin | The cell must be binary. |

# Create a
# Conditional Formula

If you only want Excel to perform a calculation when a cell contains a specific value, you can create a *conditional formula*. A conditional formula returns a one value if the condition is True, and a different value if the condition is False. For example, an analyst may ask Excel to calculate the net sales on an item only after a certain number have sold, or the Shipping department may create a formula that calculates a different shipping cost depending upon the price of the item.

You create a conditional formula using the IF function. There are three different arguments for the IF function, but only the first two are required:

`=IF(logical_test, value_if_true, value_if_false)`

For the `logical_test` argument, you must specify an argument that returns a logical value of either True or False. For example, you can see if a cell value is greater than 125 by typing **A1>125** as the argument. You can use any combination

of cell references, operators, constants, or even other functions to create the arguments. For example, you can use the SUM function to determine if the total of a series of cells is greater than 450 by typing **SUM(A1:A5)>450**.

For the `value_if_true` argument, you specify the value that the formula should return if the `logical_test` is True. You can also define an argument for the `value_if_false` argument if you want the function to return a value when the `logical_test` argument is False. With both of these arguments, if you want to return a text string value, you must place the return string in quotation marks. For example, the following formula places the value True in the formula cell if thevalue of A1 is larger than 100, and False if the value of A1 is less than or equal to 100:

`=IF(A1>100, "TRUE", "FALSE")`

Excel also has a way to build conditional formulas with the convenience of a wizard. For more on the Conditional Sum Wizard, see Chapter 11.

## Create a Conditional Formula

① Click the cell for the formula.

② In the Formula bar, type **=IF(**.

③ Type the condition you want to check.

- As you type, the syntax for the function displays under the Formula bar.

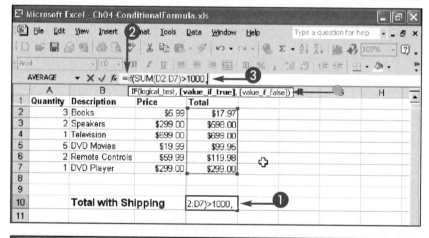

④ Type the value if the condition is True.

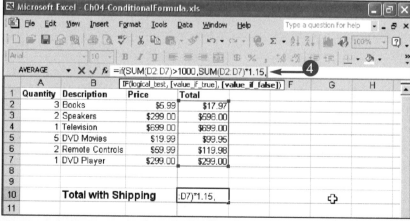

⑤ Type the value if the condition is
False.

⑥ Type ).

⑦ Press Enter.

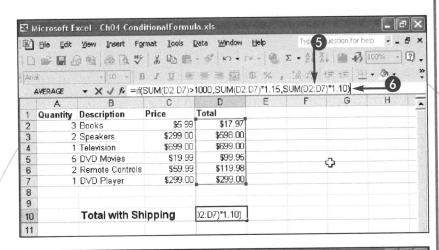

● Excel creates the formula and
displays the appropriate result
after checking the condition.

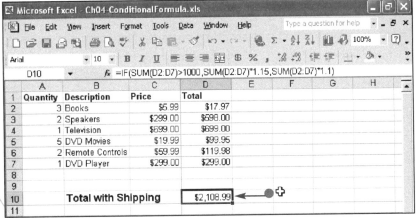

## Apply It

If you want to check for multiple conditions, you can use what is commonly referred to as *nested IF function statements*.
When you nest the IF functions, you specify an IF function as the value of either the `value_if_true` or the
`value_if_false` argument. You can combine, or nest, up to seven levels of IF functions within one formula.

The following example checks that a price falls within a specific range. The example uses two IF functions. The
value of the `Value_If_True` argument is the second IF Function. The first IF function checks A1 to see if it is
larger than 100. If so, the second IF statement checks if A1 is over 200. If this condition is met, Excel multiplies
A1 by 110%. If the value is between 101 and 200, Excel adds 25 to the value in A1. If the value is less than 100,
Excel adds 10, using the `Value_If_False` argument of the first IF statement. The following table provides a
quick look at what Excel does based upon the value in A1.

| TYPE THIS | | | |
|---|---|---|---|
| `=IF(A1>100, IF(A1<200, A11.1, A1+25), A1+10)` | | | |

→

| RESULT | | |
|---|---|---|
| **A1 VALUE** | **CALCULATION** | **RESULT** |
| 50 | 50+10 | 60 |
| 125 | 125+25 | 150 |
| 225 | 225*1.1 | 250 |

# Solve a Formula with a Data Table

If you want to compare how different values affect the results for an argument, you can do so by creating a data table. For example, an analyst can use this function to determine monthly payments on a loan at different interest rates. When you create a data table, you can use what-if comparisons to see the value of a formula when arguments contain different values.

To use a data table to solve a formula, you must create a table that contains at least two columns or two rows. If you use columns, the first column contains the values you want to substitute into an argument of the formula. The second column contains the formula in the first cell. If you use rows, you need to place the substitution values in the first row.

When you create the formula, the argument you want to substitute needs to reference the first value in the data table column. For example, if column A contains interest rates to substitute into a PMT function, the Rate argument must reference the first cell in column A as shown in the following sample formula:

`=PMT(A2/12, E3, -E2)`

In the Table dialog box, you specify the row or column containing the substitution values. You specify the substitution values by entering the first cell in the column or row. If your table contains the substitution values in a column, you place the first cell in the column in the Column Input Cell field. If values are in a row, you place the first value in the Row Input Cell field.

## Solve a Formula with a Data Table

① Type the substitution values in a column.

You can also place values in a row.

② Type the formula in the first cell of the next column.

If your values are in a row, type the formula in the first cell in the row under values.

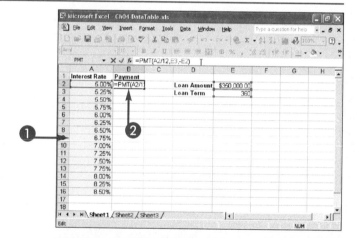

③ Select the cells containing substitution values and the formula.

**Note:** See Chapter 1 for more on selecting cells.

④ Click Data⇨Table.

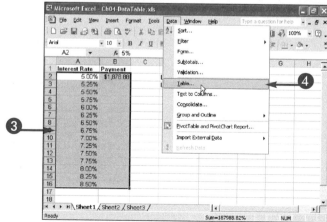

The Table dialog box displays.

⑤ Type the cell reference of the first substitution cell.

● You can type the cell reference in this field for values in a row.

⑥ Click OK.

● The comparison results display in the second column of the data table.

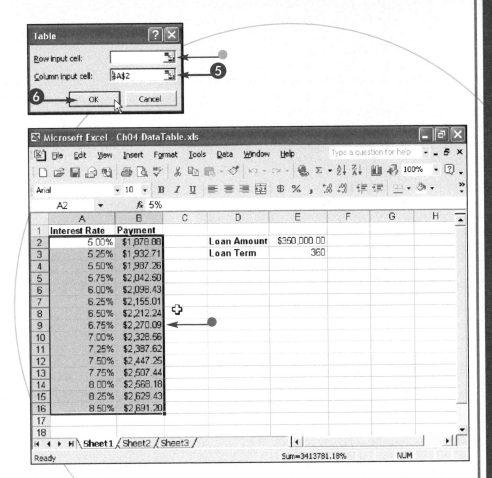

| | A | B | | C | D | E |
|---|---|---|---|---|---|---|
| 1 | Interest Rate | Payment | | | | |
| 2 | 5.00% | $1,878.88 | | | Loan Amount | $350,000.00 |
| 3 | 5.25% | $1,932.71 | | | Loan Term | 360 |
| 4 | 5.50% | $1,987.26 | | | | |
| 5 | 5.75% | $2,042.50 | | | | |
| 6 | 6.00% | $2,098.43 | | | | |
| 7 | 6.25% | $2,155.01 | | | | |
| 8 | 6.50% | $2,212.24 | | | | |
| 9 | 6.75% | $2,270.09 | | | | |
| 10 | 7.00% | $2,328.56 | | | | |
| 11 | 7.25% | $2,387.62 | | | | |
| 12 | 7.50% | $2,447.25 | | | | |
| 13 | 7.75% | $2,507.44 | | | | |
| 14 | 8.00% | $2,568.18 | | | | |
| 15 | 8.25% | $2,629.43 | | | | |
| 16 | 8.50% | $2,691.20 | | | | |

Sum=3413781.18%

## Apply It

If you want to substitute values for two different arguments in a formula, you can create a two-input data table. In a two-input data table, you specify the first set of substitution values in the column under the formula cell and the second set of substitution values in the row to the right of the formula. For example, if you want to see how both different interest rates and loan terms affect your payments, you specify the interest rates in the column under the formula and the loan term values in the row next to the formula.

When you create a two-input data table, your formula must initially reference cells outside the data table. This means if your data table contains interest rates in a column, the formula must initially reference a cell outside the column containing an interest rate value. In the Table dialog box, you specify both the row and column initial input cells.

# Trace a
# Formula Error

**W**hen you create formulas within a worksheet to analysis data, Excel evaluates all arguments of the formula and returns a value. If Excel cannot properly evaluate the formula, it displays one of the default error messages in the formula cell. Because most formula errors are a result of values in other cells, Excel lets you trace the error. Excel's Trace Error feature visually steps you through which formulas reference which cells. When you select this feature, Excel draws blue arrow lines from the formula cell to each cell that the formula references. If a referenced cell contains a formula and that formula also contains an error, Excel draws a red line between the formula cells. To view the cells that a second formula references, you can select the Trace Cells option again. By seeing which cells your formulas reference, you can often spot the cell value that produces the formula error.

Typically an error occurs when the formula refers to an invalid cell value. For example, if the cell contains the formula =A1/A2 and cell A2 contains the number 0, Excel returns the error message #DIV/0!, which indicates that the formula attempted to divide by zero. See Appendix D for a description of the Excel error messages.

If you are unable to spot the cause of the formula error with the trace arrows, you can edit the cell to display the color-coding of the formula arguments to aid in locating the cell. If the formula contains a function, as you modify the formula, Excel displays the formula syntax under the cell. You simply make the desired modifications to the formula cells to eliminate the display of the error. See the section "Edit Formulas" for more information on editing the arguments of a formula.

## Trace a Formula Error

① Click the cell containing the formula error.

- An Error button displays next to the formula error cell when you select it.

② Click Tools➪Formula Auditing➪Trace Error.

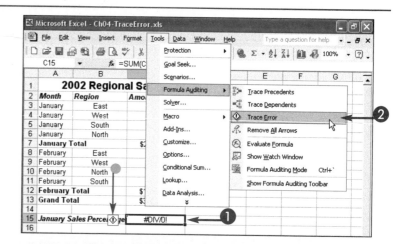

- Excel creates arrows between the argument cells and the formula cell.

③ Double-click the formula cell.

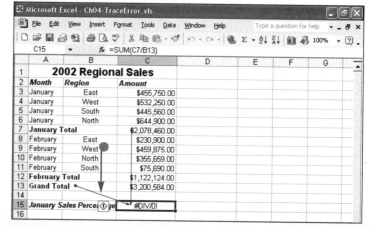

- Excel color-codes each cell in the formula.

④ Make the appropriate modifications to the correct the formula error.

**Note:** See the section "Edit Formulas" for more information.

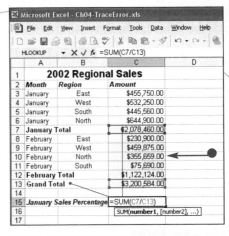

Excel removes the arrows and displays the value of the formula, if an error no longer exists in the formula.

---

## Apply It

Formula errors can occur with any formula you create. If you create a worksheet where other users input data for analysis, you may want to eliminate the display of error messages in the cells on the worksheets. By doing this, the errors still occur, but instead of displaying the error message, you can specify the value that displays in the cell. For example, you may want the cell to have a value of zero if there is an error. To control the display of the error messages, you modify each formula using the combination of the IF function, which allows you to check for a condition, and the ISERROR function, which allows you to see if a cell contains an error. For example, to return a value of 0 if there is an error, with the formula A1/A2:

| TYPE THIS |
|---|
| `=IF (ISERROR(A1/A2), "0", A1/A2)` |

| RESULT |
|---|
| With this formula, if the value that the ISERROR function returns is TRUE, a value of zero displays in the formula cell; otherwise the value of dividing A1 by A2 displays in the cell. See Appendix B for more information on using the IF and ISERROR functions. |

# Look Up a Value in a Specific Row and Column

I f part of your data analysis entails locating a specific value within a row or column of a data list, you should consider using Excel's lookup worksheet functions. Excel provides two functions you can use to locate a value in either a specific row or column: HLOOKUP and VLOOKUP. The function you select is based upon whether your data list contains column headings in the first row, or row headings in the first column.

You use the HLOOKUP function when you have column headings in the first row of the data list. Excel locates the specified column, based upon the column heading specified, and then returns the value in the specified row. The HLOOKUP function has four arguments of which Excel requires the first three arguments. The last is optional.

HLOOKUP(lookup_value, table_array, row_index_num, [range_lookup])

The lookup_table argument identifies the column heading for the desired column. You can make the value text, a number, or even a logical value. Excel does not differentiate between upper and lowercase text. The table_array argument identifies the range of cells containing the data list. Excel uses the first row in the range as the heading row. The row_index_num argument specifies the number of the row within the data list to return. If the value of the argument is 2, Excel returns the second row of the data list, not the second row in the worksheet. The optional range_lookup argument lets you define whether you want an exact match or the closest match. If the value is False, Excel only returns a value if it finds an exact match to the value that the lookup_table argument specifies.

Although the following example illustrates the use of the HLOOKUP function, the VLOOKUP works the same, with the exception that you make selections based upon a row heading in the first column of the data list.

## Look Up a Value in a Specific Row and Column

① Open a worksheet that contains the data list you want to search.

② Select the formula cell.

③ Click Insert➪Function.

The Insert Function dialog box displays.

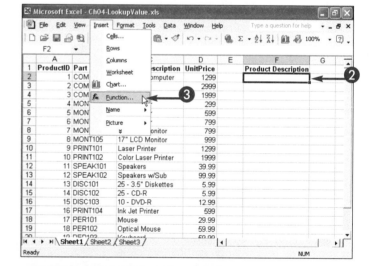

④ Select the HLOOKUP function.

To locate a value based upon the row heading, select the VLOOKUP function.

**Note:** See the section "Add a Function via the Insert Function Dialog Box" for more information.

⑤ Click OK.

The Function Arguments dialog box displays.

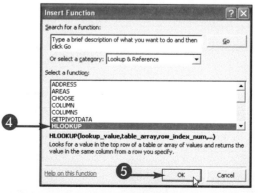

6  Specify the column heading value in the Lookup_value field.

7  Specify the range of cells for the data list in the Table_array field.

8  Specify a number representing the desired row in the Row_index_num field.

For VLOOKUP, specify the column number.

● If desired, type **False** in the Range_lookup field to find an exact match for the Lookup_value argument.

9  Click OK.

● The value in the specified row and column displays in the selected formula cell.

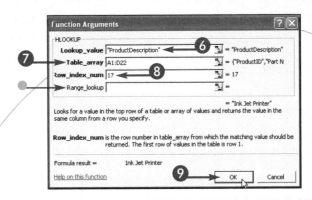

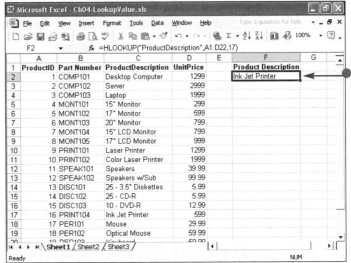

## Extra

When looking up specific values in a data list, Excel provides another function that you can use to return values called the LOOKUP function. You can use the LOOKUP function when you do not know the row or column location of the value you want to locate. The LOOKUP function provides two formats, a vector format and an array format.

With the vector format, you can specify a value you want to locate and the column or row in which you want to locate it. You also specify the column or row containing the matching value you want to return. The vector format of the function has the following syntax with an optional Result_vector parameter:

**Example:**
```
=LOOKUP(Lookup_value, Lookup_vector, [Result_vector])
```

For example, if you specify a value of 11 for the Lookup_value, with a Lookup_vector of column A and a Result_vector of column C, Excel returns the value in column C located on the same row and the value 11 in column A.

The array format finds the values you specify in the first column and returns the value on the same row in the last column of the specified range in the Array field. This version of the function has the following syntax:

**Example:**
```
=LOOKUP(Lookup_value, Array)
```

# Determine the Location of a Value

To determine the location of a specific value within a row or column of a worksheet, you can use the MATCH worksheet function. This function is important when your data analysis requires you to know the location of a specific value, or its closest match.

The Match function syntax includes three arguments, of which the first two are required. The last is optional.

```
=MATCH(lookup_value, lookup_array,
[match_type])
```

The `lookup_value` argument defines the value you want to locate within the specified range of cells. You can specify a number, text, logical value, or a cell reference containing the value you want to locate. The `lookup_array` defines a range of contiguous cells, referred to as an array, in a row or column to search.

The optional `match_type` argument defines how Excel compares the value from the `lookup_value` argument to the range of cell values if it cannot find an exact match. If you omit the argument, or if the argument contains a value of 1, Excel finds the largest value that is less than or equal to the `lookup_value`. For Excel to find the closest match, you must first sort the list of cell values in ascending order. If the value of the `match_type` argument is 0, Excel must find an exact match. If the value is -1, Excel returns the smallest value that is greater than or equal to the `lookup_value`. With a value of -1, you must sort the list of cell values in descending order. See Chapter 2 for more on sorting your data.

When you use the MATCH function, it returns an integer value that identifies the location of the value within the specified range of cells. For example, if Excel returns the value 2 and the specified range of cells in A4 through A24, cell A5 contains the value, or the closest match.

## Determine the Location of a Value

① Open a worksheet that contains the data list you want to search.

To find the closest match, sort the list in ascending or descending order.

**Note:** See Chapter 2 for more information on sorting your data.

② Select the formula cell.

③ Click Insert⇨Function.

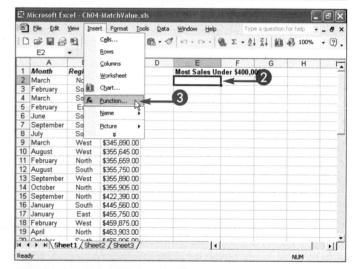

The Insert Function dialog box displays.

④ Select the MATCH function.

**Note:** See the section "Add a Function via the Insert Function Dialog Box" for more information on this dialog box.

⑤ Click OK.

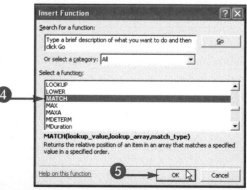

The Function Arguments dialog box displays.

**6** Specify the value to find in the Lookup_value field.

**7** Specify the range of cells to search in the Lookup_array field.

● If desired, type 0 to find an exact match, 1 to find largest value less than specified, or -1 to find smallest value less than specified.

**8** Click OK.

● Excel returns an integer value representing the cell location of the value within the range of cells.

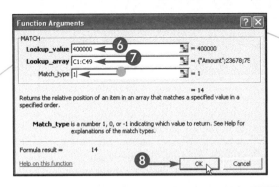

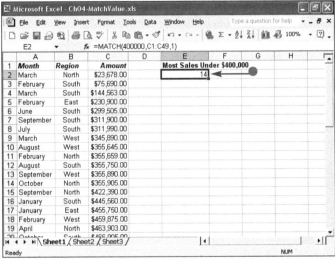

## Apply It

You can combine the results of the MATCH function with other functions to locate related values within a data list. For example, you can use the row value that the MATCH function returns to determine which month had the highest sales figures under $400,000. To do this most effectively, you combine the MATCH function with the INDEX function. The following formula has the MATCH function representing the Row_num argument of the INDEX function. See the section "Return the Value at a Specific Location in a Data List" for more information on the INDEX function.

**TYPE THIS**

```
=INDEX(A1:C49, (MATCH(400000,C1:C49,1)),1)
```

**RESULT**

The INDEX function returns a cell value from the data list range A1:C49. The MATCH function locates the row value, and 1 specifies the column number, which in this case is Column A.

To find the location of specific text within a worksheet row or column, you use the wildcard characters of an asterisk, *, to match multiple characters or a question mark, ?, to match a single character. With these characters, you must specify a value of 0 for the match_type argument.

**TYPE THIS**

```
=MATCH(ch*t, A1:A25, 0)
```

**RESULT**

Excel finds the first value in the cell range that starts with "ch" and ends with "t."

# Return a Value at a Specific Location in a Data List

If you have a data list sorted in a particular order, such as daily sales totals, you may want to find a particular value based upon its location in the list. To determine the value of a specific cell within a data list, you can use Excel's INDEX workbook function. For example, you can find the value within the second row and third column of a particular range, and have Excel place the value in the cell that you specify. If your range of cells is A2 though D10, the INDEX function returns the value in cell C3 because that is the cell in the second row and third column of the specified range of cells.

The INDEX function has two different formats: the array form and the reference form. You use the array form of the INDEX function when you want to locate values from an array, or contiguous block of cells. For example, you would consider the range A1:C10 an array of cells because it is one continuous block. The array form of the function has the following syntax:

=INDEX(array, row_num, [column_num])

The array argument denotes the range of cells. The row_num argument is an integer value of the row number within the range that the array argument specifies. The column_num argument is an integer value specifying the column number, and it is optional.

To work with multiple cell ranges that are not contiguous, such as A1:B5 and D1:E5, you use the reference version of the INDEX function, which has the following syntax:

=INDEX(reference, row_num, [column_num], [area_num])

You use the reference argument define one or more non-contiguous cell ranges. To specify multiple cell ranges, you enclose each cell range within parentheses. The optional area_num argument defines an integer value, and is the cell range where you want to find the value. For example, if the value of area_num is 2, Excel finds the value in the second range at the designated row and column. Both the column_num and area_num arguments are optional.

## Return a Value at a Specific Location in a Data List

① Open a worksheet that contains the data list you want to search.

② Select the formula cell.

③ Click Insert⇨Function.

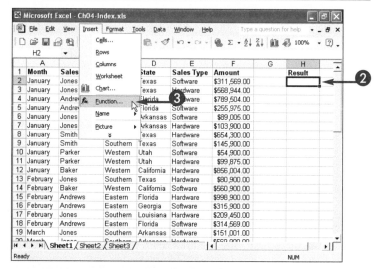

The Insert Function dialog box displays.

④ Select the INDEX function.

**Note:** See the section "Add a Function via the Insert Function Dialog Box" for more information.

⑤ Click OK.

The Function Arguments dialog box displays.

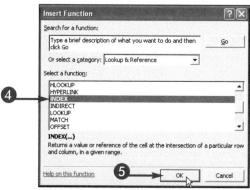

**6** Specify the cell references in parentheses with a comma between each reference.

**7** Specify the row number of the desired value in the Row_num field.

**8** Specify the column number in the Column_num field.

**9** Specify the cell reference to use. If omitted, Excel uses the first cell reference.

**10** Click OK.

● Excel returns the value of the cell within the specified location.

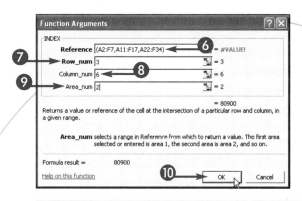

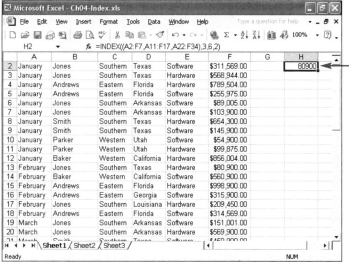

## Apply It

To quickly find a value in a data list when you do not want to manually create a formula, you can use the Lookup Wizard option, which allows you to find a value based upon the row and column labels. By selecting a particular row and column heading, Excel creates a formula that returns the intersection. The Lookup Wizard is available as part of the Add-Ins that come with Excel. See Chapter 11 for more information.

After you load the Lookup Wizard Add-in, you can click Tools⇨Lookup to run it. The Lookup Wizard consists of four different steps, or pages. On the first page, you specify the range of cells you want to search. On the second page you select the appropriate column and row labels. This wizard works best if you have unique row and column labels. If you have duplicate row or column labels, the wizard may return the wrong value.

Next, you specify the formula's cell location. Excel creates a formula with the INDEX and MATCH functions, as illustrated in the following sample. The MATCH function returns the row_num and column_num argument values for the INDEX function.

**Example:**
```
=INDEX(B1:F20, MATCH("Andrews",B1:B20,), MATCH("Amount",B1:F1,))
```

# Rank a Value within a Data List

If you want your data analysis to rank the values within a data list, you can accomplish this using the RANK worksheet function. For example, you can determine how a sales person's total sales ranks in comparison to other sales people.

The RANK function has three arguments, of which the first two arguments are required. The `order` argument is optional.

`=RANK(number, ref, [order])`

The `number` argument specifies the number you want to rank. Keep in mind, that if the list contains duplicate numbers, those numbers are assigned the same rank. For example, if you have the list 4, 6, 5, 6, 8, 9, the number 6 has a rank of 3, but the number 8 has a rank of 2 because 6 appears in the list twice. The `ref` argument specifies the list of numbers that you want to use for the ranking. Excel ignores any non-numeric values in the list.

The optional `order` argument specifies the sorting order used to rank the number specified by the `number` argument. The value of the `order` argument can be any number. Although the `order` argument specifies a sort order, the list is not actually sorted. If the value of `order` is 0, or omitted, Excel ranks the number as if the list were sorted in descending order. This means that Excel specifies how the number compares to the largest numbers in the list. For example, if you list contains the numbers 35, 56, 97, 23, 15, 25, 31, and you want to rank the number 35 in descending order, the RANK function returns the value 3. If the `order` argument is another number, Excel ranks the number as if the list were in ascending order.

Excel also has a Rank and Percentile Add-in. For more on using this feature, see Chapter 11.

## Rank a Value within a Data List

1. Open a worksheet that contains the numbers you want to rank.

2. Select the formula cell.

3. Click Insert⇨Function.

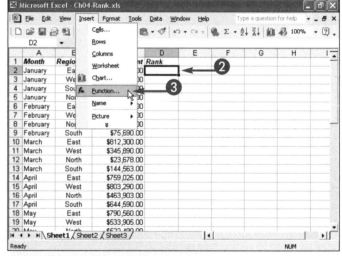

The Insert Function dialog box displays.

4. Select the RANK function.

**Note:** See the section "Add a Function via the Insert Function Dialog Box" for more information.

5. Click OK.

The Function Arguments dialog box displays.

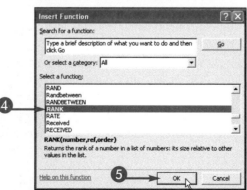

**6** Specify the number that you want to rank either as an actual number or a cell reference.

**7** Specify the reference of the range of cells containing numbers that you want to rank in the Ref field.

- You can type **0** to sort data in a descending order, or any other number to sort data in an ascending sort order.

**8** Click OK.

- Excel gives the ranking for the specified number.

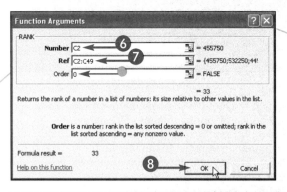

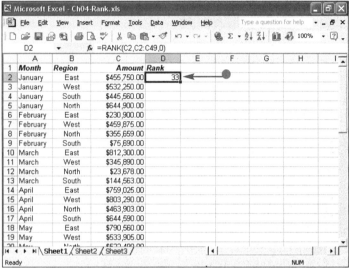

## Extra

The RANK function is one of several statistical functions that determine how a number compares to other numbers within a list:

| FUNCTION | DESCRIPTION |
|---|---|
| MEDIAN(number1, [number2]...) | Finds the middle number within a list of numbers in ascending or descending order. |
| QUARTILE(Array, Quart) | Excel displays a value for this argument between 0 and 4 where 0 is the smallest value in the list, 1 is the value larger than one-fourth of the values, 2 is larger than one-half, etc. |
| MAX(number1, [number2],...) | Finds the largest number in the list. |
| MIN(number1, [number2], ...) | Finds the smallest number in the list. |
| LARGE(array, k) | Finds the value that is a specific size in relation to the largest value. For example, a value of 3 for the k argument returns the third largest value. |
| SMALL(array,k) | Finds the value that is a specific size in relation to the smallest value. For example, a value of 2 for the k argument returns the second smallest value. |

To have Excel automatically analyze your data with 16 different statistical calculations, see Chapter 11.

# Create an Amortization Table for a Loan

A common data analysis task is to analyze the terms under which a company borrows money to acquire assets. You can use Excel to quickly figure out the monthly payment amount and to set up an amortization table so that you can quickly analyze the amount of interest and principal paid over the life of a loan. After you create the table, you can quickly change the analysis to reflect a different loan or interest rate.

Excel provides several financial functions for calculating loan information. The PMT function calculates the payment required for each period to repay the loan in a timely manner. The IPMT function determines the amount of interest paid for each period. The PPMT function finds the amount of principal paid each period. Appendix B has more information about the syntax of the PMT, PPMT, and IPMT functions, but the basic order for the PPMT and IPMT function is:

```
Function(interest rate, payment period,
total periods, loan total)
```

The data inside the parentheses is described to Excel through special arguments; for example, the payment period is `per`. The PMT function differs from the PPMT and IPMT functions in that it does not use the `per` argument.

When entering the formulas for the functions, remember to use absolute cell references for the cells in which you have entered the total loan amount, interest rate, and total number of payment periods, but a relative entry for the specific payment period. Appendix D has more information on absolute versus relative cell references. Also remember that you should make the interest rate in the formula the interest rate charged for each payment period. For example, if you have a monthly payment, you calculate the period with a formula dividing the cell with the annual interest rate by 12.

## Create an Amortization Table for a Loan

① Specify your initial loan amount, annual interest rate, and number of periods.

The loan amount is your `pv` value, and the number of periods is your `nper` value.

② In the Payment amount cell, type **=-PMT()**.

③ In the parenthesis, type in order the cell reference for the rate divided by the appropriate annualizing number, the cell for the `nper` value, and the cell for the `pv` value.

Excel calculates the payment amount.

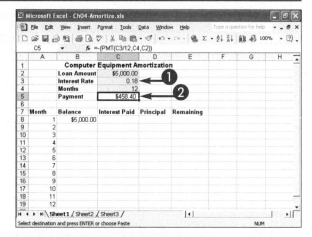

④ Create a table with the desired amortization information, including columns for period, balance, interest, principal payment, and remaining balance.

⑤ Set the initial Balance value equal to the `pv` cell reference.

⑥ In the interest cell, type **=-IPMT(rate, per, nper, pv)**, substituting with your `rate`, `per`, `nper`, and `pv` references.

**Note:** Use absolute cell references for the `rate`, `pv`, and `nper` values. See Appendix D for more on absolute cell references.

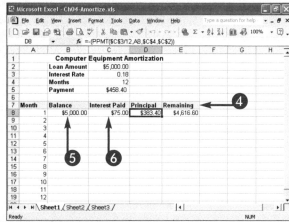

**7** In the principal cell, type **=-PPMT(rate, per, nper, pv)**, replacing the arguments with values.

Add the minus sign to the formulas to display a positive amount.

**8** In the Remaining cell, type a formula that subtracts the Principal cell from the Balance cell, in this example, =B8-D8.

**9** Set the next Balance cell equal to the result of step 8, here =E8.

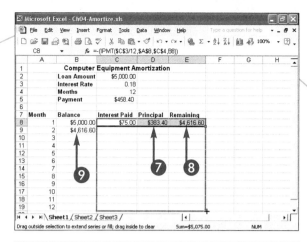

**10** Select the formula cells in the first row and copy them to the second row.

**11** Select the Balance cell and the formula cells in the second row and copy them down to the end of the table.

**Note:** See Chapter 1 for more on copying and pasting cells.

Excel duplicates the formulas in the remaining cells, and, if calculated correctly, the remaining balance for the final period displays as 0.

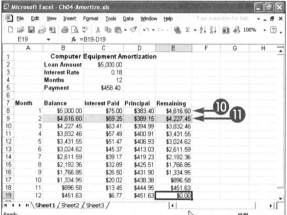

## Extra

The PMT, IPMT, or PPMT functions all have the same arguments, with the exception of the PMT function which does not use the per argument. The following table provides a description of each argument used by these functions.

| ARGUMENT | DESCRIPTION |
|---|---|
| rate | The rate charged for each period or payment. If payments are monthly, you divide the annual interest rate by 12. |
| per | The period, or payment month, for which you want to calculate the interest amount. |
| nper | The total number of periods or payments on the loan. For example, a 5-year loan with monthly payments has 60 periods. |
| pv | The total amount of the loan. |
| fv | The remaining balance on the loan when the last payment is complete. If this is 0, you can omit this argument. |
| type | An optional argument to define if payments are made at the beginning or end of each period. If omitted or 0, Excel calculates interest and payments based on a payment at the end of the period. If the value of the argument is 1, Excel calculates interest based on payments at the beginning of each period. In a table, you must use the same type value for all formulas. |

# Link Data to Other Windows Programs

You can quickly copy text and images from virtually any other Microsoft Windows document and paste them directly into Excel for analysis using the Copy and Paste commands. You can then link the Excel worksheet to the other document.

When you paste data from another program, Excel inserts the data directly into the selected cell and attempts to maintain any original formatting. Excel separates text containing hard returns and tabs into different cells starting at the location of the tab or hard return.

The Paste command only places a copy of the original selection into the worksheet. To prevent having to re-copy and re-paste any updates or modifications to the original text, you can use the Paste link option in the Paste Special

dialog box. This option creates a link from the copied data in your worksheet back to the original file. Excel monitors the original document for any changes, and reflects them immediately in the copied data in the worksheet.

Pasting data in your worksheet as a link requires that you keep all of the pasted text intact. You can apply any formatting to the pasted data, but you cannot separate any links that it may contain once you have it in Excel. For this reason, this option does not work well for data analysis.

You only use the Paste link option when you copy data from a program that supports Object Linking and Embedding (OLE), a technology that links information between different programs.

## Link Data to Other Windows Programs

① In the desired Microsoft Windows program, select the data you want to copy into Excel.

② Click Edit⇨Copy.

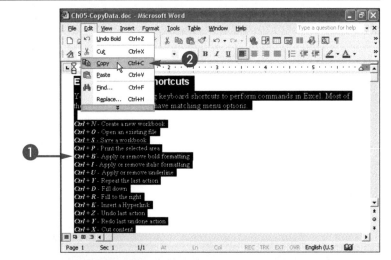

③ In Excel, select the cell where you want to paste the copied data.

④ Click Edit⇨Paste Special.

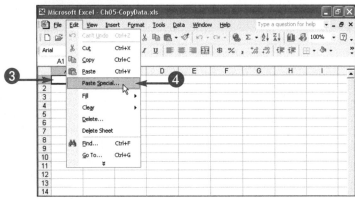

The Paste Special dialog box displays.

**5** Click the Paste link option to create a link to the original document.

● You can click the Paste option if you do not want to create a link.

**6** Click the format of the data you want to paste.

**7** Click OK.

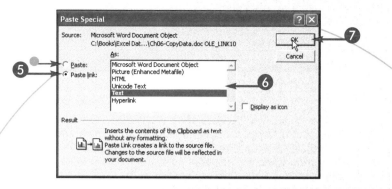

● Excel pastes the data into the selected cell.

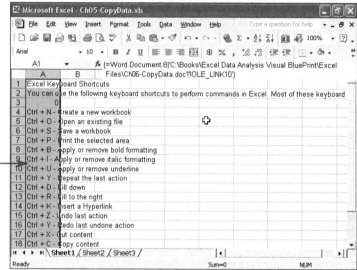

## Extra

The paste options in the Paste Special dialog box vary depending upon the original source of the copied data. For example, if you copy a picture on a Web page, you can only paste a bitmap into the worksheet. The following table lists some of the most common paste options for the Paste Special dialog box.

| PASTE OPTION | DESCRIPTION |
| --- | --- |
| Bitmap | Pastes the selected picture as a bitmap image in the worksheet. |
| HTML | Pastes the selected data in HTML format. |
| Microsoft Word Document Object | Uses OLE to paste the selected data in an object that you can modify using Microsoft Word commands. |
| Picture (Enhanced Metafile) | Smaller than a bitmap, this format pastes the selected data as a picture. |
| Text | Pastes the copied data as text only. Any formatting that existed in the original data does not transfer to the Excel cells. |
| Unicode Text | Pastes the copied data using Unicode characters. Unicode is a character set that you can use with nearly every written language in the world. |
| Hyperlink | Inserts the selected data with a hyperlink back to the original document. When you click the hyperlink, the original document opens. |

# Import a
# Delimited Text File

A data analyst commonly needs to use data from programs other than Excel. Because you can export text files with most programs, text files become the surest method for importing any data into Excel for analysis. You can import any text file directly into Excel, which allows you to open data from different programs, including those that have file formats that Excel cannot open. You create a text file by exporting only the text portion of a file, omitting any formatting and graphics in the file. After you have your data in Excel, you can edit and format it to suit your worksheet.

When you import a text file, Excel displays the Select Data Source dialog box, which you use to locate the file. After you specify the type of file you want to import, only files that match that type display in the dialog box.

Next, Excel displays the Text Import Wizard, which helps you to specify any import options you want to apply to the file. The first thing you must decide is whether you want to delimit your imported text with a character, such as a comma or tab, or organize it in fixed-width columns. Options in the Import Wizard either place the character of your choice between columns of data or align fields with spaces between them.

To aid you in laying out the file, Excel displays a preview with any changes you apply. The preview window numbers each row of data so you can determine which rows you want to import, thus eliminating the unwanted text that some programs place at the beginning of a text file. After you select a row number, Excel imports the text file from the specified row to the end of the file.

## Import a Delimited Text File

① Click Data➪Import External Data➪Import Data.

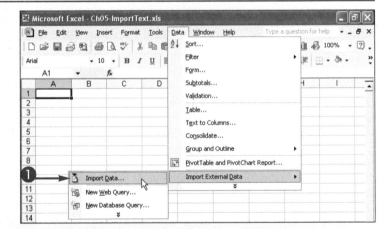

The Select Data Source dialog box displays.

② Select the Text Files file type.

● You can click New Source to start a wizard that connects to remote data sources.

③ Locate the folder containing the text file to import.

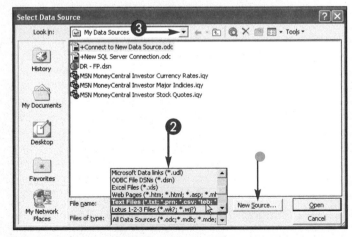

④ Click the desired text file.

⑤ Click Open.

Excel displays the Text Import Wizard.

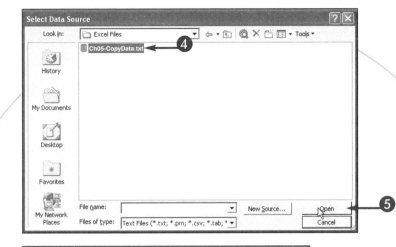

⑥ Click the Delimited option.

● If the text has fixed widths between fields, you can click the Fixed width option.

**Note:** Selecting the Fixed width option results in a different wizard.

⑦ Type the first row to import.

⑧ Click Next.

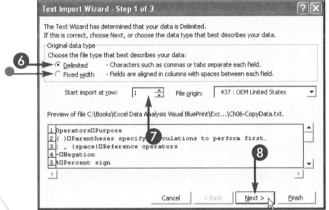

## Extra

The Select Data Source dialog box lets you import data from several different data types. Excel displays a different wizard or dialog box depending upon what you select in the Files of type field. The following table briefly describes each of the file types that Excel can import.

| FILE TYPE | DESCRIPTION |
| --- | --- |
| Office Database Connection | Microsoft Office database connection files |
| Access Databases/Projects | Microsoft Access files |
| Microsoft Data Links | Contains OLE DB data source connection information |
| ODBC File DSNs | Contains ODBC data source connection information |
| Web Pages | Connection to Web pages to import tables |
| Text Files | Text files exported from other sources |
| Lotus 1-2-3 Files | Spreadsheet files from Lotus 1-2-3 |
| Paradox Files | Spreadsheet files from Paradox |
| DBase Files | DBase database files |
| Web Queries | Files for querying data directly from the Internet |
| OLAP Queries/Cube Files | OLAP database query files |
| XML Files | XML formatted data file. |

continued →

**O**n the second page of the Text Import Wizard, you can tell Excel how to divide the text into columns. The options that display on the second page vary depending upon whether you selected the Delimited or Fixed width option.

If you select the Delimited text option, the second page of the wizard requests the delimiter characters that represent column breaks in the text file. You can select multiple column delimiters. For example, if you select Tab and Comma, Excel inserts a column break at the location of every comma and tab character in the text. As you select options, the Data Preview window moves the text into columns to illustrate how Excel will import the text file.

If you want to split the text at an exact location, for example, exactly at the fifth character, you have the option of selecting the Fixed width option on the first page of the

wizard. With this option, you manually insert breaks. See the section "Divide a Column into Multiple Columns" for more information on this option.

The final page of the Text Import Wizard shows how Excel will import the text file. By default, Excel applies the General data format to the entire text file. You can define what data format you want Excel to apply to each column. If a column contains a specific type of value, you can select the column, and then select the desired data format. For example, if one column contains date values, you can select the Date option, and then specify the format of the dates in the column.

Finally, Excel takes you to the Import Data dialog box, where you must select where you want to import the contents of the text file. You can either import the text file into the current worksheet or create a new worksheet.

## Import a Delimited Text File (continued)

Excel displays the next page of the Text Import Wizard.

⑨ Click the appropriate delimiter options for the text file.

You can click multiple delimiter options.

● The Data Preview window shows the effect of your selections.

⑩ Click Next.

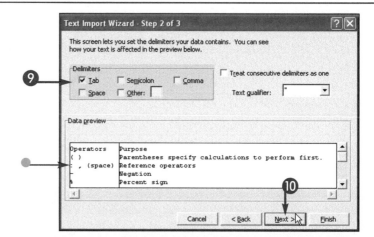

The final page of the Text Import Wizard displays.

⑪ To specify a column format, click the column, and then click the appropriate data format.

⑫ Click Finish.

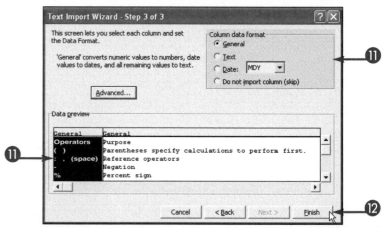

The Import Data dialog box displays.

⑬ Click an option to designate where you want your data.

⑭ Click OK.

Excel imports the data using the column break information specified.

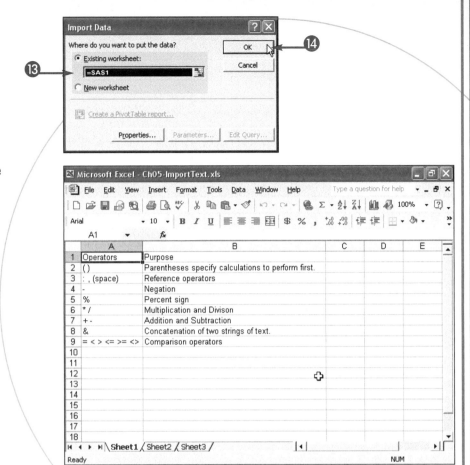

## Extra

When you import files containing numeric values, be mindful of the characters that represent the decimal and thousands separator. By default, Excel uses the Regional and Language Options in the Control Panel of your computer to determine how to interpret numbers. For example, in the United States, the default number format uses a comma as a thousands separator and a period as a decimal separator. So Excel interprets the number $1,300.45 as one thousand three hundred dollars and forty-five cents.

When you import a file containing numbers, make sure you use the same separators as those set up on your computer. If the imported file uses different separator values, you must make that distinction before importing data so that Excel can properly interpret the numbers.

To select the separators, click the Advanced button on the last page of the Text Import Wizard. This displays the Advanced Text Import Settings dialog box. Select the separator that the data file uses for both the Decimal Separator and the Thousand Separator. As Excel imports the file, it converts the numbers to match the separators specified on your computer.

# Divide a Column into Multiple Columns

You can use the Text to Columns option to easily split data in any column in your worksheet. An analyst finds this option most useful when he or she imports or pastes data, and Excel does not divide it properly into the appropriate columns. Although the option name implies the division of an entire column, you can use it with any cell selection within a column. For example, you may want to divide a column containing first and last names into two columns by using the space between the two as the delimiter.

You find the options for dividing data in the Convert Text to Columns Wizard. To divide one-column text into multiple columns, you define the delimiter that Excel will use to separate your data. If the text lines up evenly, you select the Fixed width option, and the second page of the wizard allows you to select the exact location of the split. Be aware that a fixed-width column splits at the same location throughout the column. For example, if you want to split the text after the fifth character, Excel splits every selected cell at the same location.

If your file contains a delimiter, such as a comma or tab character, you define it in the wizard. See the section "Import a Delimited Text File" for more information on working with delimited data.

When you divide the data in a column, Excel copies the data values into the corresponding columns to the right of the selection. If these columns contain data, Excel replaces them with your new data. If you do not want to overwrite the existing column data, you must insert new columns for the data before selecting the Text to Column option.

## Divide a Column into Multiple Columns

① Select the desired range of cells.

**Note:** See Chapter 1 for more on selecting a range of cells.

② Click Data⇨Text to Columns.

The Convert Text to Columns Wizard displays.

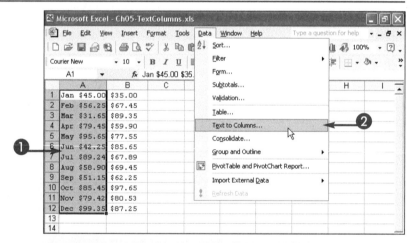

③ Click the Fixed width option.

● If the text has a delimiter between values, you can click the Delimited option.

**Note:** Selecting the Delimited option results in a different wizard. See the section "Import a Delimited Text File" for more on this option.

④ Click Next.

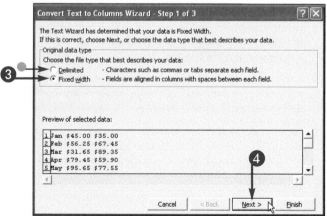

The next page of the wizard displays with break lines separating your data based on what you have in the cell.

**5** Click the Data preview window to insert a column break line.

You can click a line and drag it to a new location.

**6** Click Next.

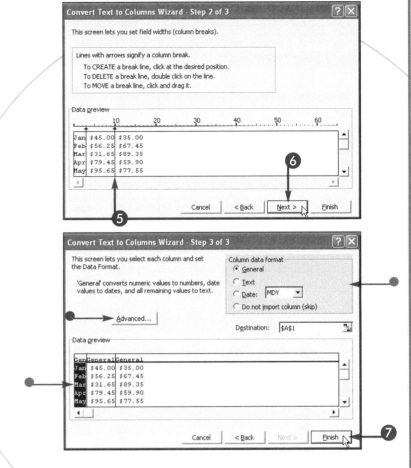

The final page of the wizard displays.

- To specify a column format, click a column and click the appropriate data format.
- You can click Advanced to define numeric separators for your data.

**7** Click Finish.

Excel breaks the specified column into multiple columns.

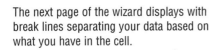

## Apply It

If you do not want to keep part of the text in your worksheet, you can eliminate it during the conversion process by skipping the corresponding column. You must place the unwanted text in a separate column on the second page of the Convert Text to Columns Wizard. In the final page of the wizard, you must select the column and click the Do not import column option (skip) (○ changes to ⦿ ). When you click Finish, all the columns marked Skip are ignored.

If you want to maintain the original column, you can paste the converted text in a separate location. In the Destination field in the last page of the Convert Text to Columns Wizard, you can specify where to locate the converted text. If you want to place the text in another location, you can type the cell reference in the field or click the Collapse Dialog button and select the new location. You only need to specify the first cell of the new location. When you paste the converted text in a new location, the original column of text remains unchanged in the worksheet.

# Create a
# Web Query

I f you want to place text from a Web site in a worksheet, you can create a *Web Query*. With a Web Query, you can copy any text into your worksheet for analysis. For example, you can copy the latest stock quote information from a financial Web site.

The New Web Query dialog box works similar to any Web browser. You type the address of any Web site and view the associated Web pages. The dialog box analyzes each Web page and breaks it into individual tables of data. Little yellow arrow buttons display next to each section of the Web page. You use the buttons to identify the portion of the Web page that you want to import. The icon changes to a green check button to identify your selections.

Keep in mind that Excel only imports the text portion of the Web page. If you want to capture any of the graphics on the Web page, you must do so using the copy and paste commands. See the section "Link Data to Other Windows Programs" for more information on copying graphics.

You must indicate the location for importing the data from the Web page. By default, Excel selects the active cell as the location for the imported data. If the existing worksheet contains data, Excel adds enough columns to contain the imported data. Any existing worksheet data moves to the right into new columns. Alternatively, you can select the New Worksheet option to create a new worksheet for the data. If you create a new worksheet, Excel inserts the worksheet in the current workbook.

## Create a Web Query

① Click Data⇨Import External Data⇨New Web Query.

The New Web Query dialog box displays.

② Type the URL of the desired Web site.

③ Click Go.

④ Click the yellow arrow button to select data for import.

- Click the button in the upper-left corner if you want to import the entire Web page.

Excel highlights the data, and the yellow button changes to a green check mark.

⑤ Click Import.

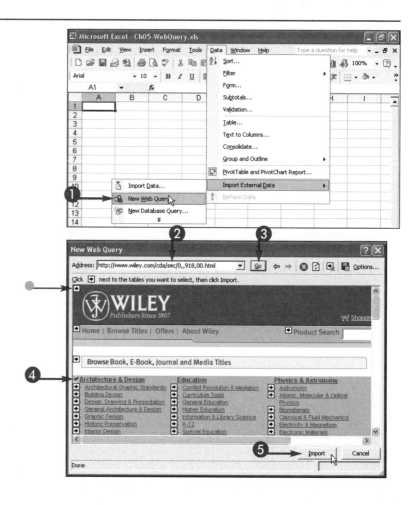

The Import Data dialog box displays.

⑥ Click Existing worksheet option to import data into the current worksheet.

⑦ Type the cell reference for the first cell of imported data, or select it with the Collapse Dialog button.

● To place the imported data in a new worksheet, click New Worksheet.

⑧ Click OK.

The worksheet contains the imported Web data.

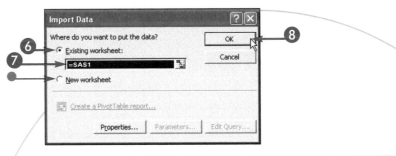

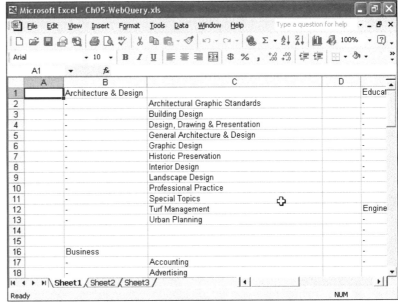

## Apply It

You can import the text formatting along with the Web page data. Click the Options button in the New Web Query dialog box. In the Web Query Options dialog box that displays, select one of the following formatting options ( ○ changes to ⦿ ).

| FORMATTING | DESCRIPTION |
|---|---|
| None | Imports the text only and applies the Normal format style. |
| Rich Text | Imports the text with the formatting on the Web page. |
| Full HTML | Imports the text with all HTML styles, including links. |

If you want to use a Web page query in other worksheets, you can save it with all of the selections specified in the New Web Query dialog box. To save a Web query, click the Save Query button (🖫) in the New Web Query dialog box. In the dialog box that displays, type the desired query name, select a folder location, and click Save.

You apply a Web query by clicking Data⇨Import External Data⇨Import Data. In the Select Data Source dialog box, select the query and click Open. In the Import Data dialog box, select the desired location for the new query and click OK.

# Import a Database Table

To prevent having to manually enter data for analysis from another program, you can copy data directly from an external database into Excel. Databases use tables to store related values, similar to the format of an Excel list. For example, a database table containing product information may have columns for the Product Name, Price, and Description. As you insert new records into a database table, the program adds a value to each column of the table. In a product database, a record exists for each product. The individual column values are fields in the database.

You can import database tables from any of the database formats supported by Excel, such as an Access database or an ODBC database. To import a table, you locate the corresponding database file in the Select Data Source dialog box.

To connect to a database table, you must have access to it. In a corporate environment, this may require changes to

database security. If you cannot do so, you may need to contact your Database Administrator.

You can only import one database table at a time into your worksheet. If you want to import the entire database, you must repeat the import process for each database table. When you select a table, Excel imports the contents of the entire table into the worksheet. If you want to import only records that match specific criteria, you must create a database query. See the section "Using Queries to Screen External Databases" for more information.

Excel imports the table data into the worksheet by placing each field in a separate column and each record on a separate row. You can use any of the formatting options to format the data values. See Chapter 1 for more information on formatting a worksheet.

## Import a Database Table

① In the Select Data Source dialog box, click the desired database.

**Note:** See the section "Import a Delimited Text File" to access this dialog box.

② Click Open.

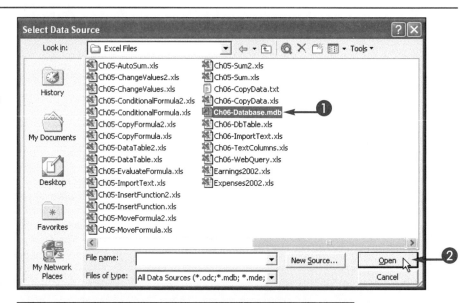

The Select Table dialog box displays a list of the database tables.

**Note:** The Select Table dialog box does not display if there is only one database table. Skip to step 5.

③ Click the desired database table.

④ Click OK.

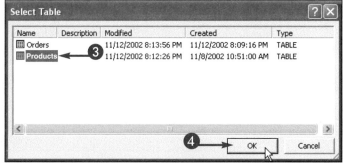

The Import Data dialog box displays.

**5** Click the Existing worksheet option to import into the current worksheet.

**6** Type the cell reference for the first cell of imported data, or select it with the Collapse Dialog button.

● To place the imported data in a new worksheet, you can click the New worksheet option.

**7** Click OK.

The worksheet contains the contents of the imported database table.

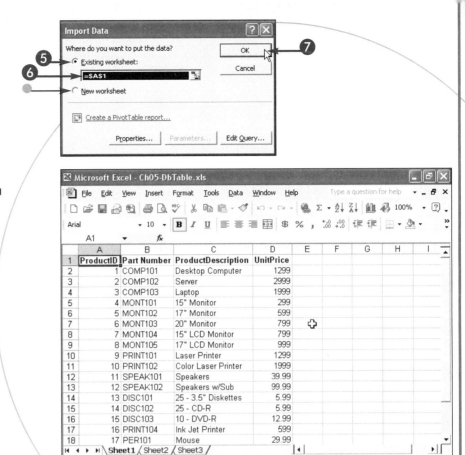

## Extra

By default, when you import data from a database table, Excel actually creates a database query definition with the specified values. For example, if you import a table called Products from the Company database, Excel creates a query file named `Company Products.odc`. The query file contains information about the database and your selected table. If you want to import the same database table again, you can simply select the query file.

You can set up a query file in the External Data Ranges Properties dialog box. This dialog box displays when you click the Properties button in the Import Data dialog box. If you type a file name in the Name field and click the Save query definition option (☐ changes to ☑ ), Excel creates the query file with your designated filename.

When Excel imports a database table, the field names appear in the first row of your worksheet. If you do not want to import the field names, you can deselect the Include field names option (☐ changes to ☑ ) in the External Data Range Properties dialog box.

# Using Queries to Screen External Databases

I f you want to import data from an external database that matches only specific criteria, you can create a database query. This allows you to import only the data records that you want to analyze, eliminating records that are of no value to you. For example, you can import all products under $1,000. You also can import data records from multiple database tables with one database query, and you can specify that you want Excel to import only specific columns. For example, you may want only product name and price columns from several database tables containing product information.

When you create a database query, you must first specify the *data source name*, or DSN, which is simply the name of the data source that you want to query and how to query it. For example, if you import data from a Microsoft Access database, you must select the MS Access Database as your data source.

The easiest way to create a database query is through Excel's Query Wizard. To activate the wizard, select the Use the Query Wizard to create/edit queries option in the Choose Data Source dialog box. The Query Wizard steps you through the process of creating the query. If you do not select this option, you must use Microsoft Query directly to create your database query. Microsoft Query is a separate program designed to create database queries. The Query Wizard links directly with Microsoft Query and simplifies the process of creating the database query by stepping you through the process.

You can select the database that matches a certain data source type in the Select Database dialog box. For example, if you select a Microsoft Access data source, you can import only an Access database. You can search for databases on any drive to which you have access.

## Using Queries to Screen External Databases

**①** Click Data➪Import External Data➪New Database Query.

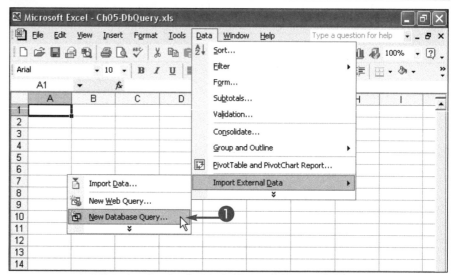

The Choose Data Source dialog box displays a list of available data sources.

**②** Click the data source for the database to query.

**③** If not selected, click the Use the Query Wizard to create/edit queries option.

**④** Click OK.

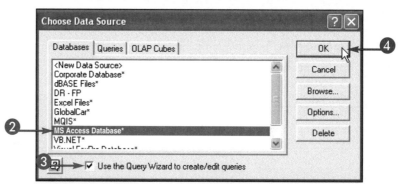

The Select Database dialog box displays.

**5** Click the folder containing the desired database.

**6** Click the database you want to import.

**7** Click OK.

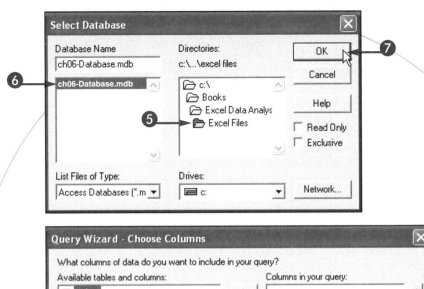

The Choose Columns page of the Query Wizard displays.

**8** Click the plus sign next to the database containing columns you want to import.

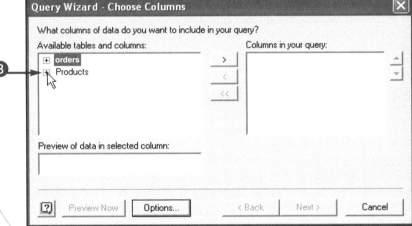

## Extra

To apply a query, you must have access to the database, and an *ODBC*, or *Open Database Connectivity*, data source for the database on your computer. An ODBC data source contains drivers to connect to the database as well as connection information, which, depending upon the database type, includes the database location and the appropriate logon information.

When you install a database application, such as Microsoft Access, on your computer, a corresponding data source is created. If you have a custom database, such as an SQL database, you may need to create a data source. To create a new data source, click the <New Data Source> in the Choose Data Source dialog box. From the Create New Data Source dialog box, select the driver that corresponds to the type of database to which you want to connect. In the Final field of this dialog box, you can also select to which default table you want to connect when you use the data source. When you click Connect, the dialog box that opens varies depending upon the database type you select. You may need to specify the required logon information.

continued →

You can use the Query Wizard to design a query definition for a selected database. The Query Wizard lets you select the columns you want to import from each table in the database. You can also create filters for the data as well as specify how to sort the data as it imports into Excel.

You can import any combination of columns from the database. Excel imports the columns into your worksheet in the order you list them in the Columns in your query box in the Choose Columns page of the wizard. The first column in the box imports as the first column in your worksheet. You can reorder the columns by moving them up or down in the list.

The most useful feature of the Query Wizard is the database filter, which limits Excel to import only those records that meet specific criteria. Although this is not a necessary step, if you do not filter the data, Excel imports the entire database. You can create up to three definitions for any of the selected columns, but if you have more than one filter, you must specify how to join the definitions.

You join definitions with either an And or an Or option. If you select And, the record value in the selected column must meet both of the filter requirements before Excel imports the data.

If you join the filter definitions with Or, only one of the definitions must be true before Excel imports it.

---

## Using Queries to Screen External Databases *(continued)*

- The columns within the table display under the selected table name.

**9** Click a column name.

**10** Click the Select button to add the column to your query box.

Repeat steps 9 and 10 for each column you want to import.

**11** Click Next.

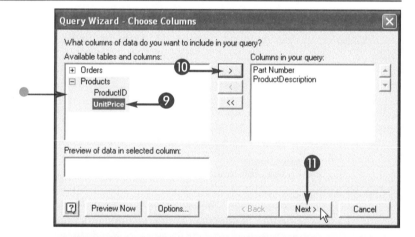

The Filter Data page of the Query Wizard displays.

**12** Click the column you want to filter.

**13** Select the desired filter operation from the available list.

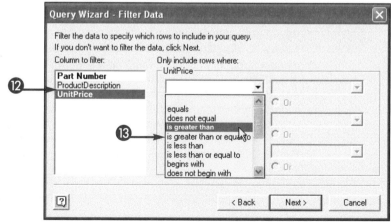

14 Type the comparison value in the field, or select a value from the existing database column values.

● You can further define your filter by clicking a join relationship and repeating steps 13 and 14 for each additional filter.

15 Click Next.

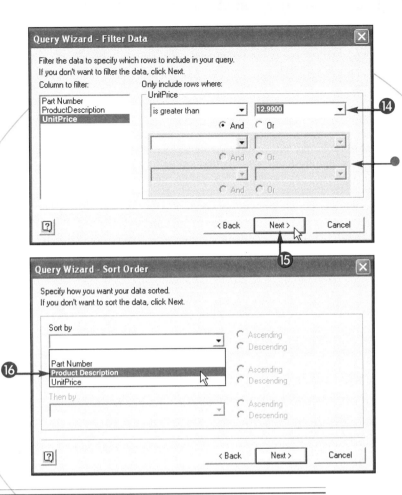

The Sort Order page of the Query Wizard displays.

16 Select a column by which you want to sort.

## Extra

In the Choose Columns page, you can view a sample of the data contained in a particular column. To do so, click the column and then click the Preview Now button. A preview displays in the Preview of data in selected column box. You must perform the same steps for each column you want to preview.

If you want to import an entire table from the database, you can do so by clicking the table name and then clicking the Select button in step 10 of this section. When you do this, the names of all columns in the table display in the Columns in your query box. Excel adds the column names in the order they appear in the database.

If the database you are querying contains several tables, you can display the table names in alphabetical order to make it easier to locate. To change the order of the tables, click the Options button in the Choose Columns page to display the Table Options dialog box. Click the List Tables and Columns in alphabetical order option (☐ changes to ☑ ). If you do not select this option, Excel lists the tables in the order specified by the database.

continued →

You can arrange your query to control how Excel orders your data as it enters your worksheet. For example, you may want to sort the data records so that they display alphabetically based upon their part name. You can sort the data in ascending or descending order by selecting any of the database columns. For more about sorting as well as Excel's built-in sorting rules, see Chapter 2.

You can specify up to three different sorts in the Sort Order page of the Query Wizard and specify a different sort order for each one. Excel sorts data records sort using the Sort by definition first. It then sorts using the Then by definitions.

The Finish page of the Query Wizard presents three options for determining where Excel imports your database. Because you want to analyze the data within Excel, you

always select the first option. The other options allow you to analyze the database data using other programs.

You must indicate where you want to place your imported data. By default, Excel designates this location as the active cell. If the active worksheet already contains data, Excel adds columns for the imported data and moves existing data to the right of these newly created columns. You have the option of creating a new worksheet for the data. With this option, Excel inserts the new worksheet in the current workbook. You can also create a PivotTable report with the imported database information. PivotTables provide an interactive table where you can quickly combine and compare large amounts of data records, making them a good tool for analyzing data imported from a database. See Chapter 8 for more information on creating PivotTables.

## Using Queries to Screen External Databases (continued)

⑰ Click either Ascending or Descending to sort the database in the order you want.

⑱ Repeat steps 15 and 16 for each sort definition.

⑲ Click Next.

The Finish page of the Query Wizard displays.

⑳ Click Return Data to Microsoft Excel.

㉑ Click Finish.

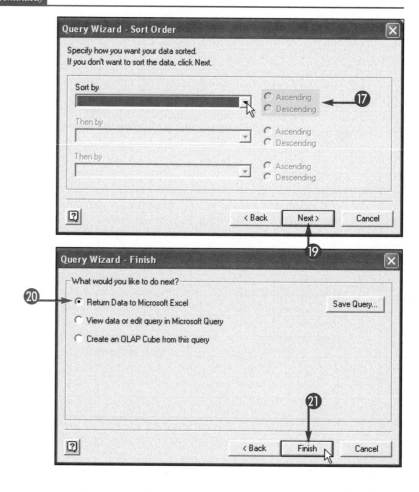

The Import Data dialog box displays.

㉒ Click Existing worksheet to import into the current worksheet.

- To place the imported data in a new worksheet, click New worksheet.

㉓ Type the cell reference for the first cell of imported data.

㉔ Click OK.

The worksheet imports the contents of the database columns.

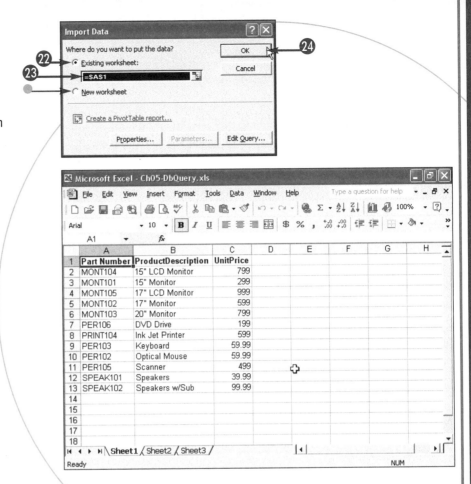

---

## Extra

You can save your database query definition so that you can reuse it to perform the same query again. You save a query by clicking the Save Query button in the Finish page of the Query Wizard. In the Save As dialog box, you can specify a name and location for the query definition file. All database query files have the extension .dqy.

You can run the saved query at any time by clicking Data⇨Import External Data⇨ Import Data. In the Select Data Source dialog box that opens, you locate the appropriate database query file and click Open. In the Import Data dialog box, specify the location for the data.

If you want to modify the database query, click the Edit Query button in the Import Data dialog box. In the Query Wizard that displays lists all of the current settings for the database query, and you can make any modifications in any page of the wizard.

If you want to keep any of the changes you make to the query definition, you must save it again by clicking the Save Query button. You can either update the current definition file or create a new file.

# Find the Average of a Database Range

To find the average of specific imported database records, you can create a formula using the DAVERAGE function in your worksheet. An analyst can use this function to average only the records that match certain criteria. For example, if you have an imported database list of computer equipment, you can find the average of the computer monitors in the list. Although Excel calls this a database function, you can use it with any data list. See Chapter 2 for more information on working with data lists in Excel.

There are three different arguments for the DAVERAGE function, and you must specify values for each of the arguments:

=DAVERAGE(database, field, criteria)

You must indicate the range that contains the imported database values for the database argument. Also, because Excel uses the column labels to match the information specified for the criteria argument, you must select the column labels as well as the database values. You reference the cell containing the label for the column of values you want to average as the field argument. You can also specify a number, identifying the column position in the selected list of the values. For example, to use the first column, you type 1 for the value of the field argument.

Finally, you must create a range of cells containing your criteria values. The criteria definition must consist of at least two rows. The first row contains the column labels that you want Excel to use for your results. The second row contains any criteria values. See p. 52–53 for more on criteria values.

## Find the Average of a Database Range

① Type the column headings for the database list.

② Type the criteria under the corresponding column label.

③ Select the formula cell.

④ Click Insert➪Function.

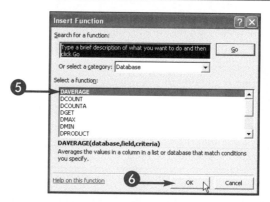

The Insert Function dialog box displays.

⑤ Select the DAVERAGE function.

**Note:** See Chapter 4 for more information on inserting functions.

⑥ Click OK.

The Function Arguments dialog box displays.

**7** Specify the reference for the `Database` argument.

**8** Specify the cell reference for the `Field` argument.

**9** Specify the range of cells containing the criteria definition.

**Note:** To learn how to specify a range, see Chapter 1.

**10** Click OK.

● The average displays for the records that meet the specified criteria.

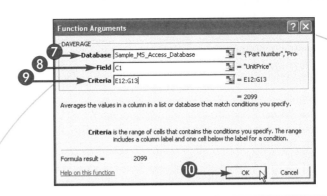

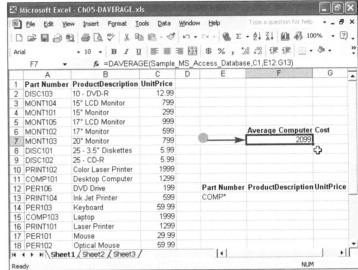

---

## Extra

The DAVERAGE function is one of twelve database functions that Excel provides to evaluate manually created or imported databases. All of the functions require the same three argument values. The following table gives a brief description of the other database functions.

| FUNCTION | DESCRIPTION |
| --- | --- |
| DCOUNT | Counts the number of cells that contain numeric values and match the criteria. |
| DCOUNTA | Counts the number of cells that contain a value and match the criteria. |
| DGET | Returns the cell value that matches the specified criteria. |
| DMAX | Finds the largest number in the column that matches the criteria. |
| DMIN | Finds the smallest number in the column that matches the criteria. |
| DPRODUCT | Multiplies the values that match the criteria and returns the product. |
| DSTDEV | Finds the standard deviation of a sample of the values that match the criteria. |
| DSTDEVA | Finds the standard deviation of the entire list of values that match the specified criteria. |
| DSUM | Totals the values that match the criteria and returns the sum. |
| DVAR | Estimates a sample variance of the values that match the criteria. |
| DVARP | Estimates a population variance of the values that match the criteria. |

# Save
# for Web

You can make your data analysis results available to other viewers by saving your worksheets and workbooks to the Web so that colleagues can view them on the Internet. When you save your data, you need to create an HTML page. HTML, *Hyper Text Markup Language,* is a standard format you can use to create Web pages and that all Web browsers can interpret. When you select that file format, Excel saves your workbook selection as an HTML page.

When you save your workbook as a Web page, you can save either the current worksheet or the entire workbook. Keep in mind, if you decide to save the entire workbook, Excel saves each worksheet as a separate HTML page. If one of the worksheets in your workbook is blank, Excel creates a blank worksheet. Therefore, you may consider removing any blank worksheets from your workbook before saving them as Web pages.

When you save in the HTML file format, you can create either a static or interactive version of your workbook. With *static* pages, users can only view the content of the workbook. You should select this option when you want to share analysis data, but you do not want other users to alter it.

With an *interactive* HTML version of the workbook, you provide each viewer the option of altering the page's contents. The Web page displays a toolbar specifically for the purpose of modifying data. If you save a PivotTable or PivotChart as an interactive HTML page, the user can apply filtering to the areas to retrieve the desired results. See Chapter 7 for more information on PivotTables. See Chapter 8 for more information on PivotCharts.

## Save for Web

### CREATE HTML FILE

①  Click File➪Save As.

The Save As dialog box displays.

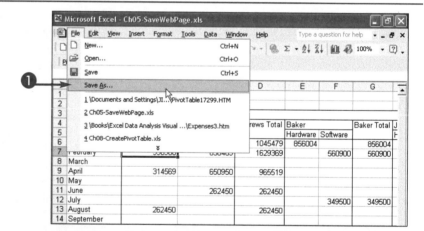

②  Select the Web Page (*.htm; *.html) option in the Save as type field.

③  Select whether you want to save the entire workbook, or just the selected worksheet.

●  You can click Add interactivity to make the HTML page interactive.

④  Click Save.

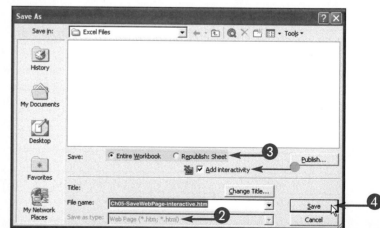

## INTERACTIVE FILE

If you selected Add interactivity, Excel allows the viewer to make modifications to the worksheet.

- You can use the toolbar buttons to modify the HTML version of the workbook.

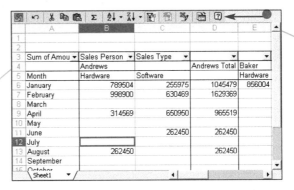

## NON-INTERACTIVE FILE

If you did not select Add interactivity, users cannot modify the worksheet within the Web browser.

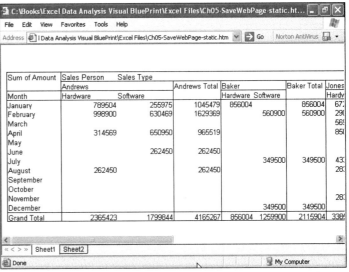

---

## Extra

If you want to query your Excel data from a Web page, you can save it as an XML file. XML, *Extensible Markup Language,* provides a structured data file that you can query from any Web file. To save an XML file, select the XML Spreadsheet (*.xml) option in the Save as type field on the Save As dialog box. Once saved, you can access your file in the same fashion as any XML file. Excel lays out all data in file based upon the values in each row and cell. For example, the following code illustrates the contents of one row converted to XML:

### Example

```
<Row>
    <Cell ss:StyleID="s21"><Data ss:Type="String">Month</Data></Cell>
    <Cell ss:StyleID="s21"><Data ss:Type="String">Sales Person</Data></Cell>
    <Cell ss:StyleID="s21"><Data ss:Type="String">ID</Data></Cell>
    <Cell ss:StyleID="s21"><Data ss:Type="String">Region</Data></Cell>
    <Cell ss:StyleID="s21"><Data ss:Type="String">State</Data></Cell>
    <Cell ss:StyleID="s21"><Data ss:Type="String">Sales Type</Data></Cell>
    <Cell ss:StyleID="s21"><Data ss:Type="String">Amount</Data></Cell>
</Row>
```

Good reference books for working with XML are *XML: Your visual blueprint for building expert Web pages*, 2001, and *XML Bible, 2001*.

# Chart Basics

You can create charts in Excel to provide a graphical representation of data within a workbook and to illustrate specific relationships between selected data values. Excel provides several different types of charts, and you can customize the attributes of each chart type for your data.

With most chart types, you can display up to 255 different data series on one chart. The only exception is a pie chart, which can only display one data series. All standard, 2D charts can display up to 32,000 individual data points, or values. All 3D charts can only display 4,000 data points.

## Column Chart

Column charts allow you to illustrate the relationship between different groups of data values. Each data point displays as a separate vertical column on the chart. With stacked charts, Excel places one set of values on top of the other within each column. Data points are color-coded to identify each data series.

Typically, you use column charts to show data changes that occur over a period of time. For example, a column chart works well for showing the sales totals for the year. You display the time values across the horizontal axis of the chart to illustrate the passage of time. For example, you can display the months of the year in chronological order on the axis from left to right.

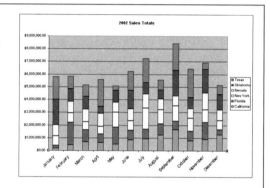

## Bar Chart

Bar charts display each data point, or value, as a separate, horizontal bar. With stacked bar charts, related data items are stacked together on a bar. Bar charts work well for showing comparisons between different sets of data values. This type of comparison is referred to as whole-to-whole comparison. For example, bar charts work well for comparing sales from different states for a corporation.

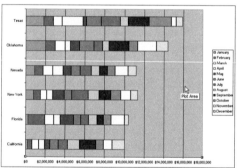

## Line Chart

Line charts create continuous lines that connect each data point within the corresponding data series. Each separate colored line represents a data series. You can select a chart sub-type that displays markers representing each individual data point on the line.

Line charts work very well for showing data changes over a period of time. Typically, the horizontal axis displays the passage of time, with the time values displayed in chronological order from left to right across the axis. For example, you would display the months of the year across the axis to show the sales for each month within your organization.

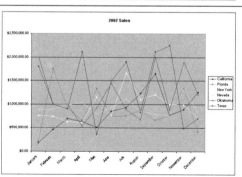

## Line Chart (continued)

You can select from seven different sub-types of line charts, with or without data markers. You can also select from line charts that display individual values or stacked line charts where the top line illustrates the total of each data series. The line chart also provides a 3D line option, but you should be careful about using this sub-type with a chart that displays several data series. Although 3D charts look more impressive, a user may find them distracting and more difficult to interpret, especially if your chart contains more than two data series lines.

## Pie Chart

Pie charts allow you to show how different data values in one data set compare proportionately to the total of the values with each piece of the pie chart representing a data value. For example, you can use a pie chart to show the proportion of sales from each location of the corporation. You can only use pie charts to show the data values from one data series because more than that creates a confusing, hard-to-interpret chart. To compare more than one data series, consider selecting either the area or doughnut chart types.

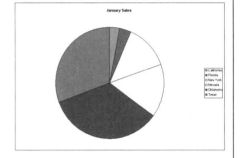

Two chart sub-types allow you to emphasize specific elements of the pie by moving them into a separate bar or pie chart. You can explode a specific piece of pie for emphasis. See the section "Explode Slices of a Pie Chart" for more information. Typically, you want to exert caution when using a 3D pie chart. Adding graphics to make a chart appear 3D often clutters the pie chart and makes it difficult to interpret.

Keep in mind that because a pie chart visually illustrates how each data value makes up a part of the total, the size of the individual slices is frequently misleading. You should select a different chart type when it is important to compare the exact size of data values.

## XY (Scatter) Chart

You can quickly analyze the correlation between two or more data series with an XY (scatter) chart because it allows you to see any trends or associations. For example, you can observe if an increasing number of mailed sales flyers increases sales of a particular item. A typical use of an XY (scatter) chart is to plot and analyze scientific data using the $x$ axis to mark some chronological time frame. When Excel charts your data, it displays each data series in a different color and marks every data point within each data series. You can select from five different sub-types of xy (scatter) charts, which allow you to display the data markers with or without connection lines, or display the connection lines without the data markers just like a regular line chart.

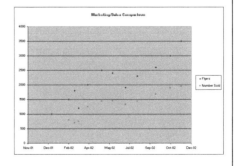

A straight line of data markers on the chart is an indication that you may have a correlation between your data series. To statistically prove or disprove this is the case, you must run a correlation and a covariance on your data sets. Excel offers these calculations as part of its Analysis Toolpack Add-in. See Chapter 11 for more information.

continued →

## Area Chart

Area charts show how values from different data series compare to a total as well as how the data series relate to each other. Each data series appears in a different color to emphasize how large one data set is compared to another. For example, if the Texas sales team sells significantly more than a team in California, the Texas sales show more visibly than the California sales.

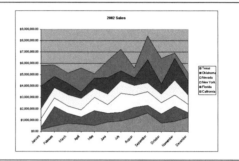

## Doughnut Chart

Doughnut charts allow you to show how different data values compare proportionately to the total of the values in the corresponding data series. Each data series displays as a separate ring within the doughnut chart, with individual data values displayed in different colors.

Because a doughnut chart visually shows how each data value makes up the total, the size of the individual data values is frequently misleading. For example, a value in an inner data series may appear smaller than the same value in an outer ring representing a different data series. You should select a different chart type when it is important to compare the exact size of data values.

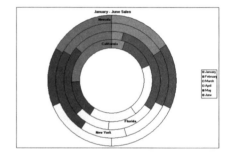

## Radar Chart

With radar charts, you can analyze each data series on a separate axis of the chart. Each axis extends from the center of the chart, creating a chart that resembles a radar screen.

Although radar charts create an interesting way to compare data values, they are typically more difficult to analyze. Usually, you can illustrate your data values better using a standard chart type, such as a column, bar, or line chart.

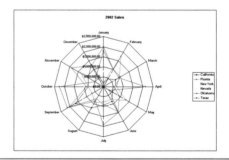

## Surface Chart

You can use surface charts to make a geographical comparison of the data values. A surface chart creates a chart that resembles a topographical map. Although this type of chart provides an interesting visual effect, it gives limited information when you analyze data using it.

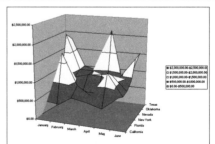

### Bubble Chart

Bubble charts allow you to quickly analyze the correlation between three data series. By looking at the correlation between the data values, you can view any trends or associations between the changes of one data series compared to another data series. For example, you can compare the cost of the items to the number of items sold and show the total revenue for each price as individual bubbles.

A bubble chart resembles an xy (scatter) chart by displaying the correlation of the data series. Each axis represents a different data series, with the size of the bubble showing the data value of the third data series.

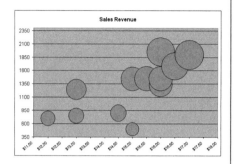

### Stock Chart

You plot stock charts for the sole purpose of analyzing data values related to the stock market. Each of the four sub-types of stock charts requires at least three different data series arranged in the appropriate order. Excel creates the selected chart only if the data has the appropriate layout.

The stock chart sub-type names correspond to the required data series layout. For example, if you select the High-Low-Close chart sub-type, you must provide three data series in the order of the high price, low price, and close price. You can use dates, stock symbols, or stock names as labels for each chart sub-type.

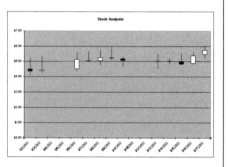

### Cylinder, Cone, and Pyramid Charts

You use the cylinder, cone, and pyramid charts to plot your data as 3D objects either horizontally or vertically. You can select from three different horizontal chart options and four different vertical chart options. This allows you to display individual data values or stacked values. You can also select a 3D vertical chart option.

You use the horizontal versions of the charts to display each data point as a separate, horizontal bar, or with stacked bar charts. Related data items are stacked together on a bar. The horizontal charts work well for showing comparisons between different sets of data values. This type of comparison is referred to as whole-to-whole comparison. For example, the charts work well for comparing sales from different states for a corporation.

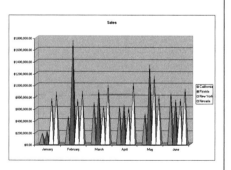

# Modify a Chart Type

To emphasize a different aspect of your data or to apply a different type of comparison, you can change your chart type. See the section "Chart Basics" for more information on the available chart types.

You change the chart type for any chart in a workbook using the Chart Type option. The only thing you need to keep in mind is that some chart types require specific types of data. For example, if you convert an exploded pie chart to a column chart, the individual data will not be emphasized.

When you switch to a different chart type, by default, Excel maintains any special formatting from the existing chart. For example, if you have modified font types or colors, those options apply to the new chart type. If you want to use the default formatting of the new chart type, you must select the Default formatting option.

## Extra

You use the Chart menu, which appears when you select a chart and you have the Data menu open, to make modifications to an existing chart. Depending upon the current chart type, some menu options may appear grayed out. For example, the 3D View option becomes available only when you select a 3D chart.

If you have an embedded chart in a worksheet, the Chart menu displays when you have any portion of the chart object selected. If your worksheet contains multiple chart objects, the changes made from the Chart menu only affect the selected chart.

When you select a Chart Sheet, the Chart menu always displays in the Menu bar. Any changes made from the Chart menu affect the chart on the Chart Sheet.

## Modify a Chart Type

① Click anywhere on the chart object to select an embedded chart.

For a chart sheet, click the tab of the chart you want to modify.

② Click Chart⇨Chart Type.

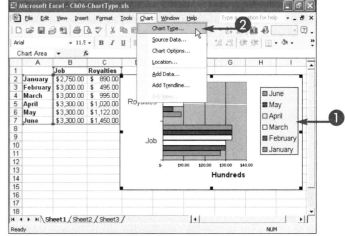

The Chart Type dialog box displays.

③ Click the desired chart type.

④ Click the appropriate chart sub-type.

⑤ Click the option for Default formatting to replace custom formatting.

⑥ Click OK.

The selected chart updates to the new chart type.

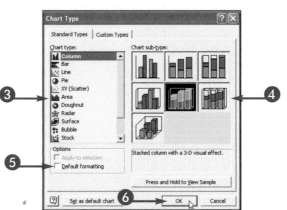

# Explode Slices of a Pie Chart

I f you consider one piece of information more crucial than any other in your pie chart, you can emphasize it by exploding its corresponding piece of pie. Remember that the purpose of a pie chart is to show the relationship between individual values and the entire chart. After you create a pie chart, and apply this feature, you can move each element of the chart individually within the chart object to emphasize your specific data values. For more on the various types of charts that Excel provides, see the section "Chart Basics."

You can explode all pieces of a chart by selecting the entire pie chart and dragging toward the outside of the Chart object. As you drag, each piece moves an equal distance from the center of the pie chart.

## Extra

You can rotate the pie chart so that the exploded piece appears at a specific angle in the chart. To rotate the chart, click the piece of the pie chart and click Format⇨Selected Data Point to display the Format Data Point dialog box. Click the Options tab. In the Angle of first slice field, specify the degrees of rotation for the pie chart. The Preview window in the dialog box shows the effect of rotating the chart. Keep in mind that the selected piece remains in the same location in the chart. Excel rotates the entire chart.

By default, Excel displays each piece of the pie chart in a different color. If you want to make the entire chart the same color, you can deselect the Vary colors by slice option (☑ changes to ☐).

## Explode Slices of a Pie Chart

**1** Click a piece of the pie chart.

**2** Drag the piece toward the edge of the chart object.

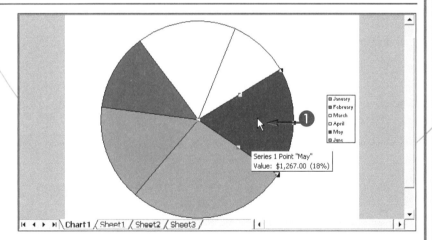

The piece moves away from the pie chart.

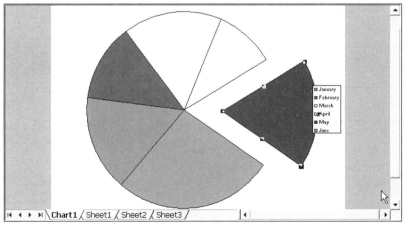

# Create a Custom Chart Type

**W**hen creating charts to show analyzed data, you save time and effort by designing a custom chart that you can reuse. To use the same chart in multiple workbooks, or in multiple projects, you can create a *custom chart type*, or user-defined chart type, which is simply a template for a chart layout. When you create the custom chart type, Excel stores all information about the appearance of the chart, including the chart type, color changes, fonts, legends, and even data tables. After you create a custom chart type, you can save it and select it from the Custom Types tab in any workbook. The Custom Types tab maintains a list of both built-in custom chart types that come with Excel and any user-defined chart types.

To create a custom chart type, you must first select the default chart type. For more about the various types of

charts available in Excel, see the section "Chart Basics." You can create a chart using the Chart Wizard, and then format it to meet your specifications. You can also adjust the scaling of the axes, add gridlines, and specify whether the chart includes a legend or data table. All formatting and layout changes become part of the chart type template.

When you save a custom chart type, you must give it a unique name. You can also create a description of the chart. Any description you specify displays in the box under the sample chart window.

You can eliminate any unwanted user-defined chart types from the Custom Types by deleting them. You can only delete the User-Defined chart types; you cannot remove any of the Built-in chart types.

## Create a Custom Chart Type

① Create and customize a chart.

② Click Chart➪Chart Type.

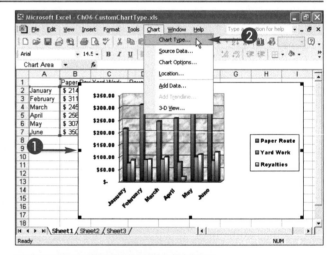

The Chart Type dialog box displays.

③ If not visible, click the Custom Types tab.

④ Click the User-defined option.

⑤ Click Add.

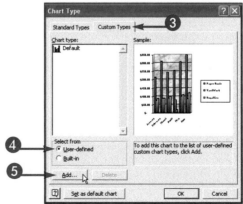

The Add Custom Chart Type dialog box displays.

**6** Type a unique name for the chart type in the Name field.

**7** If desired, type a description for the chart type.

**8** Click OK.

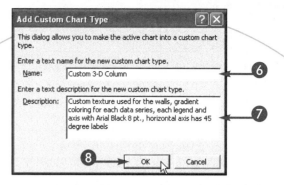

The custom chart type displays on the Custom Types tab.

● The custom description displays when you select the chart type.

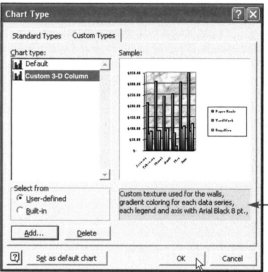

## Extra

When you select a range of cells in a worksheet and press F11, Excel creates a chart using the default chart format. To determine what the default chart type is, click Chart⇨Chart Type⇨Custom Types. In the Custom Types tab, click the User-defined option (○ changes to ⦿). Click the Default option in the Chart Type list to view a sample of the custom chart type. Excel's default chart type is a standard bar chart.

You can change the default chart type to any of the chart types listed on either the Standard Types or Custom Types tabs. To change the default chart type, select the desired chart type and click the Set as default chart option. Keep in mind that if you select one of the chart types on the Standard Types tab, you need to also specify the sub-type.

You can change the formatting for any of the chart elements. Depending upon the element selected, there are different formatting options available in the Format dialog box. To change the formatting, select the desired chart element and click Format⇨Selected Element, where Element becomes the name of the selected chart element. There are different tabs that display for formatting the appearance of the selected chart element.

# Add a Trendline to a Chart

To illustrate trends that occur in your data, you can apply a trendline to your chart. *Trendlines* are helpful in analyzing data because they forecast future data values based upon your current data. For example, if you have net sales data for a particular sales team for an entire year, you can predict how the team may perform in the upcoming year.

Forecasts are only accurate if you select the appropriate trendline. To do so, observe the shape of your charted data, and then select a trendline type that best fits the general trend you see in the Add Trendline dialog box. You can confirm that you have selected the correct trendline by looking at the R-squared value. The *R-squared value*, which ranges from 0 to 1, identifies how closely the values on the trendline match the actual values in the data series. The closer the R-squared value is to 1, the more reliable your trendline.

To forecast either future or past data values, you use the Forecast options. When Excel adds the trendline, it extends the line to match the number of future or past periods you specify. The forecast is based solely upon the values in the selected data series and the trendline type.

Although you can add trendlines to each data series in the chart, Excel only allows you to add trendlines to certain types of charts. You can add trendlines to bar, column, unstacked 2D area, line, stock, xy (scatter), and bubble charts. Trendlines do not work with 3D charts. If you change a chart containing trendlines to a chart type that does not support them, Excel removes them. If the chart type does not support trendlines, Excel grays out the option on the menu. For more about the various chart types available in Excel, see the section "Chart Basics."

## Add a Trendline to a Chart

① Click the tab of the chart to which you want to add a trendline.

For an embedded chart, click anywhere on the chart.

② Click Chart➪Add Trendline.

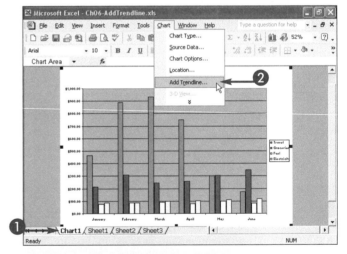

The Add Trendline dialog box displays.

③ Click the series to which you want to apply the trendline.

④ Click the desired trendline type.

- If you select Polynomial, specify the Order number.

- If you select Moving Average, specify the number of periods.

⑤ Click the Options tab.

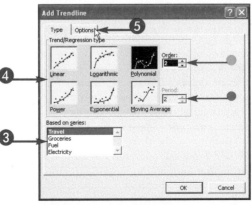

The Options tab displays.

**6** If desired, click Custom and type the custom trendline name.

**7** Type the number of periods to use to determine future trend.

- You can type values in the Backward field to forecast previous values.

**8** Click the Display R-squared value on chart to display the R-squared value.

**9** Click OK.

The trendline displays on the chart for the selected data series.

You can repeat steps 3 to 9 to create additional trendlines.

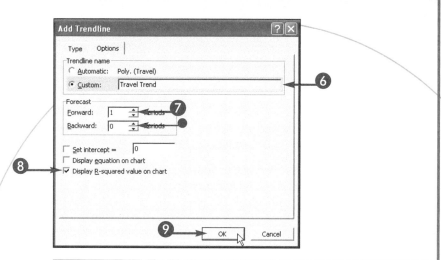

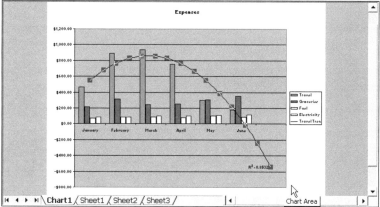

## Extra

The Type tab on the Add Trendline dialog box provides six different types of trendlines, each with a different type of comparison of the values in the data series. To more accurately predict future events, you can observe the shape of your charted data, and then select a trendline type that best fits the general trend you see:

| TRENDLINE | DESCRIPTION |
| --- | --- |
| Linear | Creates a best-fit straight line that shows how values in a data series increase or decrease at a steady rate. |
| Logarithmic | Creates a best-fit curved line that illustrates how data values increase or decrease and then level out. You can use both negative and positive values with a Logarithmic trendline. |
| Polynomial | Creates a curved line illustrating fluctuations in the data values. You specify an Order value to indicate the maximum number of fluctuations, or bends, that occur on the line. |
| Power | Creates a curved line to compare measurements that increase at a specific rate. You cannot use a Power trendline with a data series that includes negative or zero values. |
| Exponential | Creates a curved line that shows data values that increase or fall at increasingly higher rates. You cannot use an Exponential trendline with a data series that includes negative or zero values. |
| Moving Average | Reduces the fluctuations in the trendline to show a smoother pattern. You use the Period field to specify the number of data values to create the line. Excel creates the line by averaging the specific data values. For example, if the Period value is 2, the first two values are averaged and that value is the first point on the line, and then the second and third values are averaged and become the second point. |

# Add or Change
# New Data to a Chart

f you change the range of values for your data analysis, you can redefine the range of data Excel uses to display values on the chart. You can either expand the range of values on the chart, or you can add an additional data series. You use the Source Data dialog box to both expand a data range and add a new data series. When you expand a data range, you typically expand the range of values that each data series uses in the chart. For example, if your chart contains the monthly expenses for January through June, to add the expenses for July you expand the data range to include July.

Excel groups related data values together in a data series. Typically, a data series refers to the data values that appear in rows or columns on a worksheet. If your chart uses

columns as the data series range, you can add a new data series by selecting a new column. For example, if you create a new column containing Landscaping expenses, you can create a new data series on the chart.

If you expand a data range to include an additional data series, Excel automatically creates a new data series. You can customize any data series name or range in the Series tab.

Excel allows you to add a maximum of 255 data series to most of the default chart types. The only exception is the pie chart, which only allows you to use one data series. If you create a pie chart using multiple data series, Excel ignores all but the first data series. For more information about the various chart types in Excel, see the section "Chart Basics."

## Add or Change New Data to a Chart

### CHANGE THE DATA RANGE

① Click the chart's tab.

  For an embedded chart, click anywhere on the chart.

② Click Chart⇔Source Data.

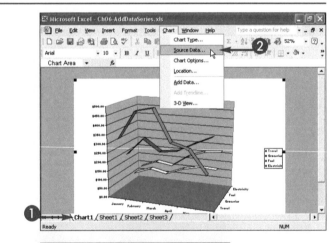

  The Source Data dialog box displays.

③ Click the Data Range tab.

④ Specify the range of data.

**Note:** See Chapter 1 for more on selecting a range of cells.

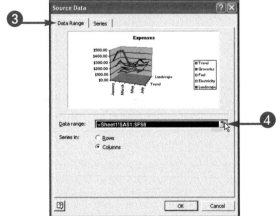

## ADD A DATA SERIES

**5** Click the Series tab in the Source Data dialog box.

**6** Click Add.

Excel creates a new data series.

**7** Specify the name of the new data series.

**8** Specify the range of the new data values.

**9** Click OK.

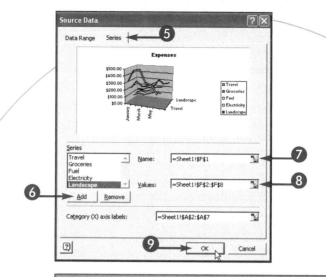

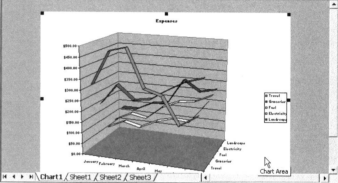

The chart displays the new data.

---

### Extra

The Data Range tab in the Source Data dialog box allows you to only specify a range of contiguous cells for your chart. If you want to add data values from another location, you use the Add Data option. With this option, you can add data values from another worksheet, or even another open workbook. However, if you add data values from another workbook, you must make sure that workbook remains in the same location so that Excel can locate the linked data in the future.

To add data from another worksheet location, select the chart and click Chart⇨Add Data to display the Add Data dialog box. Specify the range for the new data values in the Range field. See Chapter 1 for information on how to specify a data range.

When you click OK, the Paste Special dialog box displays. In this dialog box, you indicate how to add the new data to the chart. If you select the New series option, Excel creates a new data series. If you select the New points option, Excel adds the new data values to the existing data series. You must specify whether the data series are located in rows or columns within the newly selected data.

# Create a Chart with Multiple Chart Types

You can create charts that apply different chart types to each data series. For example, you may want to create a column chart to display one data series and then include another data series as a continuous line. Combining chart types allows you to create more complex charts.

To create a chart with multiple chart types, you must first create the main chart type specifying all data values for the chart. You then select the chart type for the selected data series. You can only change the data type for one series at a time.

The *legend* reflects any changes made to the chart type for a data series. For example, if a data series changes from a bar chart to a line chart, a colored line displays as the key for the data series on the legend.

There are some chart types that you cannot combine. For example, Excel does not allow both a column and bar chart.

If you attempt to combine non-compatible charts, an error message displays and the charts are not combined. To verify that you can add a new chart type to the existing chart, preview the chart selection in the Chart Type dialog box. If Excel has any problems, messages display in the Preview window.

You cannot combine 2D and 3D chart types. In fact, most 3D chart types must be the chart type of the entire chart. Attempts to combine 2D and 3D chart types results in a warning message: You must either change both chart types to 3D or cancel your work. Although you have the option of creating a different chart type for each data series on the chart, avoid using more than two different chart types, because too many chart types can make your chart confusing and difficult to interpret.

## Create a Chart with Multiple Chart Types

**1** Create the main chart.

**2** Click the data series you want to change.

**3** Click Chart➪Chart Type.

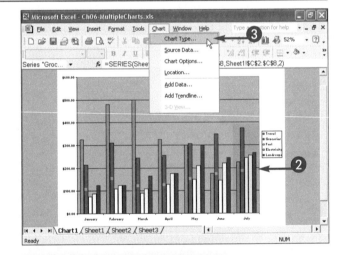

The Chart Type dialog box displays.

**4** Click the desired chart type.

**5** Click the desired sub-type.

**6** Click Press and Hold to View Sample to preview the chart.

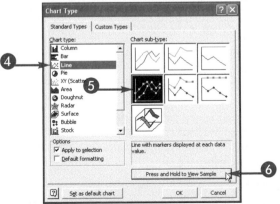

- A preview of the chart displays.

If the chart types are not compatible, an error message displays instead of the preview.

⑦ Click OK.

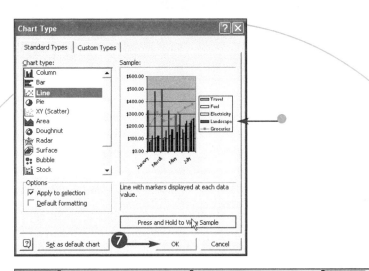

The selected data series displays in the new chart type.

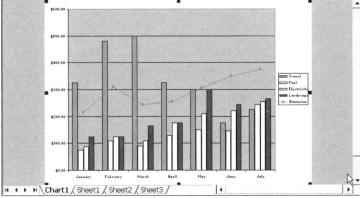

## Extra

If you have a range of data in a combined chart with different data types, you can add a secondary axis to help identify the chart values. Depending upon the chart type, you can typically add both a secondary $x$ and $y$ axis. For example, if your main chart is a column chart, the $x$ axis displays at the bottom of the chart and the $y$ axis displays on the left of the chart. If you add secondary axes, the secondary $y$ axis displays at the right side of the chart, and the $x$ axis displays at the top of the chart.

To add secondary axes to a chart, click Chart⇨Chart Options. In the Chart Options dialog box, click the Axes tab. If your chart contains multiple chart types, the Secondary Axis options display in the bottom-left corner of the Axes tab.

To display a secondary axis, click the corresponding check box option. The number of axes available varies depending upon the chart types selected. Some chart types, such as pie and doughnut charts, have no axes.

# PivotTable Basics

**U**sing a PivotTable, you can create a dynamic and immediate summarization of your Excel list or external database. PivotTable Reports allow you to *cross-tabulate*, or summarize data records in two or more ways by combining values from different fields. For example, you can analyze the order amounts for salespeople from each state, find the total sales per salesperson, and then rank the salespeople by total sales amounts. You can accomplish all of this by simply changing the location of fields on the report and applying filtering options. PivotTables are dynamic because you can change a report's appearance instantaneously as well as create links to the original data to refresh the table when your data changes.

You can use any Excel-accessible database to import data values and create a PivotTable report. See Chapter 5 for more information on importing data values from external sources.

## Filtering and Grouping Data

Large lists work well in PivotTables, because you can quickly filter them to show specific values, and group them to hide or reveal sections of data. To construct your PivotTable, you drag fields — basically the labels of your data — to a layout. The field essentially acts as a filter for your data in that you can select which data values you want to display for each field. Excel includes the All option with each field, which you can use to display all possible values for that field. For example, if you select All for the Months row field, the PivotTable displays all values from each month. If you only want to select specific values, you can select them individually from the Column and Row fields. The Page field only allows the selection of one value and that value matches all data records that display on the page. See the section "Filter a Field" for more information on filtering.

Once you construct your PivotTable, you can use Excel's Group option to combine items together into one value or to show a specific relationship. See the section "Group PivotTable Data Items" for more information on the grouping option.

## PivotTable Restrictions

To have your PivotTable work properly, consider the following guidelines and restrictions:

- You must label each column because Excel will make them into the field names on the PivotTable report.

- Because a PivotTable report creates the necessary totals based upon the fields you have in the report, you must remove any automatic totals from the list.

- Excel uses the entire list, even hidden cells. If you do not want hidden data in the PivotTable, you must filter the list to another worksheet using the Advanced Filter. See Chapter 3 for more information.

- Excel allows you to create a PivotTable that contains a maximum of 8,000 total items. You can only have 256 fields in the Page area and 256 fields in the Data area. The other areas are only limited by the overall size limitation.

## PivotTable Data Types

No matter what the data source, you must make your data source fields one of the following types:

| TYPE | DESCRIPTION |
|------|-------------|
| Category | Contains a text value that describes the data. You use category type values as labels for the Row, Column, and Page fields. |
| Data | Contains a value to summarize. Typically the data values are numbers, but you can also summarize text values. |

# A View of the PivotTable Report Fields

Y ou add imported fields to your PivotTable report by dragging them onto one of four different areas: Page, Column, Row, and Data. Although you can add a field to any of the four PivotTable areas, the placement determines the layout of the report.

One nice feature of a PivotTable report is that Excel automatically inserts a row and a column to provide a total for the values in the corresponding rows and columns of the PivotTable report.

## Ⓐ PAGE FIELD

An optional field that filters the values on the page. Only records containing matching values display on the page.

## Ⓑ ROW FIELD

Identifies the values from the source data assigned to the row orientation.

## Ⓒ ITEMS

Identifies a sub-category for a row or a column that identifies the corresponding data area values.

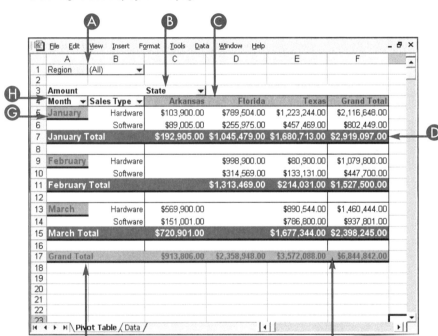

## Ⓓ SUBTOTAL

A row or column that summarizes cells within the corresponding detail fields.

## Ⓔ GRAND TOTAL

A row or column that provides a total for all cells in the cells of the data area.

## Ⓗ DATA FIELD

Identifies the values from the source data that are summarized in the Data area.

## Ⓖ COLUMN FIELDS

Values from the source data assigned to the column orientation.

## Ⓕ DATA AREA

Summarizes the data values using the assigned summarization function or custom formula.

# Create a PivotTable Report from an Excel List

**P**ivotTables provide an excellent tool for quickly analyzing data values from an Excel list or an external database by creating a cross-tabulated summary of the data values. With a PivotTable Report, you can dynamically customize which columns from the list that you want to summarize.

You create a PivotTable Report using the PivotTable and PivotChart Wizard, which allows you to place the Excel list in the current worksheet or another accessible workbook. If you select a cell for a list in the current workbook before accessing the wizard, Excel automatically displays the range of cells in the Range box. Alternatively, you can manually enter the cell references for the range of cells.

If your list is not in the current worksheet, you must specify its exact location, including the workbook and worksheet name, in the Range box. You do this by enclosing the workbook and worksheet names in single quotes, and

placing the workbook name in square brackets. For example, if you want to retrieve a list from Sheet1 in the workbook ExcelList.xls, you enter the following:

`'[ExcelList.xls]Sheet1'$A$1:$G$100`

You must indicate the worksheet location for the PivotTable report, which can either be in the current worksheet, or a newly created worksheet within the current workbook. If you decide to place the PivotTable report in the current workbook, you must specify the first cell for the report. You should specify a cell that does not contain data values. If you select a cell that contains data, Excel gives you the option of replacing the current cell values.

Although this task illustrates how to create a PivotTable from an Excel list, you can also create one by importing the data from an external database. See Chapter 8 for more on creating a PivotChart with your PivotTable using an external database.

## Create a PivotTable Report from an Excel List

① Select a cell in the list of data values.

② Click Data⇨PivotTable and PivotChart Report.

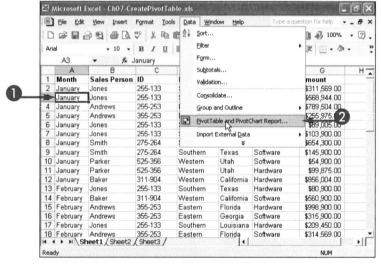

The PivotTable and PivotChart Wizard displays.

③ Click the Microsoft Excel list or database option.

④ Click the PivotTable option.

⑤ Click Next.

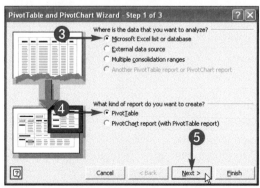

The second page of the wizard displays.

**6** Verify that the correct range of cells appear in the Range field.

If the range of cells you want does not appear in the Range field, click Collapse Dialog Box button and select the range.

**7** Click Next.

The third page of the wizard displays.

**8** Click the New worksheet to place the PivotTable report on a new worksheet.

- You can click Existing worksheet to place the PivotTable report in the current worksheet and specify the starting cell.

**9** Click Layout.

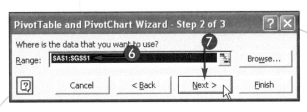

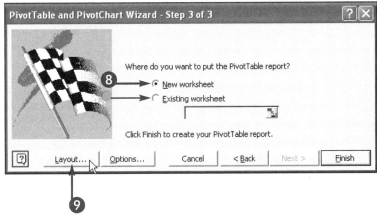

## Extra

You can select data for a PivotTable from multiple sources using the PivotTable and PivotChart Wizard. The type of data you select determines which page displays as the second page of the wizard. See Chapter 8 for more on this option. The following table provides guidelines for the different data types:

| DATA TYPE | DESCRIPTION |
|---|---|
| Excel List | Limited to the size of 65,536 records, or rows. Each record can have up to 256 fields or columns. The first row of an Excel list must contain the column labels. |
| Database | When you select the Database option on the first page of the wizard, the second page lets you select the external database you want to import into the data fields. See Chapter 5 for more information on importing from a database. |
| Consolidation Ranges | To use data values from multiple worksheets, you select this option. On the second page of the wizard, you specify each data range separately. See Chapter 2 for more information on consolidating data. |
| PivotTable or PivotChart | You select this option to use the same data that another PivotTable or PivotChart has. Excel only stores the data values once when both share the same data, making the memory usage more efficient. |

continued →

Y ou build your PivotTable report by dragging the appropriate column names and fields to a diagram until you have your desired layout. The column names and fields appear as field buttons, which you can use in any combination. If you do not include a field button on the layout, the corresponding data values do not display on the PivotTable report.

Any buttons that you drag to the Row area of the diagram appear on the PivotTable as separate rows. Any buttons in the Column area become columns. When you drag a field button to the Data area, by default the wizard applies the Sum function if the values are numeric. If the values that correspond to the field button are not numeric, the wizard automatically applies the Count function. If you want to summarize the data differently, you can select a different Excel function. See the section "Change the Calculation of a Data Field" for information on applying a different summarization function.

You can place multiple field buttons in the same section on the diagram. For example, if you place the Month field button in the Row section followed by the Sales Person field button, Excel displays the amounts for each month broken down into Sales Person sub-categories. You can also specify a value that all data records must contain by dragging a field button to the Page section. For example, if the Page area contains the State field button, only data from the selected state appears in the PivotTable. See the section "PivotTable Basics" for more on the elements of a PivotTable.

After you create the PivotTable, you can quickly change the layout by dragging fields from one section of the PivotTable report to another. See the section "Change the Layout of the PivotTable" for more information.

### Create a PivotTable Report from an Excel List *(continued)*

The Layout page of the wizard displays.

⑩ Click a field button.

⑪ Drag the selection to the Row section.

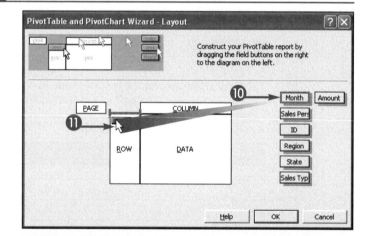

⑫ Repeat steps 10 to 11 for the Column and Area field locations.

⑬ Click OK.

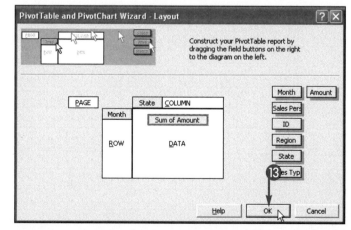

The third page of the wizard displays.

- You can click Options to select a wide variety of formatting and data options for your PivotTable.

⑭ Click Finish.

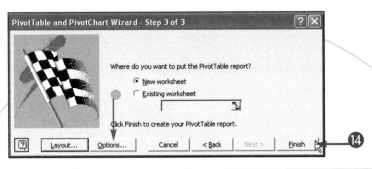

Excel creates the PivotTable report in the specified location.

The PivotTable toolbar appears with options for changing the PivotTable.

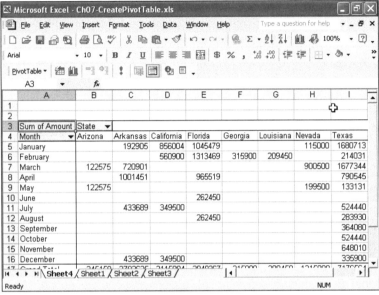

## Extra

When you create or view a PivotTable, Excel displays the PivotTable toolbar. The following table describes the most important toolbar buttons:

| BUTTON | DESCRIPTION |
| --- | --- |
| 📊 | Displays the AutoFormat dialog box. See Chapter 1 for more information. |
| 📈 | Creates a PivotChart using the default Pivot Chart format. |
| 🔲 | Hides the items in a group. See the section "Group PivotTable Data Items" for more information. |
| 🔲 | Shows all hidden items in the PivotTable report. |
| ❗ | Updates the PivotTable report with the current data values. |
| 🔲 | Hides or reveals the PivotTable Field List. |

You can use the Page field, on the top-left corner of the PivotTable, to help filter data from a large list. This field breaks the report into separate pages and only displays records that meet your specifications. You can view either all values or a specific value. See the section "Filter a Field" for more on working with the Page field.

Although you can change the layout of a PivotTable, you cannot add or remove rows or columns, or modify cell values on a PivotTable report. To change a value in a PivotTable cell, you must make modifications to the source data.

# Change the Layout of a PivotTable

**P**ivotTables work well for data analysis because they allow you to quickly add, move, and even remove fields from the report, thus quickly changing the values in the data field. If you want to change the layout of a PivotTable, you can quickly drag the fields to different locations. For example, you can move the fields in the row section to the column section, or even add additional fields to a section. You can also change the layout of the PivotTable by adding more fields to either the Row or Column sections.

You add new fields using the PivotTable Field List. The PivotTable Field List displays all of the fields that were part of the PivotTable when you first created it in bold. If you add a field to an area of the report that already contains a field, the new field becomes a sub-category of the original field.

You can move any fields on the PivotTable report from one area to another. When you move a field, the filter selections remain the same for the field. For example, if you are only viewing values for the months of January and February and you move the Month field to the Column area, the filter selection for the Months field or January and February remains the same. See the section "Filter a Field" for more information on filtering fields.

When you move or add fields on a PivotTable chart, Excel identifies the location for the field with a thick broken line as you drag it. If you drag the field to the Row area, Excel inserts the new field to the left of the line. If you drag the field to the Column area, Excel adds the new field below the line. For more about the elements of a PivotTable, see the section "PivotTable Basics."

---

### Change the Layout of a PivotTable

#### ADD FIELDS

① Select the desired field in the PivotTable Field List.

● You can click the Show Field List button to display the PivotTable Field List.

② Drag the field to the desired PivotTable area.

● A broken line indicates the area that will receive the new field.

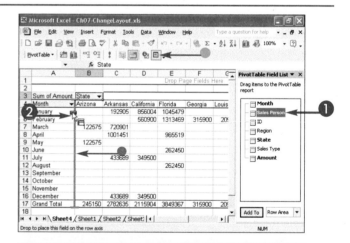

● The selected field appears in the corresponding area of the PivotTable report.

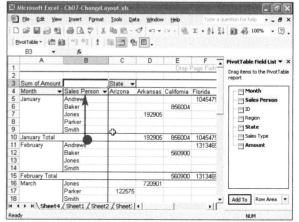

## MOVE FIELDS

**1** Select the desired field on the PivotTable.

**2** Drag the field to the new area.

- A broken line indicates the area that will receive the new field.

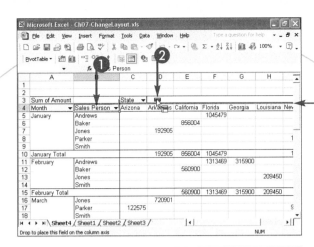

- The PivotTable updates to show the field in the new area.

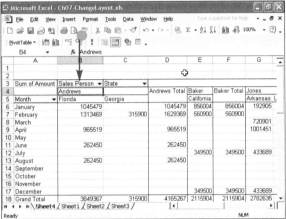

## Extra

You can change the layout of a PivotTable with the PivotTable and PivotChart Wizard. To display the wizard, select a cell from the PivotTable and click Data⇨PivotTable and PivotChart Report. This displays the third page of the PivotTable and PivotChart Wizard. To learn more about the wizard, see the section "Create a PivotTable Report from an Excel List."

If you have multiple fields in the Column area, you can change their order on the PivotTable. To move a column, on the PivotTable toolbar, click PivotTable⇨ Order to view a menu of move options. Click the location where you want to move the selected column. For example, Move to Beginning places the selected column as the first column on the left side of the PivotTable report.

You can remove any field from the PivotTable. To remove a field, click on it and drag it back to the PivotTable Field List. As you drag the selected field, the mouse pointer changes from an arrow to a button image, and a red X indicates that Excel is removing the button. Keep in mind, when you remove a field you are simply removing it from the PivotTable report display. It still remains in the list and you can add it again at any point.

# Filter
# a Field

Y ou save time and effort analyzing your data by filtering each field on a PivotTable to only display records that meet specific criteria. By default, when you add a field to a PivotTable report, all items display in the row or column. You can filter the fields to display only certain items, or any combination of the items that display on a list in the Row and Column areas. For example, if the Row area contains a Cities field, you can filter the field to only display records for specific cities, such as Dallas and Houston. You must select at least one item for each field. If you try to close the list without selecting an item, an error message displays.

The items that display for each field come from the data you used to create the PivotTable report. If you created your PivotTable report from an Excel list, the items on the list are the actual labels from the corresponding Excel column. If you do not see the appropriate item on the list, you must verify your original data values. If you created your PivotTable report from another Excel worksheet, you need to check the original values on the worksheet. If you used an external database, you can review the data by importing it into another worksheet. See Chapter 5 for information on working with external databases.

If you assign a field to the Page area, the field in the top-left corner of the PivotTable, you can either select all items or just one individual item. If you specify a single item for the field, only records that contain that item value display on the entire PivotTable. See "PivotTable Basics" for more information about the Page area and other elements of a PivotTable.

## Filter a Field

① Click the down arrow next to the field you want to filter.

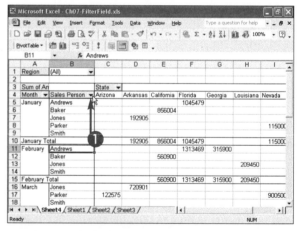

A list displays the available items.

② Click the Show All option to remove the selection (☑ changes to ☐).

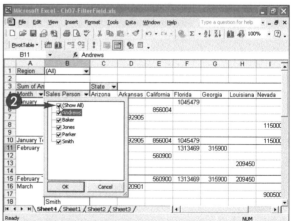

Excel removes all of the checkmarks.

③ Click each item you want on the PivotTable
(☐ changes to ☑).

④ Click OK.

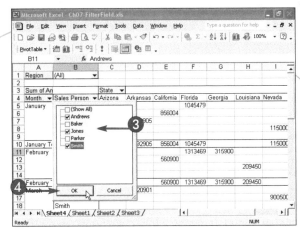

● The PivotTable updates automatically
to display only the selected items.

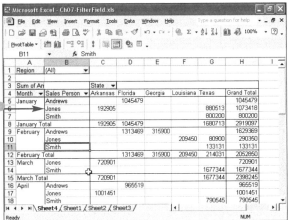

## Extra

If the list of available items is longer than
the space allotted for it, a scroll bar displays
on the right side so you can scroll through
the list. You can also resize the list box by
dragging on one of the sides so that you can
view more of the available items.

If you resize the list box and click OK, Excel
remembers the size and displays the list box
that same size the next time you view the
field values.

If you filter multiple fields, the values in the
Data Area update automatically to reflect
the changes. Only records that match each
of the field filters display on the PivotTable.
For example, if you filter the Row field to
display only the items January and February
and filter the Column field to display the
items Texas and Florida, only values that
match these criteria display in the Data area.
Keep in mind, filters do not remove the data
values from the PivotTable report, they
simply hide your data. If you select different
items on the list box for a field, Excel
updates the PivotTable report immediately
to show the new selections.

# Change the Calculation of a Data Field

hen you create a PivotTable report, Excel performs *Standard calculations* by summarizing the data values that appear in the Data area. For example, if the cell contains all sales in Arkansas during January, Excel determines the cell value by summing all of the matching sales totals from the original data. If you have sales from four different sales people, Excel totals all four amounts and places them in the cell.

You can change your data's summary to something other than the default Sum function. Excel lets you select from eleven different functions to summarize the original data values, such as counting the values or finding the maximum value. For example, if you selected the Count function, each cell contains a number representing the number of values in the original data. If you had four sales amounts for Arkansas, the cell contains the number 4 and not the total amount.

When you change the function, the Data area reflects the selection. For example, if the selected function is Count and the field in the Data area is Amount, the name of the Data area becomes Count of Amount.

You can also customize the selected function by adding some calculation options available on the PivotTable field dialog box. For example, you can determine what percentage a sum is of a total amount by combining the Sum function with the % of calculation option.

Some of the custom calculations options require more information about the calculation. You must define the field that you want to use for the calculation as well as the value for the field. For example, to determine the difference between the current month and the previous month sales, you select the Month field and Previous in the Base item box.

## Change the Calculation of a Data Field

① Right click on the Data field.

A menu of options displays.

② Click Field Settings.

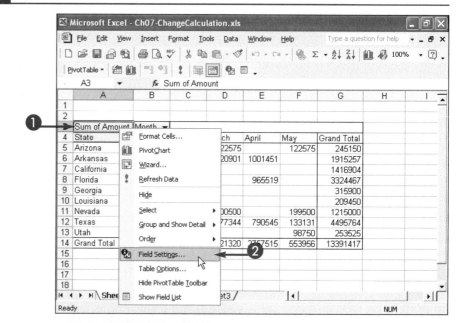

The PivotTable Field dialog box displays.

③ Click a new summary function.

④ Click Options.

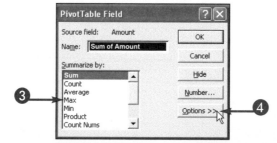

The dialog box expands.

**5** Click a custom calculation option in the Show data as field.

**6** Click OK.

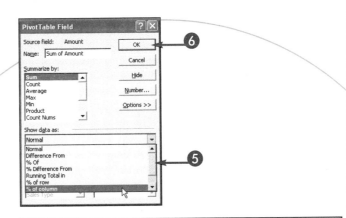

The values in the Data area update using the new calculation.

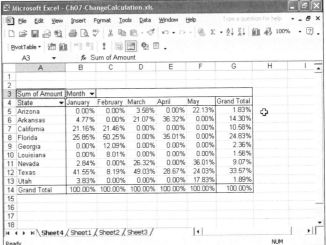

## Extra

You can access a variety of custom calculations in the Show data as field. The following table describes the different custom calculations and their descriptions:

| OPTION | DESCRIPTION |
| --- | --- |
| Difference From | Calculates the difference between two PivotTable cells. |
| % Of | Determines the percentage of the current PivotTable cell to the selected base value. |
| % Difference From | Determines the percentage difference between two cell values. |
| Running Total in | Shows the running total in each cell. |
| % of row | Finds the percentage of the cell value to the total row. |
| % of column | Finds the percentage of the cell value to the total column. |
| % of Total | Finds the percentage of the cell value to the grand total value. |
| Index | Finds an index value of the cell value. |

# Group PivotTable Data Items

A s you analyze your data on a PivotTable report, you can combine items together into one value or to show a specific relationship. The Excel's Group option is helpful for organizing and presenting your analysis, especially when you have a large amount of data. For example, you can group months together to illustrate sales by quarters. You can then collapse the group to show only the group's summary information, such as total sales for the quarter.

As you divide a field into different groups, Excel creates new field items that contain the group names as the filter selections on the box. When you finish grouping the items, you can remove the original field. You can change the Excel default name for the group and apply formatting options to the cell.

You cannot group items that belong to different fields. For example, if the Row area contains both a Month and Sales Person field, you can group Month field items, but cannot include Sales Person field items in the same group. You can even select and group items from the same field that are not adjacent in the PivotTable report. To select non-adjacent items, see Chapter 1. See "PivotTable Basics" for information about the areas and fields of the PivotTable report.

When you create groups on your PivotTable, Excel does not automatically calculate group subtotals. To see the totals for a group, you need to collapse it. When you collapse or hide the detail of the group, Excel combines the values of the items within the group and displays the corresponding totals. You can also obtain totals for a group by filtering the field to only display the group. See the section "Filter a Field" for more information about filtering options.

---

## Group PivotTable Data Items

### GROUP ITEMS

1 Select the items you want to group on the PivotTable.

2 Click Data⇨Group and Outline⇨Group.

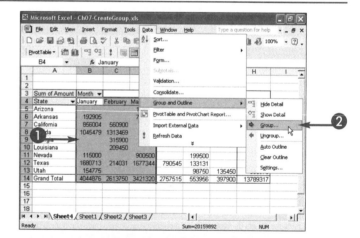

● Excel creates a new group.

● You can rename the group by selecting the group cell and typing a name for your group in the cell.

The groups display on the PivotTable report.

You can repeat steps 1 to 3 to create more groups.

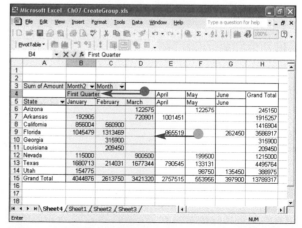

## COLLAPSE GROUP AND CREATE SUBTOTALS

① Select the group.

② Click Data⇨Group and Outline⇨Hide Detail.

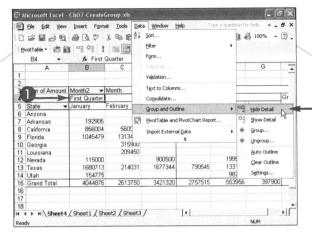

Excel hides all items within the selected group, and only the group totals display.

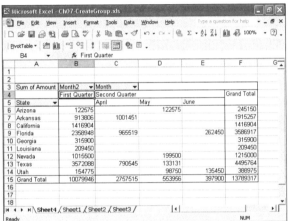

---

## Extra

If you have a series of dates in a field, you can use the Grouping dialog box to specify the way you want to group the items in the field. With this dialog box, you can have Excel create multiple groups with one step. For example, if you have dates from five different months, you can group the dates by Months, and Excel creates a separate group for each month, automatically naming the group to match. For example, Excel places all dates from January in the January group and names the group Jan.

You can remove any grouping from a PivotTable. To do so, select the group and click Data⇨Group and Outline⇨Ungroup. When you remove a group, it no longer exists as part of the PivotTable. If you want to view the group again, you must re-create it.

If you just want to hide a group, you can click the corresponding field and deselect the name of the group. If you select the items of the group from the box, the individual items display on the PivotTable without the corresponding group.

# Add Another Data Area Calculation

I f you want to show multiple calculations in the Data Area, you can do so by adding additional fields. Perhaps you want to analyze the sales figures by showing both the amount of the sales and the percentage of sales each sale represents. You can either add a different field to the Data area, or you can add another copy of the same field and apply a different summary calculation.

Excel automatically names each Data area field based upon the name of the field and the calculation that the field uses. For example, if your Data area field name is Amount, the first instance of the field is named Sum of Amount; if you add another instance of the same field, Excel names the second field Sum of Amount2. The field name is important because it provides the description necessary to interpret the PivotTable results. Therefore, you should adjust the

field names on the PivotTable Field dialog box to reflect information you want to convey in your analysis.

Each field in the Data area uses some type of summary calculation to display the results. The default summary calculation is the Sum function. You can change the summary function to any of the functions available on the PivotTable Field dialog box. You can also create custom summary calculations. See the section "Change the Calculation of a Data Field" for more information on customizing a Data field calculation.

You can change the summarization calculation for each data field. For example, you can have the first item sum the amounts and the second item determine the percentage of the amount in relation to the other sums in the column. See the section "Change the Calculation of a Data Field" for more information.

## Add Another Data Area Calculation

① In the PivotTable Field List, select the field to add.

● You can click the Show Field List button to display the PivotTable Field List.

② Drag the field selection to the Data area of the PivotTable Report and release the mouse button.

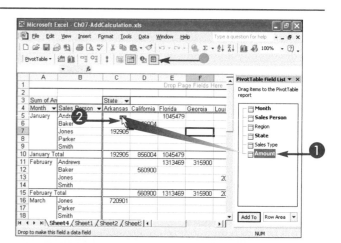

● The selected field displays as the second row in the Data area.

③ Right click the new Data field and click Field Settings from the options that display.

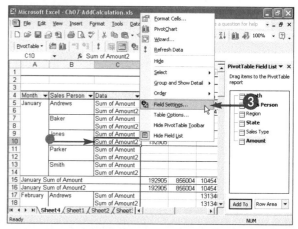

The PivotTable Field dialog box displays.

④ Create the new summary function.

**Note:** See the section "Change the Calculation of a Data Field" for more information.

⑤ Type a name for the field.

⑥ Click OK.

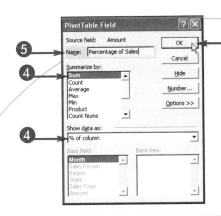

● The PivotTable updates to use the new summary calculation.

---

**Extra**

When there are two or more Data area fields, Excel creates a separate Data field in the Row Area. Excel places the new field on a separate row below each instance of the first field's data values. Excel allows you to place a maximum of 256 fields within the Data area. Because you can add multiple fields to the Data area, as with other areas of the PivotTable, you can change the analysis by using filtering to hide some of the Data area calculations. See the section "Filter a Field" for more information on selecting fields.

This process allows you to create one PivotTable containing all of your different calculations, but use filtering to only display the values relevant to the viewers. For example, an individual sales person may be interested in seeing how his or her sales total relates to the overall percentage of sales.

Excel allows you to change the order of the information on a PivotTable report by using the Sort option that displays when you click Data➪Sort. You can sort a PivotTable report by any field. See Chapter 2 for more information on sorting.

# Add a Calculated Field

Frequently your data analysis requires special calculations. If you want to include a field that contains a calculation based upon other fields or customized values in the PivotTable, you can create a *calculated field*. A calculated field is simply an inserted row or column containing a formula that you create. For example, you can create a calculated field to determine the amount of commission paid for each type of sales. The formula uses the value of the Sales field and multiplies it by the commission amount, similar to the following:

`=-(SALES * .10)`

You can use any of the standard Excel formula options on the Insert Calculated Field dialog box to create the formula for the calculated field. This includes built-in Functions and mathematical operators, such as *, +, and (). If you use a built-in function, you must make your arguments the

constant values or any of the PivotTable report fields in the Fields box. You cannot use cell references or range names within a formula for a calculated field.

You can create multiple calculated fields for each PivotTable report. Each field that you create displays as a separate Data field. As you create new calculated fields, Excel adds them to the Fields list on the dialog box. You can use a calculated field as an argument in a new calculated field. For example, you can determine the total earnings by subtracting the calculated commissions from the sales:

`= Amount - Commission Paid`

Although the calculated fields look like any other field, and appear in the PivotTable Field list once you create them, you can only place them in the Data area. You cannot move them to the Page, Row, or Column areas. For more on the different areas of a PivotTable, see the sections "PivotTable Basics" and "A View of the PivotTable Report Fields."

## Add a Calculated Field

① Select a cell within the PivotTable report.

② Click Insert⇨Calculated Field.

The Insert Calculated Field dialog box displays.

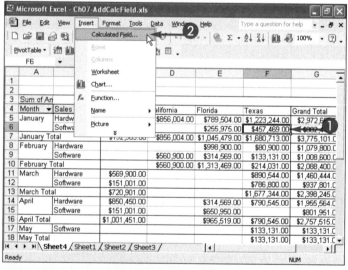

③ Type a label for the calculated field.

④ Type the formula for calculating the field values.

**Note:** See Chapter 4 for more on creating formulas.

● You can add a field to the formula by selecting one in the Fields list and clicking Insert Field.

⑤ Click Add.

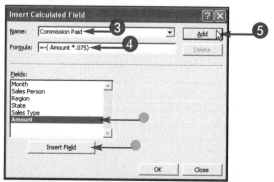

● The new calculated field displays in the Fields list box.

Repeat steps 3 to 5 to create additional calculated fields.

**6** Click OK.

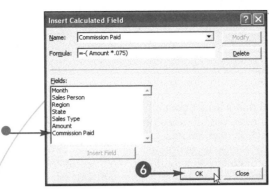

● The new calculated field displays in the PivotTable.

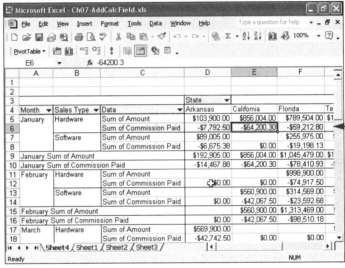

## Apply It

If you no longer want to include a calculated field in your PivotTable report, you can delete it. To remove a calculated field, select the calculated field label on the PivotTable report and then click Insert⇨Calculated Field. In the Insert Calculated Field dialog box, click the Name field and select the name of the calculated field you want to remove. If the Name field contains the calculated field, click Delete.

Keep in mind, if your PivotTable contains other calculated fields that rely on the deleted field, your PivotTable may not return the desired results. In fact, in most cases Excel displays an error message, such as #NAME?, in the cells that contain a formula that references the deleted calculated field. See Appendix D for information on formula errors.

If a calculated field does not return the results you want, you can modify the field. To modify it, click Insert⇨Calculated Field. In the Insert Calculated Field dialog box, click the Name field and select the name of the calculated field you want to modify. Make the appropriate changes in the Formula field and click Modify.

# Add a
# Calculated Item

To insert a new item in a field that was not part of the original source data, you can create a *calculated item*. A calculated item contains a user-created formula to determine the value of the item in a particular field. You create a calculated item by adding a new item to a field and then defining a formula that calculates the individual values for the item.

You create a calculated item on the Insert Calculated Item dialog box. When you display the dialog box, Excel shows where it will add the new calculated item as part of the dialog box title. For example, if you selected the Sales Type field or corresponding item, the title of the dialog box is, Insert Calculated Item in "Sales Type".

You can use any of the standard Excel formula options to create the formula for the calculated item. This includes using built-in Functions and mathematical operators, such

as *, +, and (). If you use a built-in function, you must make your arguments the constant values or field items listed in the Items list box. You cannot use cell references or range names within a formula for a calculated item. See Chapter 4 for more information on creating formulas. For example, you can type the following formula to calculate a Maintenance Fee for computer hardware sales:

```
=Hardware * 0.0125
```

You can create multiple calculated items for each field. Each item that you create displays as a row or column on the PivotTable. As you create new calculated items, Excel adds them to the Items list for the corresponding field on the dialog box. You can use a calculated item as an argument in a new calculated item. For example, you can determine the total amount earned for hardware and maintenance fees:

```
= Hardware + Maintenance
```

## Add a Calculated Item

① Select an item within the field where you want to add an item.

② Click PivotTable➪Formulas➪Calculated Item.

The Insert Calculated Item dialog box displays.

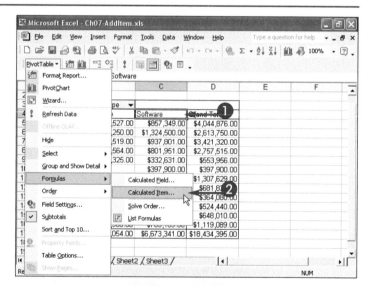

③ Type a label for the calculated item.

④ Type the formula for calculating the item values.

**Note:** See Chapter 4 for more on creating formulas.

● You can add an item to the formula by selecting one in the Items list and clicking Insert Item.

⑤ Click Add.

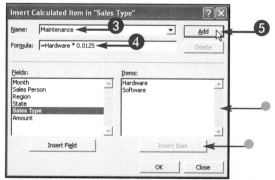

- The new calculated item displays in the Items list box.

Repeat steps 3 to 5 to create additional calculated items for the selected field.

6 Click OK.

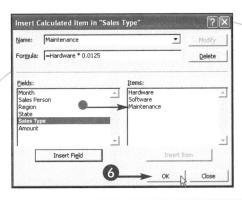

- The new calculated item displays in the PivotTable.

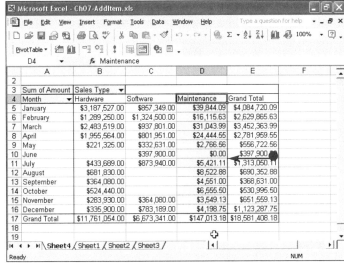

After adding a calculated item, you can have Excel automatically sort the PivotTable report so that it displays in ascending or descending order based upon the items in a particular field. To do so, click PivotTable➪Sort and Top 10 on the PivotTable toolbar to display the PivotTable Sort and Top 10 dialog box. The default AutoSort option is manual, which means the report only sorts when you use the Data➪Sort option. To sort it automatically, click either the Ascending or Descending options ( ○ changes to ● ), and select the field to use for the sort. Click an option in the Using field and select the PivotTable report field with which you want to sort. When you click OK, Excel sorts the PivotTable using the specified sort key field. To turn off the AutoSort, click the Manual option in the PivotTable Sort and Top 10 dialog box.

If you have calculated items whose formulas rely on another calculated item, you can make sure that Excel calculates them in the right order by viewing how Excel solves the formulas. To do so, click PivotTable➪Formulas➪Solve Order. In the Calculated Item Solve Order dialog box that displays, click a formula and then click Move Up or Move Down to change its order in the list.

# Retrieve a Value from a PivotTable Report

You can add PivotTable values to other worksheets containing data analysis by creating a separate formula to retrieve values from the PivotTable. If you want to retrieve a value from a PivotTable into a worksheet cell location, you can use the GETPIVOTDATA function. You use this function, instead of a simple cell reference, to dynamically display the values of a PivotTable based upon the filters on the PivotTable. For example, when you view the entire PivotTable report, cell E4 may contain the total sales in California in January. But, if you filter the report to only show sales from California and Texas, that value may now display in cell B4. See the section "Filter a Field" for more information on filtering.

To use the GETPIVOTDATA function, you must provide descriptive information about the PivotTable value you want to retrieve, including the name of the Data area field, and the corresponding Column area and Row area items. For

example, if you wanted the hardware sales for Texas, you need to specify that information as arguments for the GETPIVOTDATA function.

The GETPIVOTDATA function has two required arguments and up to 28 pairs of optional arguments. The `Data_field` argument expects the name of the Data area field for the value you want to retrieve enclosed in quotes. For example, if you want to retrieve a Sales amount, and the Data field is Sales, you specify a value of `"Sales"` in this field.

The next argument is `Pivot_table`, which requires a cell reference to the PivotTable. Remember, if the PivotTable is in a different worksheet, the reference must include the worksheet name.

The remaining arguments identify the value you want to retrieve. You must define the field and item. For example, to retrieve sales total from January, you specify a Field value of "Month" and an Item value of "January".

## Retrieve a Value from a PivotTable Report

① Select the formula cell.

② Click Insert⇨Function.

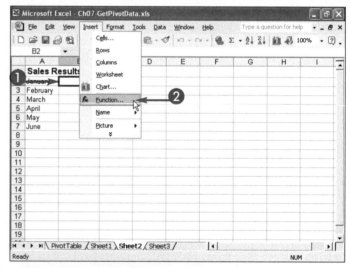

The Insert Function dialog box displays.

③ Select the GETPIVOTDATA function.

**Note:** See Chapter 4 for more information on inserting functions.

④ Click OK.

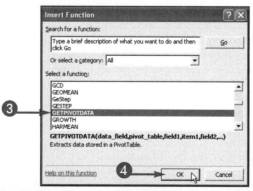

The Function Arguments dialog box displays.

**5** Type a name for the data field.

**6** Specify a cell reference to the PivotTable.

**7** Type the name of an associated field.

**8** Type the name of the item.

**9** Repeat steps 7 and 8 for all fields and items associated with the value.

**10** Click OK.

- The PivotTable value displays on the worksheet.

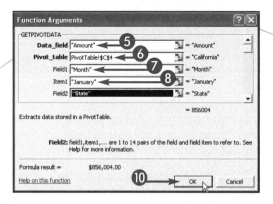

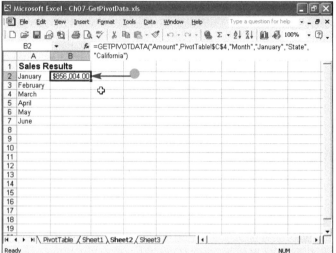

---

## Apply It

If you want to copy all values from a PivotTable, you can use the Paste Special option. To copy the PivotTable, click PivotTable➪Select➪Entire Table to select the entire PivotTable. After the PivotTable is selected, click Edit➪Copy to copy the selection. Select the first cell in the worksheet where you want to paste the copy of the PivotTable and click Edit➪Paste Special to display the Paste Special dialog box. Click the Values option (○ changes to ⦿) and then click OK. Excel pastes all of the visible values from the PivotTable in the new location. Excel does not copy any values that were hidden due to filtering to the new location.

If you want to see what values create a data value on the PivotTable report, you can view a summary of the original data values used to create the value. To view a summary, double-click the cell containing the data value on the PivotTable. Excel creates a separate worksheet that shows the records from the original database or Excel list that were used to create the data value.

# Create a PivotChart from an External Database

**A** *PivotChart* combines the dynamic, cross-tabulation ability of the PivotTable with the visual aspect of a chart. This allows you to dynamically analyze your data values in a chart format and to quickly spot any trend. Although you can use PivotCharts with data from any source, they are best suited for smaller sets of data, because if you try to show too much data on a chart, it becomes difficult to interpret. For more on PivotTables, see Chapter 7.

You create a PivotChart using the PivotTable and PivotChart Wizard, which gives you the option of creating just a PivotTable, or a PivotTable with a PivotChart. With the latter option, Excel creates a PivotChart placing each of the fields you add to the chart on the corresponding PivotTable. You can change field locations either on the PivotChart or PivotTable.

You can use any external database that Excel supports to create a PivotChart. When you do so, you actually import the data fields from the selected database. Therefore, you must use a database that you can access and have clearance from the database administrator. If you intend to share the workbook containing the PivotChart with other people, make sure that they can also access the database. If not, you should consider importing the database table into the workbook before creating the PivotChart. See Chapter 5 for more information on importing an external database table.

You must specify the location of the external database, on the second page of the PivotTable and PivotChart Wizard. You specify the database information with the Query Wizard, which displays when you import a database table. You specify the data source, or the type of database. You can open only databases that match the data source that you select. After locating the database, you can select the fields that you want to include in your PivotChart.

## Create a PivotChart from an External Database

① Click Data➪PivotTable and PivotChart Report.

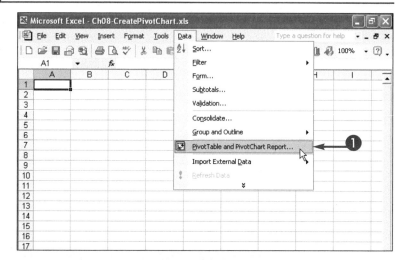

The PivotTable and PivotChart Wizard opens.

② Click the External data source option.

● Alternatively, you can select an Excel list or database.

③ Click the PivotChart report (with PivotTable report) option.

④ Click Next.

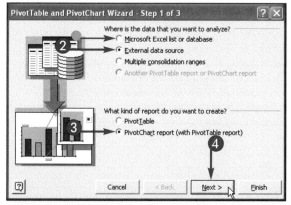

The second page of the wizard appears.

**5** Click Get Data.

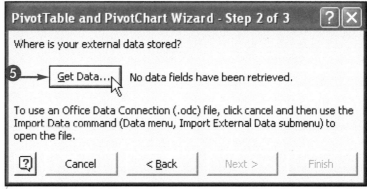

**PivotTable and PivotChart Wizard - Step 2 of 3**

Where is your external data stored?

**5** → [ Get Data... ]   No data fields have been retrieved.

To use an Office Data Connection (.odc) file, click cancel and then use the Import Data command (Data menu, Import External Data submenu) to open the file.

[?]   Cancel   < Back   Next >   Finish

The Choose Data Source dialog box opens.

**6** Select the data fields from the appropriate database.

**Note:** See Chapter 5 for information on importing data fields from a database table.

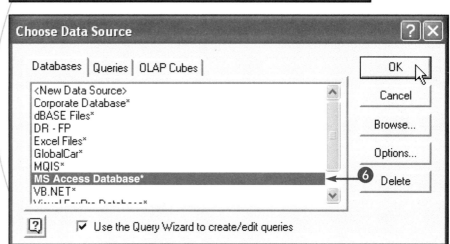

**Choose Data Source**

Databases | Queries | OLAP Cubes |

<New Data Source>
Corporate Database*
dBASE Files*
DR - FP
Excel Files*
GlobalCar*
MQIS*
**MS Access Database*** ← **6**
VB.NET*
Visual FoxPro Database*

OK
Cancel
Browse...
Options...
Delete

[?]   ☑ Use the Query Wizard to create/edit queries

## Extra

When you use the Query Wizard to select the database table fields to import for the PivotChart, you have the option of filtering the data based on a specific data value. If you want to import a large database table, consider filtering out only the desired range of data values. For example, if the database contains sales information for the last year, but you only want to show the sales for the last three months, you can use the Filter Data page of the Query Wizard to filter out the excess data records. By filtering the data records, you reduce the number of records that you need to work with in the PivotChart.

The Query Wizard lets you sort the database fields as it imports. You can skip this step when importing database table fields for use with a PivotTable or PivotChart. Because both report types are dynamic, Excel sorts the records based on the report selections. You can customize the sorting of the values displayed on the PivotChart by clicking Data⇨Sort within Excel.

continued →

**E**xcel always creates a new chart sheet for each PivotChart that you create. You cannot embed a PivotChart in a worksheet, as you can with regular charts. Although you cannot specify the PivotChart location, when you use the PivotTable and PivotChart Wizard, you still have to specify a worksheet location for the PivotTable report associated with the PivotChart. You can either place the report in the current worksheet or create a new worksheet within the current workbook. If you decide to place the PivotTable report in the current worksheet, you must specify the first cell for the report. You should specify a cell that does not contain data values. If you do so, Excel gives you the option of replacing the current cell values.

By default, Excel always creates a Stacked Column chart for the PivotChart. You can change the chart type with the Chart Type dialog box. See the section "Change the Chart Type of a PivotChart" for more information about changing the chart type.

You create the PivotChart report by dragging the appropriate fields onto the Data, Categories, Series, and Page areas. All the database fields appear on the PivotTable Field List box. As you add fields to the PivotChart, Excel adds the same fields to the associated PivotTable report. You can use any combination of the available fields, but if you do not use a field on the layout, the corresponding data values do not appear on the PivotChart.

Fields that you drag into the Category area of the PivotChart become the specific categories for the corresponding data points. The Category field corresponds to the Row field on the PivotTable. Fields that you place in the Series area identify the different data series for the chart. The Series fields correspond to the Column fields on the PivotTable report.

---

### Create a PivotChart from an External Database *(continued)*

- The wizard indicates that external database fields have been imported.

**7** Click Next.

The third page of the wizard appears.

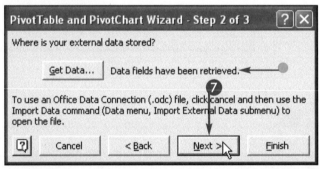

**8** Click Existing worksheet to place the associated PivotTable report in the current worksheet.

- You can click New worksheet to place the PivotTable in a new worksheet.

**9** Specify the starting cell.

**10** Click Finish.

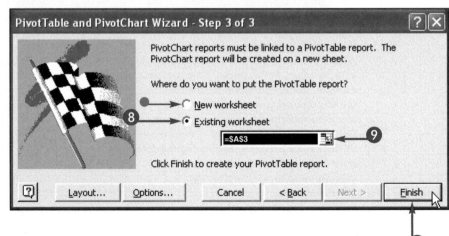

Excel creates the PivotChart with the
selected database fields listed in the
PivotTable Field List.

⑪ Click a field and drag it to the Data area.

⑫ Repeat step 11 for the Category, Series,
and Page areas.

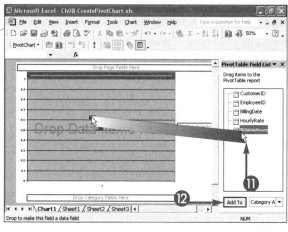

Excel displays the completed PivotChart.

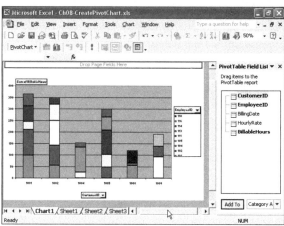

---

## Extra

When you create or view a
PivotChart, Excel displays
the PivotTable toolbar.
The toolbar has options
for quickly modifying
the PivotChart and its
corresponding PivotTable.
Excel grays out all
unavailable options.
You can display the
toolbar by clicking View⇨
Toolbars⇨PivotTable.

You can determine the
layout of a PivotChart by
selecting the Layout option
on the third page of the
PivotTable and PivotChart
Wizard. With the Layout
page that opens, you can
construct the PivotTable
report as well as the
PivotChart. You just need to
keep two things in mind:
Any field buttons that you
drag to the Row area
become the Category fields
on your PivotChart, and the
field buttons that you add
to the Column become the
Series fields.

Instead of dragging fields
from the PivotTable Field
List to the PivotChart, you
can use the Add To option
at the bottom of the list.
To add a field to an area
of the PivotChart, select the
field and then select the
location for the field from
the list next to the Add To
option. When you click
Add To, the selected field
appears on the PivotChart.

# Change the Layout
# of a PivotChart

You can visually analyze data in a different fashion by altering the layout of a PivotChart. If you want to change the layout of a PivotChart, you can quickly drag the fields to different locations. For example, you can move the fields in the Category area to the Series area or even add additional fields to an area. Keep in mind that when you change the Category fields, the number of data points on the chart changes to reflect the new category. The Category fields also determine the labels that appear on the Category axis. On the Stacked Column chart, the category axis is the horizontal or X axis.

You can add new fields using the PivotTable Field List, which shows all the fields that were selected when you created the PivotChart. The list displays the currently used

fields in bold. If you add a field to the Categories area, Excel creates a subcategory for the field on the right.

You can also move any fields on the PivotTable report from one area to another. When you move a field, the filter selections remain the same for the field. For example, if you are only viewing values for the months of January and February and you move the Month field to the Series area, those months remain the selections. See the section "Filter a PivotChart Field" for more information on filtering fields.

When you move or add fields on a PivotChart, Excel identifies the location for the field as you drag it. For example, if you drag the field to the Categories area and in front of the current fields, Excel inserts the new field to the left of the line. The field listed on the left of the Category area becomes the main category.

## Change the Layout of a PivotChart

### ADD FIELDS

**1** Click the desired field in the PivotTable Field List.

- You can also click the Show List button to display the PivotTable Field List.

**2** Drag the field to the desired area and release the mouse button.

A broken line indicates the area that will receive the new field.

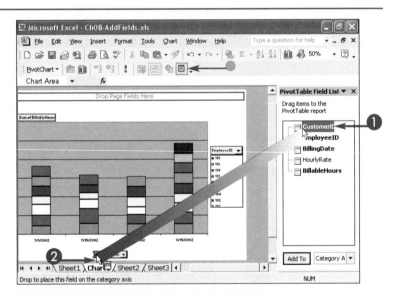

- The selected field appears in the corresponding area of the PivotChart.

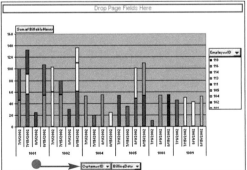

## MOVE FIELDS

① Select the desired field on the PivotChart.

② Drag the field to the new area and release the mouse button.

● A broken line indicates the area that will receive the new field.

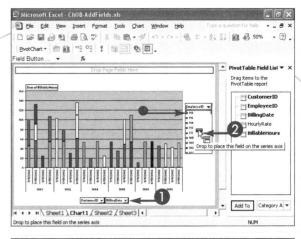

● The PivotChart updates to show the field in the new area.

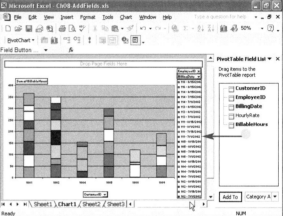

---

## Extra

When you change data in the original Excel list, Excel does not automatically update the values in the PivotChart. To automatically update the PivotChart and associated PivotTable values, you need to refresh your chart. Excel provides three different methods of updating a PivotChart. You can click the Refresh button ⬚ on the PivotTable toolbar, you can choose the Refresh option on the PivotTable menu, or you can right-click the PivotChart and select Refresh from the menu that displays.

You can remove any field from the PivotChart. To do so, click and drag it back to the PivotTable Field List. As you drag the selected field, the mouse pointer changes from an arrow to a button image and a red X indicates Excel is removing the button. When you remove a field, you simply remove it from the PivotChart display. It still remains in the list, and you can add it again at any point. Also, Excel removes any unwanted fields from both the PivotChart as well as from the corresponding PivotTable report.

Even if you do not have the PivotTable Field List displayed, you can still remove fields from your PivotChart by clicking on the desired field and dragging it off the chart.

# Change the Chart Type of a PivotChart

Y ou can use a different chart type with a PivotChart to aid in emphasizing different values in your data analysis. For example, if you want to analyze sales for each state over a year, you probably want to select a line or column chart. Whereas, if you want to compare sales within the state of Texas with the entire country, you want to select an area or pie chart. See Chapter 6 for more information about when to use different chart types to show data analysis.

If the default Stacked Column chart does not illustrate the PivotChart fields as desired, you can change the chart type using the Chart Type dialog box. With the exceptions of XY (Scatter), Stock, or Bubble chart types, which Excel does not allow you to use, you can use almost any of the chart types and associated subtypes on your PivotCharts.

You need to consider what types of data your specific chart type requires. For example, a Pie chart can display only one data series, so if your PivotChart contains multiple data series, not all data display on a Pie chart. To ensure that you can use a specific chart type with your PivotChart, you should preview the new chart type from the Chart Type dialog box. When you preview the PivotChart, Excel creates a sample chart using the data from your PivotChart.

When you switch to a different chart type, by default Excel maintains any specially applied formatting. For example, if you have modified font types, colors, and so on, Excel applies those options to the new chart type. If you want to use the default formatting of the new chart type, you must select the Default formatting option.

## Change the Chart Type of a PivotChart

❶ Click the entire PivotChart.

❷ Click Chart➪Chart Type.

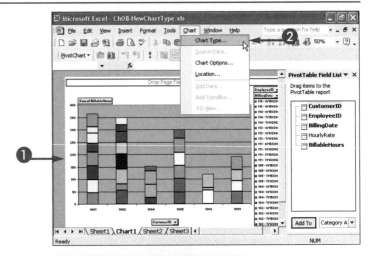

The Chart Type dialog box opens.

❸ Click the desired chart type.

❹ Click the appropriate chart subtype.

❺ Click Press and Hold to View Sample option to preview the chart.

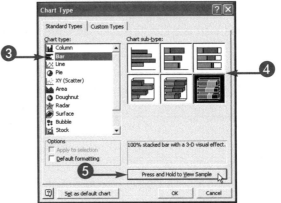

A preview of the PivotChart with the new chart type appears in the Sample box.

If the chart type is not valid, an error message appears in the Sample box.

⑥ Click OK.

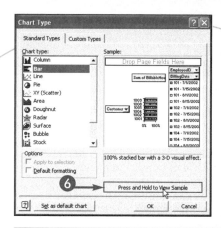

Excel updates the PivotChart to the new chart type.

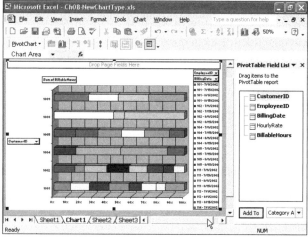

---

## Extra

You can create a custom chart type to use for your PivotCharts. A custom chart type, or *user-defined,* is a template for the layout of your PivotChart. When you create a custom chart type, Excel stores all the information about the appearance of the PivotChart, including the chart type, color changes, fonts, legends, and even data tables. After you create a custom chart type, you can select it from the Custom Types tab of the Chart Type dialog box when you create a PivotChart. To view the custom chart types that you have created, click User-defined ( ◯ changes to ◉ ). You can view a sample of the custom chart type with your data in the Sample box. See Chapter 6 for more information on creating a custom chart type.

If you do not like the appearance of the chart elements on your PivotChart, you can change the formatting. To do so, select the desired chart element and click Format⇨Selected *Element,* where *Element* is the name of the selected chart element. Depending on the element selected, different formatting options are available on several tabs in the Format dialog box.

# Filter a
# PivotChart Field

The filtering options available with PivotCharts simplify the process of analyzing the data displayed on the PivotChart; if you only want to see specific values on your PivotChart, you can filter the corresponding field. You can filter each field on a PivotChart to show only those records that meet your criteria. For example, if the Category area contains a Customer field, you can filter specific customer numbers and view sales from only specific customers.

By default, when you add a field to a PivotChart, all items display in the row or column. You can opt out of the default to display only certain item values. You can select any combination of the items in the menus for both the Categories and Series areas. If you assign a field to the Page area, you can either select all items or just one individual item. If you specify a single item for the field, only records

that contain that item value display on the entire PivotChart. You must select at least one item for each field or Excel displays an error message when you try to close the box. See the section "Create a PivotChart from an External Database" for more information on the Page, Categories, and Series areas of the PivotChart.

The items for each field come from the data that generated the PivotChart. If you created your PivotChart using an Excel list, the items in the box are the actual labels from the corresponding Excel column. If you created the PivotChart from an External database, the fields correspond to the names of the data fields. If you do not see the appropriate item in the box, check your original data values from the original Excel list or database. See Chapter 2 for information on data lists and Chapter 5 for information on databases.

## Filter a PivotChart Field

① Click the down arrow next to the field that you want to filter.

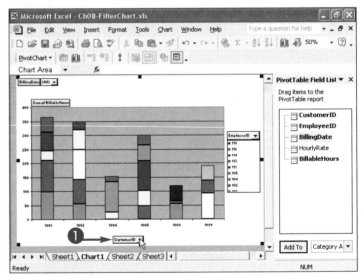

A list box displays the available items.

② Click Show All to remove the selection from the check boxes.

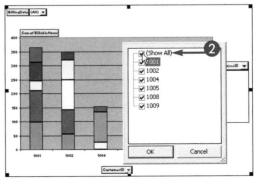

③ Click each item that you want on the PivotChart.

④ Click OK.

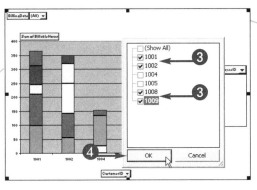

The PivotChart updates automatically to display only the selected items.

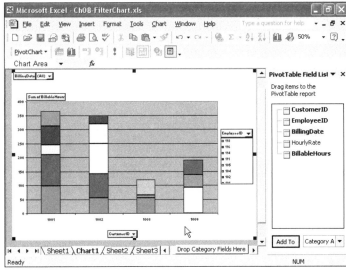

## Extra

Although a PivotChart works well for moving around fields to create a desired analysis, once you have the chart laid out and established the way you want, you may consider removing the field buttons that display in the Page, Category, Data, and Series areas. When you do so, the chart looks like a standard Excel chart and becomes more presentable for printing or display purposes. Hiding buttons also protects your chart from unwanted changes; users cannot change the layout of your chart when they cannot access buttons. See Chapter 1 for information on protecting a worksheet.

When you hide the field buttons that display on your PivotChart, Excel removes all buttons as well as the PivotTable Field List. To hide buttons, click PivotChart➪Hide PivotChart Field Buttons. To restore the buttons, click the option again. You can find the PivotChart option on the PivotTable toolbar. The toolbar displays when you view a PivotTable or PivotChart. If you cannot find the toolbar, you can display it by clicking View➪Toolbars➪PivotTable.

# Group Items in a PivotChart Field

f your PivotChart contains a lot of different data values, you may find it confusing to interpret all the information as part of your data analysis process. Instead of eliminating values from the chart by filtering, you can create smaller groups of items on the PivotChart. You group specific items to illustrate their relationship on the PivotChart, thus reducing the number of displayed data items. For example, if you have a Date field on the Categories axis, with specific dates as the items, you can group the dates together by month or quarter. See the section "Filter a PivotChart Field" for more information on filtering, and "Create a PivotChart from an External Database" for more on available fields.

You can group only items that contain numeric values, dates, or times directly on a PivotChart. And you can group only the fields that are part of either the Categories or Series fields. If you attempt to group another type of data on the PivotChart, Excel displays an error message.

In the Grouping dialog box, you must indicate where you want to start and end the grouping as well as how to group the data. For example, if you group a field that contains dates, you must specify the first date to group, the last date to group, and whether to group the dates by day, month, quarter, or year.

When you create a group, Excel changes the corresponding Series or Categories label to represent the group. If you attempt to filter the PivotChart, the new groups display as the filter items in place of the original items. For example, if you combine the dates 1/15/2002, 1/20/2002, and 1/25/2002 into a Month group, Excel displays the Month group as the label and places the individual items in the filter box.

---

## Group Items in a PivotChart Field

### GROUP ITEMS

1 Right-click the button for the field that you want to group.

2 Click Group and Show Detail⇨Group in the menu that appears.

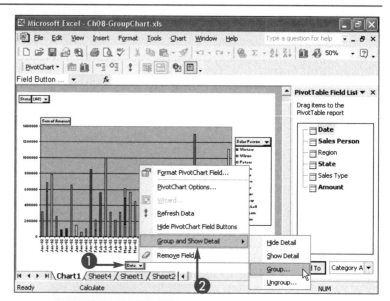

The Grouping dialog box opens.

- If desired, type a new start range value.

- If desired, type a different end range value.

3 Click the desired grouping.

4 Click OK.

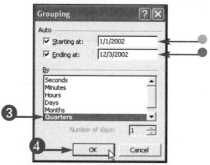

Excel groups the items from the selected field and changes the labels.

## VIEW THE NEW GROUPINGS

**⑤** Click the field button.

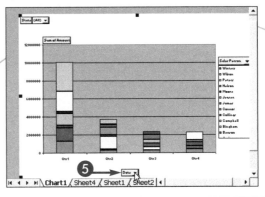

● The new groupings appear as the available filter items.

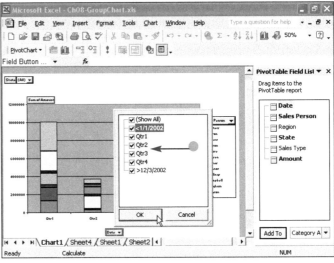

---

### Extra

If you want to group fields that do not contain numeric, dates, or time values, you can do so using the associated PivotTable report. Click the tab of the PivotTable report. On the PivotTable, click the items in the field that you want to group together and then click Data⇨Group and Outline⇨Group. When you switch back to the PivotChart, Excel groups the items together. Keep in mind that you do not need to have adjacent items to select them. See Chapter 1 to select items and Chapter 7 for more information on grouping items from a PivotTable.

When grouping together dates and times, you can use multiple groupings. For example, you can create a Months grouping and a Quarters grouping. To use multiple groupings, click each desired grouping in the By list in the Grouping dialog box. As you click each grouping selection, Excel highlights it in the list.

If you want to remove all groupings from a field, click Data⇨Group and Outline⇨Ungroup. Excel removes the groupings. The original data that you used to generate the PivotChart field items appears on the PivotChart.

153

# Add a Data Table to a PivotChart

**W**hen analyzing data using a PivotChart, you can make the data easier to interpret if you know what values display on the chart. If you want to see the exact value of each data point on a PivotChart, you can include a data table. A data table contains all numeric values shown on a PivotChart. Excel typically places the data table at the bottom of the chart sheet.

When you add a data table to an Excel chart, you have the option of displaying the legend keys next to the row labels in the table. The Legend keys are the colored squares that display next to each value name to identify how the value appears on the chart. If you select this option, the same keys on the Legend appear in the data table, making the use of the Legend redundant on the PivotChart. Therefore,

if you decide to use a data table, you should consider removing the Legend from the PivotChart display.

Excel frequently uses the Category axis as the column labels for the data table. For example, if you use the default PivotChart chart type of a stacked column chart, Excel attaches the data table to the Categories axis with the axis labels also being the column headings. However, if you create any type of bar chart, the data table becomes a separate element in the chart.

Data tables dynamically update when you change the values displayed on the PivotChart. For example, if you are analyzing the sales in different states within your organization, and you specify that you only want to view sales from California, Texas, and Florida, Excel updates the data table to show only those values.

## Add a Data Table to a PivotChart

① Click Chart⇨Chart Options.

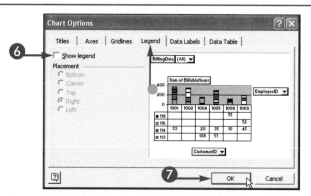

The Chart Options dialog box opens.

② Click the Data Table tab if it is not displayed.

③ Click the Show data table option.

④ Click the Show legend keys option.

⑤ Click the Legend tab.

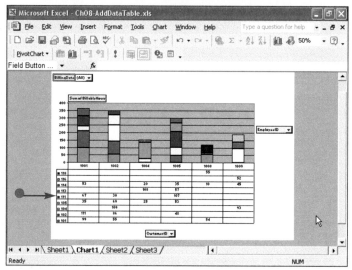

- The Legend tab displays options for customizing the legend.

**6** Deselect the Show legend option if it is selected.

**7** Click OK.

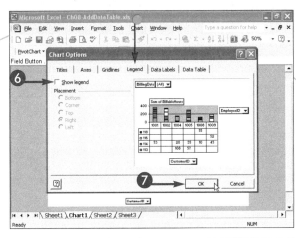

- The PivotChart updates to include the data table.

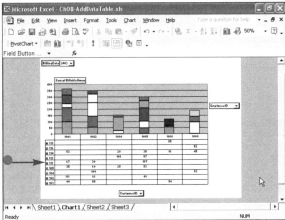

## Extra

You can customize the appearance of a PivotChart with the Chart Options dialog box. As you make changes to the options on the different tabs, the window displays a preview of how the PivotChart will appear. See Chapter 6 for more information on customizing a chart.

Instead of creating a data table to show the data point values, you can have Excel label the data items directly on the chart. This option works well if your chart does not include too many data values. To insert data labels, click Chart⇔Chart Options and click the Data Labels tab. You can select three types of data labels: Series Name, which displays the value from the Series axis directly on the data point; Category Name, which displays the value from the Category axis directly on the data point; and Value, which displays the actual value of the data point. You can use any combination of the three types of data labels on your chart. If you use more than one type, you must specify how to separate the different labels by selecting a Separator value, such as a comma.

# An Introduction to Macros

A *macro* is a set of instructions that you use to automate a task. Using macros enables you to repeat tasks much more efficiently than tediously performing each step over and over. When performing repeated data analysis steps, creating macros allows you to quickly perform the same steps in multiple worksheets. For example, if you want to take each column of numbers in a worksheet, convert them to currency, and then add them together, you can create a simple macro to perform this task. In other worksheets, you simply apply the macro, and Excel performs the corresponding steps. As an Excel user who analyzes data, you probably have a series of tasks that you perform frequently. By creating a macro to perform complex or repetitive tasks, you can save time by pressing a simple keystroke each time you want to perform the tasks.

You can create a macro to perform a task as simple as adding two numbers or as complex as creating a whole user interface within Excel. To do so, you can employ one, or a combination, of two different methods: You can use the Macro Recorder, or you can manually write a macro using the Visual Basic Editor (VBE). Although many macro users rarely venture past the Macro Recorder, you can harness the power of Visual Basic for Applications, or VBA, to create more complex macros. No matter how simple or complex the macros, they are all written in VBA.

Macro is a common term in the spreadsheet world. All spreadsheet packages enable you to create macros to automate tasks, and Excel is no exception. Although you can create macros with all Microsoft Office products, macros are often best suited for Microsoft Excel.

## Macro Recorder

Using the Macro Recorder is a great method for creating a macro without writing VBA code directly. The Macro Recorder holds true to its name. When you turn it on, like a tape recorder, it records all the events that occur within Excel. Excel takes the recorded events and creates the VBA code necessary to re-create the events. The Macro Recorder works well for creating simple macros, such as a macro that adds a column of numbers or changes the layout of the page. But because the Macro Recorder creates a macro by recording your actions, it cannot create a complex macro, such as one that repeats a process until meeting a specific condition or one that displays a custom dialog box. More complex Excel macros require the use of VBA.

The Macro Recorder does work well in conjunction with the Visual Basic Editor: You can modify all macros that you create with the Macro Recorder in the VBE. For example, if you want to create a macro that sums each column of data in your worksheet, you record the macro that sums a column. You then edit the macro in the Visual Basic Editor, modifying it to run the macro until Excel processes all columns. Combining the use of the Macro Recorder and the Visual Basic Editor simplifies the macro creation because Excel codes part of it for you. See the section "Record a Macro" for more information on recording a macro in Excel.

You write the Visual Basic for Applications, or VBA, code required to create complex macros using the Visual Basic Editor, accessible via all Microsoft Office applications, including Excel. Arranged in a series of windows, which you can move around with your mouse to obtain the desired development layout, the VBE contains project information.

The Visual Basic Editor remembers the window locations that you set up each time you open it. By default, not all windows are displayed when you initially open the Visual Basic Editor, but you can select the windows that you want to view from the View menu.

**Ⓐ PROJECT EXPLORER**

Displays a list of the open projects and corresponding modules, objects, and forms, using different nodes to represent each item type.

**Ⓑ OBJECT LIST BOX**

Lists objects associated with the selected project.

**Ⓒ PROCEDURE LIST BOX**

Lists the procedures associated with the selected object.

**Ⓓ CODE WINDOW**

Displays the VBA source code in the selected module.

**Ⓔ IMMEDIATE WINDOW**

Provides immediate results for statements typed in the window.

**Ⓕ WATCHES WINDOW**

Shows the set watches during debugging.

**Ⓗ PROPERTIES WINDOW**

Displays properties for the currently selected object.

**Ⓖ LOCALS WINDOW**

Shows values of local variables during debugging.

continued →

## Understanding VBA

You use the Visual Basic for Applications programming language to create all macros within Excel. VBA enables you to add complex functionality to a macro. To create a VBA macro, you need to be familiar with common VBA terminology.

### Variables

*Variables* are essentially just user-defined storage spaces. You can declare a variable to contain a specific type of data value.

You can make variable names almost anything including any combination of alphabetic characters, numbers, and some punctuation — such as #, $, %, ., and ! — as long as the first character is alphabetic. You cannot use spaces as part of the name.

VBA is not case-sensitive when it comes to variable names. You can make the names any combination of upper- or lowercase characters. Keep in mind that the name cannot exceed 254 characters.

### Data Types

A *data type* refers to how VBA stores data in memory. VBA provides an assortment of built-in data types that you can use to handle your macro data, along with user-defined data types that you create.

With VBA, you do not need to specify the type of data stored in a variable when you declare it. You can enable VBA to automatically determine the data type, but doing so can slow down your code for a large macro.

The size of a data type is the number of bytes required to store it. A *byte* is a group of bits, with a *bit* being the smallest storage unit and having a binary value or either 1 or 0. Knowing the number of bytes you need to store a data type can help you use memory more efficiently. Although storage issues are rarely a problem with most macros, keep them in mind when you create complex macros.

### NUMERIC

VBA provides several different numeric data types, categorized by the type of numeric value that you want to save. VBA provides three integer data types for numeric values that do not include a decimal portion and uses three floating-point data types. The one that you select depends on the size of the numeric values you want to store in the variable. The following table lists the various numeric data types:

| DATA TYPE | BYTES | RANGE OF VALUES |
| --- | --- | --- |
| Byte | 1 | 0 to 255 |
| Integer | 2 | -32,768 to 32,767 |
| Long | 4 | -2,147,483,648 to 2,147,483,647 |
| Single | 4 | -3.402823E38 to -1.401298E-45 for negative values |
|  |  | 1.401298E-45 to 3.40283E38 for positive values |
| Double | 8 | -1.79769313486232E308 to -4.94065645841247E-324 for negative values |
|  |  | 4.94065645841247E-324 to 1.79769313486232E308 for positive values |
| Currency | 8 | -922,337,203,685,477.5808 to 922,337,203,685,477 |

### BOOLEAN

You use a `Boolean` data type to store a logical value of `True` or `False`. A `Boolean` data type takes up two bytes of data storage. The keywords `True` and `False` are predefined as `Boolean` values in VBA. To assign them to a variable, you simply specify the value `BoolValue = True`.

### DATE

You can use the `Date` data type to store dates and times so that you can use them in calculations. VBA accepts a date range from January 1, 100 to December 31, 9999. Unfortunately, the date range within Excel is much smaller — January 1, 1900 to December 31, 9999. If you place a date value in an Excel worksheet that is outside this range, Excel produces an error message.

The `Date` data type is an 8-byte value that is stored as a decimal number. Because dates are numeric, calculations can use them.

When you specify dates and times in VBA, you enclose them in pound signs instead of the quotation marks used by strings:

Example:
```
Const StartDate As Date = #6/12/2001#
```

### OBJECT

You use the `Object` data type to define a variable as one of the objects that are part of the Excel Object Model. These data types are four bytes in size.

Excel provides an abundance of objects, including `Workbook`, `Window`, `Chart`, and `PivotTable`. Each of the objects provided by the Excel Object Model can be assigned as a data type — for example:

Example:
```
Dim chrt as Chart
Dim sheet1 as Worksheet
```

### STRING

You can use a `String` data type to store a sequence of characters. A string can contain any combination of letters, numbers, punctuation marks, and spaces. In order for VBA to recognize the start and stop of your string, you must enclose it in quotes — for example:

Example:
```
SampleString = "This is a sample"
```

You can declare strings using one of two different types: variable length and fixed length. As the names state, you declare *fixed-length* strings with a maximum number of characters and *variable-length* strings with as many as 2 billion characters.

To declare a fixed-length string, you need to specify the string length as part of the definition. When you declare a string length, the string is always that size, even if you assign a smaller string to it. For example, a string of 25 characters is declared as follows:

Example:
```
Dim FixedString As String * 25
```

On the other hand, variable-length strings have no length specified:

Example:
```
Dim VarString As String
```

## Variant

The `Variant` data type is the default data type that VBA uses. Because a variant can contain any type of data, VBA treats all variables that you do not assign a data type as variants. But because of the processing required by VBA to determine the data type, it is a good idea to use variants only for values that you cannot type with the standard VBA data types.

| DATA TYPE | BYTES | RANGE OF VALUES |
|-----------|-------|-----------------|
| Decimal | 14 | +/-79,228,162,514,264, 337,593,543,950,335 |
| Variant | 16 | -1.79769313486232E308 to -4.94065645841247E-324 (with numbers) for negative values 4.94065645841247E-324 to 1.79769313486232E308 for positive values |
| Variant | 22 + string length | 0 to 2,000,000,000 (with characters) |

## User-Defined

You can create user-defined data types to describe specific types of data. User-defined data types resemble an array because you can store multiple values using one variable name. But unlike arrays, which must contain values of the same data type, you create user-defined data types as a combination of standard VBA data types.

You specify a user-defined data type with the `Type` and `End Type` statements followed by the name of the new data type definition. For example, this data type stores information about individual books:

**Example:**
```
Type BookReview
     Title as String
     Pages as Byte
     ReviewDate as Date
End Type
```

## Arrays

An *array* is a group of variables with the same name and data type. For example, if you have a list of the 50 U.S. states, you can place the state names in an array called `States`. You refer to each value in an array as an *element*. You access elements of the array using index numbers that correspond to their positions in the array.

Using an array reduces the number of variables in your code because you declare only one variable to manage all your data values. Otherwise, storing all 50 states requires declaring and managing 50 different variables.

**Example:**
```
Dim States(50)
States(43) = "Texas"
```

An array with one list of data is called a *one-dimensional array.* With VBA, you can declare multidimensional arrays in which each array element has a corresponding array. For example, with the aforementioned `States` array, you can have a corresponding list of cities in each state. If a user selects Texas, a list of the cities in Texas becomes available:

**Example:**
```
States(43,5) = "Dallas"
```

VBA allows for up to 60 dimensions in an array, but most developers rarely use more than two or three dimensions.

You can declare an array either as *fixed-length,* where you specify the number of elements, or as *dynamic,* with an unknown number of elements:

**Example:**
```
Dim States()
```

## Constants

*Constants,* as the name implies, represent specific values that do not change within your code. You declare constants using the `Const` keyword. If you do not specify the data type for the constant, Excel treats the constant as a variant.

Using constants enables you to have only one place in the code to modify if the value of the constant changes. For example, suppose that you have the following constant declaration:

**Example:**
```
Const SalesTax As String = ".075"
```

If your state raises the sales tax, you simply have to modify the constant value — .075 in the example — and not each calculation. Using constants helps eliminate potential errors that can arise from mistyping a value.

## Operators

VBA provides several different operators that you can use in your code. You can group these operators into four general categories: arithmetic, concatenation, comparison, and logical. You should find most of these operators quite familiar.

## Arithmetic Operators

VBA accepts seven different arithmetic operators. When a statement, a single VBA expression or definition, contains multiple arithmetic operators, VBA uses precedence order to determine how to evaluate the statement. For example, VBA always calculates exponents first. The only exception to the precedence order are parentheses; when parentheses separate portions of a statement, VBA evaluates the contents of the parentheses first, still using the precedence

order within the parentheses and for the rest of the statement. In the following statement, `Val2` is added to `Val3`, and then the sum is multiplied by `Val1`:

**Example:**
```
Value = Val1 * (Val2 + Val3)
```

The following table lists arithmetic operators in their precedence order:

| OPERATOR | PRECEDENCE | PURPOSE |
|---|---|---|
| ^ | 1 | Raises the number before the operator to the power of the exponent — for example, $2^3 = 8$. |
| – (before a number) | 2 | Denotes a negative value. |
| * | 3 | Multiplies two numerical values. |
| / | 3 | Divides two numerical values and returns the entire result, including any decimal places — for example, $5 / 2 = 2.5$. |
| \ | 3 | Divides two numerical values and returns the integer portion of the result — for example, $5 \setminus 2 = 2$. |
| Mod | 4 | Divides two numeric values and returns the remainder — for example, $5\ MOD\ 2 = 1$. |
| + | 5 | Adds two numerical expressions. |
| – (minus sign) | 5 | Finds the difference between two numerical expressions by subtracting the second expression from the first. |

continued ➔

### Concatenation Operator

You can use the concatenation operator (&) to join together two or more strings. For example, ap & ple creates a new string, apple. VBA also enables you to use the + operator for concatenating strings, but for consistency purposes you should always use the & operator with strings.

### Comparison Operators

You use comparison operators between two expressions to determine if the expressions are equal, greater than, or less than each other.

VBA uses these operators to compare numerical or string values. If comparison operators compare a numerical and string value, Excel always evaluates the numeric expression as less than the string expression.

If you compare two string expressions, Excel looks at the characters in the string and not the string length. For example, if you compare abcd with cd, cd is considered to be greater because the letter C comes after A. This is true even though cd has fewer characters.

The following table lists comparison operators:

| OPERATOR | PURPOSE |
|---|---|
| = | Determines if the expressions are equal. |
| > | Determines if the first expression is greater than the second expression. |
| < | Determines if the first expression is less than the second expression. |
| <> | Determines if the expressions are not equal. |
| >= | Determines if the first expression is greater than or equal to the second expression. |
| <= | Determines if the first expression is less than or equal to the second expression. |

## Logical Operators

Logical operators evaluate expressions and return a logical value of True or False. For example, you can use a logical operator to compare two comparison expressions, as shown in the following:

**Example:**
```
If val1 > 10 And val2 = 5 Then
```

With this expression, the If statement can execute only if both expressions are true.

VBA supports six different logical expressions, and the following table lists their logical operators:

| OPERATOR | PURPOSE |
|----------|---------|
| Not | Negates the value of the expression. If the expression is True, the operator causes it to be False, or vice versa. |
| And | Performs a logical conjunction of two expressions. If they are both True, the result is True. If either of the expressions is False, the result is False. If either expression is Null, the result is Null. |
| Or | Performs a logical disjunction of two expressions. If the value of either expression is True, the result is True; otherwise, the result is False. Just like the And operator, if either expression is Null, the result is also Null. |
| Xor | Performs a logical exclusion (exclusive Or) on two expressions. The result is the converse of the Eqv operator. If both expressions are True or if both are False, the result is False. If one expression is True and the other is False, the result is True. |
| Eqv | Performs a logical equivalence on two expressions. If both expressions are True or if both are False, the result is True; otherwise, the result is False. |
| Imp | Performs a logical implication on two expressions. If both expressions are True or if both are False, the result is True. If the first is True and the second is False, the result is False, but if the first is False and the second is True, the result is True. |

# Record a Macro

You can use macros to automate a series of steps used to analyze data within a worksheet. For example, if you repeatedly sort and sum a series of values, you can create a macro to perform that task. The easiest way to create a macro is to use the Macro Recorder, which captures everything that you do and saves the steps in a macro with a name that you specify. After you create a macro, you can run the macro again, modify it, or delete it.

Because the Macro Recorder records every action that you perform when you use it, consider planning your steps before creating a macro. When you plan out the macro steps beforehand, you can save yourself some recording time, and the macro will run faster and more effectively. When you name a macro, use a name that starts with a letter and has no spaces in it; you can, however, use the underscore character to separate words.

Excel creates the macro with either relative or absolute reference to the cell where you apply it. To use a *relative reference*, meaning that the macro is performed based on the location of the cell, specify the cell reference by selecting the Relative Reference button on the Stop Recording toolbar. For example, you can create a macro that adds the values in the four cells above and places the total sum in the selected cell. With *absolute positioning*, however, the macro records in absolute mode and remembers the specific recorded cells. For example, the macro remembers always to add the same cells (such as A1 through A5) and place the total sum in cell A6. You can toggle between relative and absolute referencing while recording your macro by selecting the Relative Reference button. For more on relative and absolute cell references, see Appendix D.

---

## Record a Macro

① Click the worksheet cell to contain the results of the macro.

**Note:** If you intend to use other worksheet cells in your macro, make sure that the cells contain the desired values.

② Click Tools➪Macro➪Record New Macro.

The Record Macro dialog box opens.

③ Type a unique name for the macro.

- You can create a keyboard shortcut for your macro by typing the desired key in the Shortcut Key box.

④ Select where you want to store the macro.

⑤ Click OK.

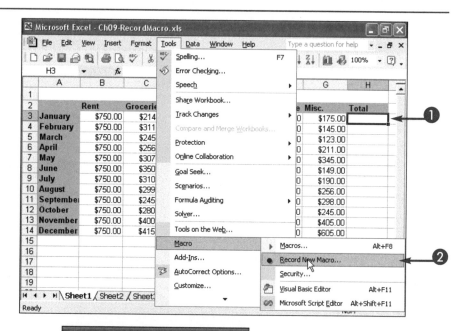

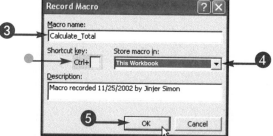

164

The Stop Recording toolbar appears.

● The status bar reminds you that a macro is recording.

❻ Perform the appropriate keystrokes to record the macro.

❼ When complete, click the Stop Recording button.

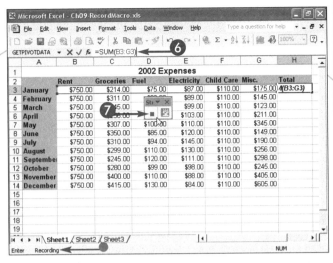

Excel records the macro.

The Stop Recording toolbar no longer displays on the screen.

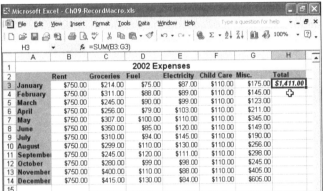

## Extra

You can use the Store Macro In option to store your macros in the current workbook, a new workbook, or the Personal Macro Workbook. You can store the macro in your current workbook, commonly referred to as the *active workbook*, by selecting the This Workbook option. Use this option if you want the macro available to anyone who opens the workbook. You can record the macro to a new workbook by choosing the New Workbook option. Excel creates the workbook automatically and adds the new macro to it. If you store a macro in another workbook, you need to open that workbook whenever you want to use that macro. You store macros in separate workbooks when you want to store specific types of macros in different workbooks. You can record a global macro by selecting Personal Macro Workbook, which serves as a common storage location for macros that you expect to use with other workbooks. Excel stores your Personal Macro Workbook as Personal.xls in the XlStart folder. This workbook does not exist until you store a macro in it. After you create the workbook, it loads as a hidden workbook whenever you run Excel.

# Run a Macro

You can run a macro to perform a repetitive data analysis task that normally would require multiple steps to save yourself some time. You can run macros in a worksheet that exist either in the current workbook or in any other Excel workbook, as long as the corresponding workbook is open. When you run a macro, Excel re-creates the recorded steps that you performed to create it or runs the VBA code that you created in the Visual Basic Editor. See the section "Create a Macro Using the Visual Basic Editor" for more information on the Visual Basic Editor.

You select macros to run from the Macro dialog box, which lists all currently available macros — those that Excel can locate in an open workbook. Because you can access only macros in open workbooks, you must open the workbook containing the macro that you want to run first.

When you create a macro, Excel stores it in one of three locations: the current workbook, a new workbook, or the Personal Macro Workbook. Excel opens the Personal Macro Workbook as a hidden file each time that you run Excel and makes all the macros that you store there available to run with any workbook. You can learn more about creating a macro in the section "Record a Macro."

To run a macro from another workbook, the macro must be from a signed source, or you must set your macro security to either Medium or Low. The default macro security level, High, requires that all macros from other sources be signed. Setting your macro security to Medium or Low enables you to run unsigned macros. See the section "Set Macro Security" for more information about macro security.

## Run a Macro

① Click File➪Open.

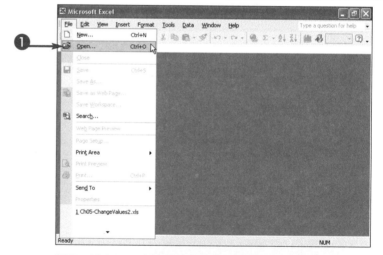

The Open dialog box opens.

② Click the workbook containing the macro that you want to run.

③ Click Open.

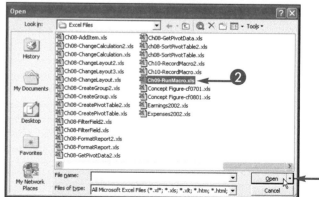

The selected workbook opens.

④ Click the cell in which you want the macro to execute.

⑤ Click Tools➪Macro➪Macros.

The Macro dialog box opens and displays a list of available macros.

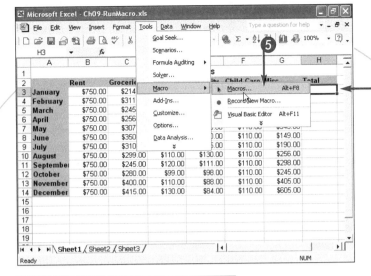

● If the macro is not listed, you can select the location of the macro.

⑥ Click the macro that you want to run.

⑦ Click Run.

The selected macro executes and makes the appropriate changes to the worksheet.

To run the macro again, repeat steps 4 to 7.

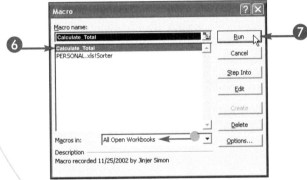

## Extra

You can use the Macros In field to limit the number of macros that are displayed in the Macro dialog box. To see the macros in any open workbook, including the Personal Macro Workbook, you can select the All Open Workbooks option. If you want to see only the macros from a specific workbook, select the name of the workbook in the Macros In drop-down list. For the global macros stored in the Personal Macro Workbook, you need to select the PERSONAL.XLS option.

Excel differentiates between macros listed in the Macro dialog box by placing the name of the workbook that contains the macro in front of the macro name. For example, Excel lists a macro named Sum_Expenses in the Personal Macro Workbook as PERSONAL.XLS!Sum_Expenses. Because of this naming scheme, two workbooks can have macros with the same name. In other words, if the macro Sum_Cells exists in both the Budget.xls and Expenses.xls workbooks, Excel treats them as two different macros because they are stored in two different locations. The Macro dialog box lists the macros as Budget.xls!Sum_Cells and Expenses.xls!Sum_Cells.

# Activate the
# Visual Basic Editor

With the Visual Basic Editor, you can create and modify Excel macros using Visual Basic for Applications, or VBA. Using the Visual Basic Editor, you can create more complex macros for analyzes data within Excel. You can run the Visual Basic Editor only from a Microsoft Office application. You can activate the Visual Basic Editor by editing a macro that you recorded with the Macro Recorder, or you can open the editor directly from the Tools menu by clicking the Visual Basic Editor option. Whether you create a macro using the Macro Recorder or in the Visual Basic Editor, you write all source code using VBA. Of course, with the Macro Recorder, Excel takes the keystrokes that you record and converts them to VBA.

When you open the Visual Basic Editor, the Project Explorer, if displayed, indicates your location within the project. If you open an existing macro from the Macro dialog box, the Project Explorer highlights the corresponding module in the tree, and the VBA code for the macro displays in the Code window. When you select the Visual Basic Editor directly, however, the Project Explorer highlights the name of the current project, which is the name of the workbook open in Excel. The Visual Basic Editor refers to each entry in the Project Explorer as a *node*. The top nodes, which are displayed in bold, represent the Excel VBA projects currently open. You can select a specific module in a project by double-clicking the module node in the Project Explorer.

Keep in mind that if the Personal Macro Workbook, Personal.xls, contains macros, the project for the Personal.xls project always opens when you access the Visual Basic Editor. Although the Personal Macro Workbook is hidden within Excel, in the Visual Basic Editor you can view and modify all its macros.

## Activate the Visual Basic Editor

### OPEN THE VBE USING THE TOOLS MENU

① Click Tools⇨Macro⇨Visual Basic Editor.

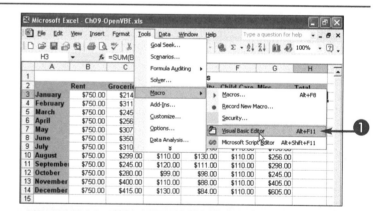

The Visual Basic Editor opens with the window layout that you last used.

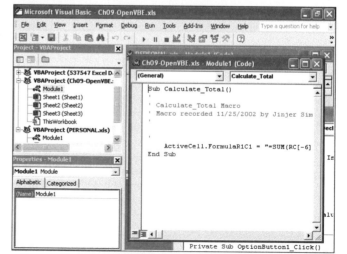

## OPEN THE VBE FROM THE MACRO DIALOG BOX

**1** Click Tools⇨Macro⇨Macros.

The Macro dialog box opens.

**2** Click the macro that you want to modify.

**3** Click Edit.

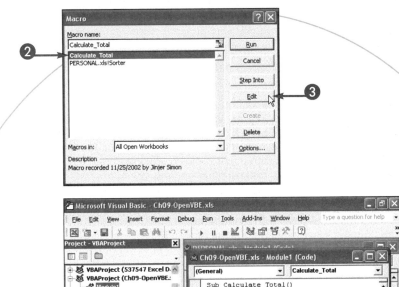

The Visual Basic Editor displays the code for the selected macro in the Code window.

● The module containing the macro is highlighted in the Properties window.

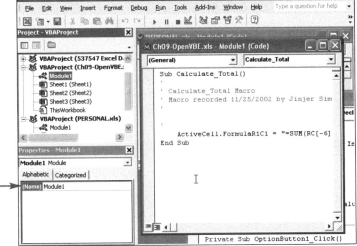

---

### Extra

For easier navigation in the Visual Basic Editor, you can use shortcut keys. These shortcuts work when the Visual Basic Editor window has focus, or is the selected window.

| SHORTCUT KEY | FUNCTION |
|---|---|
| F7 | Switches to the Code window for the object (node) that is selected in the Project Explorer. |
| F4 | Switches to the Properties window and displays the properties for the selected object. |
| Ctrl + R | Switches to the Project Explorer. |
| Alt + F11 | Toggles between the Visual Basic Editor and Excel. This shortcut is useful when trying to step through a macro. |
| F1 | Displays online help on the item selected in the Code window. |
| Shift + F2 | Displays a definition of the selected function or subroutine in the Code window. |

# Create a Macro Using the Visual Basic Editor

To create a macro in the Visual Basic Editor, you need to create a subroutine. You can easily create a subroutine within the Visual Basic Editor that executes a series of VBA commands. Each macro that runs in Excel is actually just a subroutine that contains blocks of VBA code. A single subroutine can call other subroutines and functions, so you can create a macro that is much more complex than just a simple subroutine.

VBA provides essentially two different types of subroutines: private and public. When you create a macro with the Macro Recorder, the subroutine it creates is *public,* meaning that all procedures, including the Macro dialog box, can access and see it. Conversely, only other procedures within the same module can access a *private* subroutine. Excel hides all private subroutines from the Macro dialog box, so you cannot activate them with key combinations. You should mark subroutines as private if you do not want

them accessible as macros. You do so by placing `Private` before the `Sub` statement, such as `Private Sub SampleSub()`. Typically, other subroutines within the same module call private subroutines. A subroutine is called using the `Call` statement — for example, `Call SampleSub()`. Excel considers any subroutines that do not have the `Private` keyword to be public; the use of the `Public` keyword is unnecessary because a subroutine with no keyword is the same as one with the `Public` keyword.

VBA does allow a subroutine to be called without the `Call` statement. However, even though the `Call` statement is not required, you should always use it to remind you that another procedure is being called. Using the `Call` statement makes your code much more readable because another user can quickly look at the code and see that another subroutine is being called.

## Create a Macro Using the Visual Basic Editor

① In the Project Explorer, click the project to which you want to add a new macro.

**Note:** The project is the name of the workbook in which you want to store the new macro.

② Click Insert➪Module.

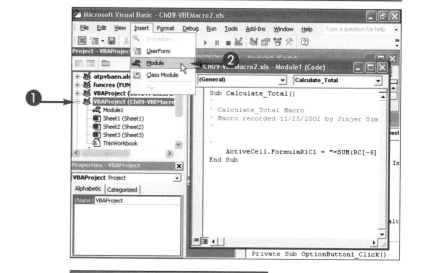

Excel opens a blank Code window.

③ Type **Sub**.

④ Type the name of your subroutine.

⑤ Type **()** after the name of the subroutine.

⑥ Press Enter.

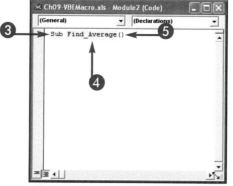

● The Visual Basic Editor inserts the
End Sub command when you press
Enter.

**7** Type the macro code.

**8** Switch to Excel and open the Macro
dialog box.

**Note:** See the section "Run a Macro" to open
the Macro dialog box.

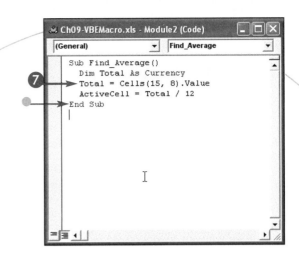

● The new subroutine appears as a
macro along with the other available
macros.

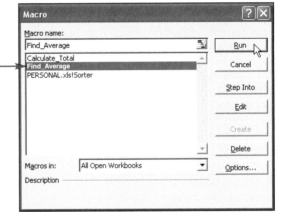

## Extra

You may have situations in which you want to pass parameters to subroutines. A *parameter* is essentially
a variable that receives an argument from the statement that you use to call the subroutine. Just like
standard variables, you want to specify the data type for the subroutine parameters to avoid their being
converted to variants.

In the following example, the Call statement in the TotalValues subroutine calls the AddValues
subroutine and passes in the values contained in the Value1 and Value2 variables. A subroutine that
has parameters cannot be called from the Macro dialog box. Other procedures typically call subroutines
with arguments. Therefore, you would run the macro TotalValues and it would call the subroutine
AddValues by passing the required parameter values.

**Example:**
```
Sub TotalValues
  Dim Value1, Value2 As Integer
  Value1 = 5
  Value2 = 7
  Call AddValues (Value1, Value2)
End Sub
Sub AddValues (Val1 As Integer, Val2 As Integer)
   Dim Total As Integer
   Total = Val1 + Val2
   MsgBox (Total)
End Sub
```

# Update a
# Recorded Macro

**A**s your data analysis needs change, you may find that a macro needs updating because you want it to perform additional or different steps. You can update a macro at any time by adding or removing VBA code. Of course, after you record a macro, you can record over the top of it to replace it, but you cannot modify it directly within Excel. The only way to actually modify the macro code is to change the corresponding subroutine in the Visual Basic Editor. If you do not know how to read and write the VBA code required for the step that you want to add to the macro, this can become quite an undertaking.

Typically, modifying a macro, even one that you create with the Macro Recorder, requires manually specifying the new VBA code that you want to add. A quick-and-dirty method for updating a macro involves recording another macro

containing the steps that you want to add to the first one and then using the Copy and Paste buttons in the Visual Basic Editor to add the new steps to the old macro. For example, if you create a macro to sum up a column of values but forget to change the formatting of the column to Currency, you can record a second macro in Excel that formats the column. After you do this, you open the Visual Basic Editor and copy the formatting code of the second macro and paste it into the subroutine for the first macro. Keep in mind when you copy the code that you want to copy only the portion of the subroutine between the `Sub` and the `End Sub` statements.

After you copy the code from the new macro into the old macro, you should delete the new macro from the Macro dialog box.

## Update a Recorded Macro

① In the Macro dialog box, click the macro that contains the source code that you want to add to the original macro.

**Note:** To open the Macro dialog box, see the section "Run a Macro."

② Click Edit.

The Visual Basic Editor displays the code for the selected macro.

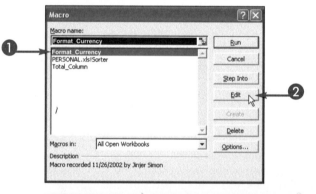

③ Click the start of the source code that you want to copy.

④ Press the Shift key and click the end of the source code to copy.

Excel highlights the code that you selected.

⑤ Click the Copy button.

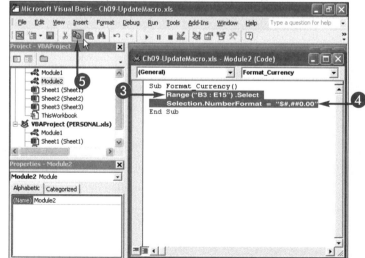

⑥ Click the module that contains the code for the macro you want to update.

⑦ Place the cursor between the last line of code and the End Sub command.

**Note:** You may need to insert a blank line.

⑧ Click the Paste button.

⑨ Close the Visual Basic Editor.

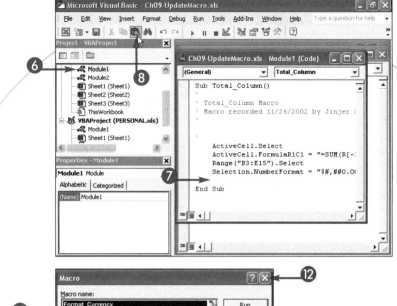

⑩ In the Macro dialog box, click the macro from which you copied source code.

⑪ Click Delete to remove the macro.

⑫ Close the Macro dialog box.

When you run the updated macro, Excel executes the original and copied code.

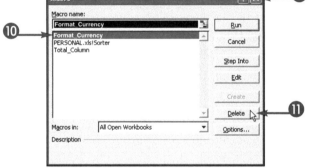

## Extra

When you view the VBA code for your macro, you may notice that a single quote ( ' ) precedes several lines. These lines are called *comment lines;* programmers use these lines to provide information about the code, such as what the code does, when it was created, or even who coded it. When you use the Macro Recorder to create a macro, by default Excel adds several comment lines. These comment lines always indicate the name of the macro, the creation date, and the programmer. If the programmer created a keyboard shortcut for the macro, the comments contain this information as well. Making modifications to the comment lines does not affect the macro execution. In fact, Excel ignores any line of text or code preceded by a single quote when the macro executes.

**Example:**
```
Private Sub add()
'
' add Macro
' Macro recorded 5/19/2001 by Jinjer Simon
'
' Keyboard Shortcut: Ctrl+d
'
    ActiveCell.FormulaR1C1 = "=SUM(RC[-6]:RC[-1])"

End Sub
```

# Set Macro Security

**W**hether you create your own macros for data analysis, or open workbooks created by other users containing macros, you need to specify your macro security settings. Due to the increasing problem with computer viruses, specifically macro viruses, by default Excel disables all macros in worksheets that you open except ones with digital signatures from trusted sources.

Digital signatures, which macro creators use to verify their macros' safety, remain attached to a macro or other file as long as no one modifies the macro or file. Macro modifications require you, as the creator, to reattach the signature. A macro with a valid digital signature confirms the macro's origins and that no one altered it.

There are three different security settings you can select for macros:

- High: The default security level for Excel. This level disables all unsigned macros, even ones that you

create. You have the option of selecting macros from other trusted sources when you run Excel.

- Medium: This level of security enables you to specify whether you want to run macros from trusted and unsigned sources when you load Excel. Select this level if you want to eliminate the hassle of signing the macros that you create.

- Low: With this level, Excel automatically loads all workbooks and macros without checking to see if they are from trusted sources. With this setting, the only protection from macro viruses is a good virus scanner.

To eliminate the hassle and expense of acquiring a digital certificate, you can personally sign your macros by running `selfcert.exe`, an Office XP program. Creating and attaching your personal signature indicates that you certify the security of a macro, identifies the macros that you create, and distinguishes your macros from other macros.

## Set Macro Security

### SET SECURITY

**1** Click Tools⇨Macro⇨Security.

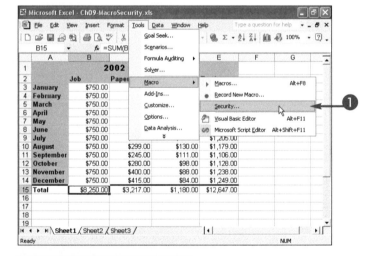

The Security dialog box opens.

**2** Click the Security Level tab.

**3** Click the desired security level.

**4** Click OK.

Excel assigns a security level.

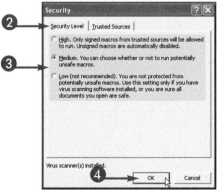

## CREATE A PERSONAL SECURITY CERTIFICATE

1. Open Microsoft Windows Explorer.

2. Click the Office10 subfolder of the Microsoft Office folder.

**Note:** Office XP typically locates your program files in C:\Program Files\Microsoft Office.

3. Double-click the SelfCert.exe program file.

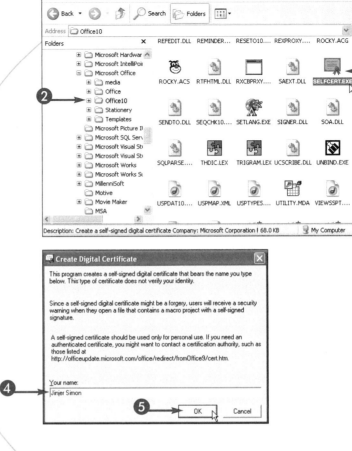

The Create Digital Certificate dialog box opens.

4. Type your name.

5. Click OK.

SelfCert.exe creates a digital certificate.

---

## Extra

Assigning a certificate you create with SelfCert.exe to a project indicates that the project is self-signed and not authenticated. This option works well for personal workbooks. However, if you plan to distribute your workbook to other users, you probably want to consider acquiring a true digital signature file. When you use a commercial digital signature file, the digital ID attaches to the macro and remains with it; if the macro is altered in any way, the user is notified that the macro has been changed and should not be trusted. This ensures that a macro you create is not altered to harm another person's machine.

The most common source of digital certification is VeriSign, Inc. Of course, to obtain a commercial certification, you have to submit an application and pay the appropriate fee. You can find out more about obtaining a digital certification for your macro at www.verisign.com. Another company that you can contact for a digital ID is Thawte Consulting. You can find out about their digital signature options at www.thawte.com.

continued →

I f you create a data analysis workbook containing macros that you want to distribute to others, you should consider assigning a digital signature to the workbook. As previously discussed, a digital signature provides you assurance that the workbook file is valid and has not been altered by other sources.

You can assign a digital signature to any of your macros. You attach signatures to code in a macro, or file, to signify that the code is valid and that no one has modified it since you applied the signature.

No matter what type of digital signature you choose to assign to your macro, a certified digital signature or personal digital signature, you follow the same steps. You must acquire the digital signature before you can assign it to the macro. Personal digital signatures work well for indicating that no one has altered the macro since you

assigned the signature, but they do not certify it like the ones you acquire from a commercial agency.

After you acquire a digital signature, you need to attach it to your macros. Attaching a digital signature is similar to sealing an envelope: If an envelope arrives sealed, no one has tampered with its contents. Keep in mind that the digital signature stays attached to the macro only until someone modifies it. Excel even removes the digital signature if you modify the VBA code. Therefore, if you make any modifications at all to the macro code, you need to re-attach the digital signature.

If you are not sure whether you have modified a macro since attaching the digital signature, you can check if the signature is attached in the Digital Signature dialog box. If a digital signature is attached, the name of the signature displays in the Certificate Name field in the dialog box.

### ASSIGN A DIGITAL SIGNATURE TO A MACRO

**1** Select the module that contains the macro you want to sign.

The macro code is displayed in the Code window.

**2** Click Tools⇨Digital Signature.

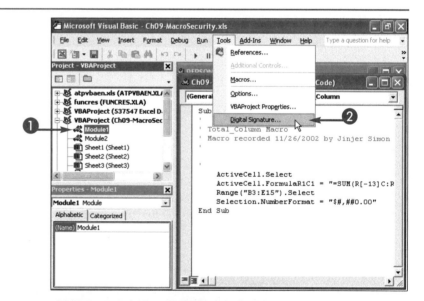

The Digital Signature dialog box opens and indicates whether a digital signature certificate is currently assigned to the selected macro.

**3** Click Choose.

The Select Certificate dialog box opens and displays a list of available digital signature certificates.

④ Click the desired certificate.

⑤ Click OK.

⑥ Click OK in the Digital Signature dialog box.

⑦ Close the workbook in Excel.

⑧ Reopen the workbook containing the macro.

Depending on the type of certificate loaded, you see a message indicating that a signed macro is being loaded.

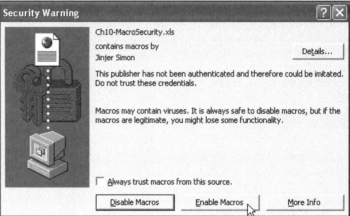

## Extra

When a worksheet containing a signed macro loads, you can indicate that you trust the source by clicking the Always Trust Macros From This Source check box (☐ changes to ☑ ). If you select this option, Excel saves the name of the trusted source in the Trusted Sources tab of the Security dialog box. You can view the list of trusted sources by clicking Tools➪Macro➪Security to display the Security dialog box and then selecting the Trusted Sources tab.

If you no longer want to trust macros from a source listed on the Trusted Sources tab, you simply highlight the name of the source and click Remove. If you remove the source from the list, the next time you open a workbook with a macro from that source, Excel again warns you about its macros.

On the Trusted Sources tab, you have two other options. To have Excel also warn you before opening installed add-ins and templates, remove the check mark from the Trust All Installed Add-ins and Templates check box. To allow Excel to access all macros with your project without warning you, select Trust Access to Visual Basic Project.

# Create a Custom Function

I f you cannot find an Excel function to accomplish a desired data analysis task, you can create a custom function within the Visual Basic Editor. You can also create functions to use with your other VBA subroutines.

When you create a public function in the Visual Basic Editor, it appears in the Insert Function dialog box within Excel under the User Defined category. You can use these VBA functions directly in your worksheet to create formulas in the same fashion that you use the built-in functions that come standard with Excel. Keep in mind that a VBA function that you create is only available when the corresponding workbook containing the function is open in Excel. Therefore, if you create a specific function that you want to use with all your workbooks, you must add it to the Personal Macro Workbook — Personal.xls, which always opens with Excel — to ensure that it is always available.

You can also use functions with the code you create for a macro within the Visual Basic Editor. You can create functions to return a value to the procedure that calls them. Unlike subroutines, you cannot call functions directly from the Macro dialog box. When working with macros, only a subroutine can call a function. Like subroutines, functions consist of blocks of VBA code grouped together to perform a common task or series of tasks.

At first glance, the value of a function may appear somewhat limiting. But unlike subroutines, which do not return a value, functions always return a value, making them ideal for performing calculations. For example, you can create a function that always calculates the sales tax for an item and returns that amount.

## Create a Custom Function

① Click Insert⇨Module to create a blank module in a project.

**Note:** For a worksheet function, place the module in the Personal.xls project.

② Type **Function**.

③ Type the name of your function.

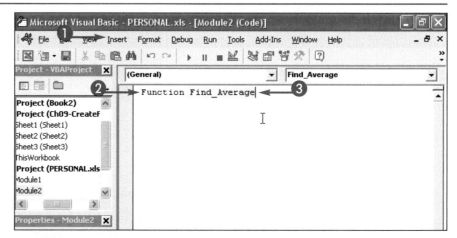

④ In parentheses, type the names of the function parameters.

⑤ Type **As**.

⑥ Type the data type to be returned by the function.

⑦ Press Enter.

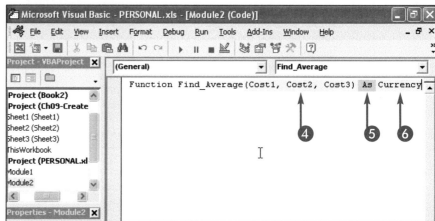

- The Visual Basic Editor inserts the `End Function` command when you press Enter.

**8** Set the function name equal to the value of the function.

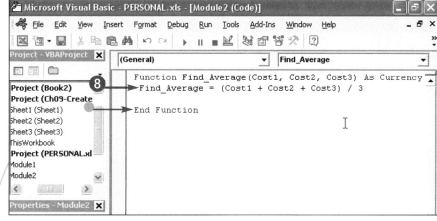

The Visual Basic Editor creates a new Excel function.

- The new function appears in the Insert Function dialog box.

**Note:** See Chapter 5 for information on working with Excel functions.

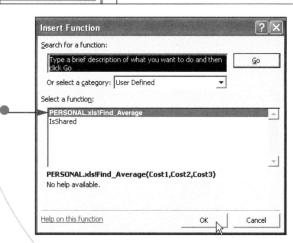

## Extra

There are essentially two different types of functions: private and public. All modules within the workbook can access a *public* function. However, only other procedures within the same module can access a *private* function. You mark a function as private by placing `Private` before the `Function` statement as in the example `Private Function SampleFunc(Param) As Integer`. Excel considers any functions that do not have the `Private` keyword to be public. Therefore, using the `Public` keyword is unnecessary because a function with no keyword is the same as one with the `Public` keyword.

Other functions and subroutines within the same module typically call private functions. Because functions return a value, they are typically called as part of an expression. For example, you can assign the value returned by a function to a variable: `FunctionValue = SampleFunc(Param)`. This line of code exists in a subroutine that calls the function. When Excel encounters this code, the function executes using the value of the `Param` parameter, and the result of the function is placed in the `FunctionValue` variable.

# Declare a Variable

Y ou can use variable declaration to make your VBA code run more efficiently. *Variable declaration* means that you specify the data type of the variable when you declare it. For example, if you intend for the variable to contain only integer values, you declare an integer variable.

Unlike some programming languages, VBA enables you to use variables that have not been declared. However, if you misspell a variable within your code, VBA may treat the misspelled variable as a totally different variable. For example, if you use the variable MthRent throughout your code and inadvertently type it as MnthRent, VBA sees MnthRent as a new variable and assumes that MthRent and MnthRent are two different variables. To ensure that variables are always properly declared, use the Option Explicit statement as the first statement in a module before you type any procedure code.

You can select the Require Variable Declaration option in the Editor dialog box in the Visual Basic Editor to ensure that variables are always declared for all created procedures. If you select this option, the Visual Basic Editor places the Option Explicit statement at the top of each created module.

Even if the variable is declared, you should also assign a data type to it as part of the declaration. VBA treats all variables without a data type as *variants.* A variant is VBA's catchall data type because it can essentially contain any type of data. In fact, the same variable can contain an integer value at one point and a string value at another location within the same module. Because VBA is forced to interrogate the value in the variant variables to determine the type of data, your code becomes less efficient when you do not explicitly specify the data type.

## Declare a Variable

① Type **Option Explicit** at the top of the module.

② Position the cursor after the Sub statement.

③ Type **Dim**.

④ Type the name of the variable.

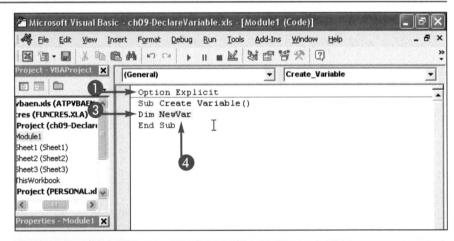

⑤ Type **As** after the variable name.

⑥ Type your variable data type.

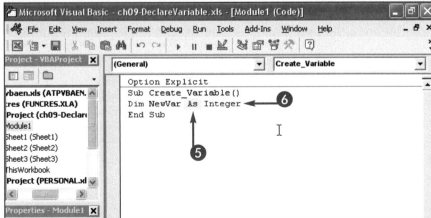

**7** Press Enter.

**8** Type your variable name.

**9** Type an equal sign (=) and a starting value for your variable.

**10** Set the cell location equal to the name of your variable.

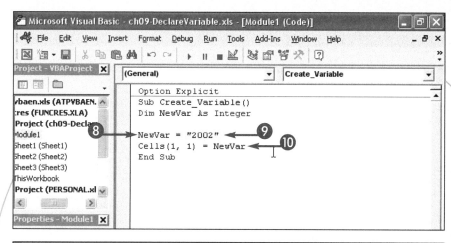

**11** Switch to Excel and run the corresponding macro.

● The declared value displays in the cell specified in step 10.

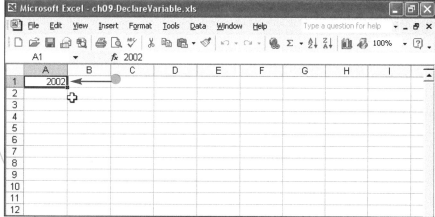

## Extra

You can reference a specific cell in a worksheet with the Cells property using one of two methods. The first method enables you to specify the row and column number of the appropriate cell. For example, to specify the row and column number to reference cell A5, you type Cells(5,1). This is interpreted as the cell in the fifth row and the first column. Using the cell reference method, you can reference rows from 1 to 65,536 and columns from 1 to 256.

The second method numbers each cell on the worksheet between 1 and 16,777,216 (65,536 rows by 256 columns). With this method, you specify one numeric value for the cell, which may confuse you at first. For example, cell M1 is referenced as Cells(13).

| EXCEL CELL | COLUMN/ROW REFERENCE | NUMERIC REFERENCE |
|------------|---------------------|-------------------|
| A1 | Cells(1,1) | Cells(1) |
| A2 | Cells(2,1) | Cells(257) |
| C5 | Cells(5,3) | Cells(515) |

# Execute a Task a Specific Number of Times

t is quite common to perform the same data analysis tasks repeatedly within the same worksheet. For example, you may want to summarize each column of data values. Instead of manually rerunning a macro, you can set up a macro to repeat the same tasks a specific number of times. You can use the For Next loop to execute a statement or a series of statements a specific number of times in your macro. For example, using a For Next loop enables you to add the values in a specific number of cells.

The For Next loop consists of four basic parts. The For statement initiates the loop. You specify a counter variable with an initial and a maximum value, such as A = 1 To 5. The inside of the body of the loop consists of a series of statements that performs until the counter meets the maximum value of the loop. Finally, you mark the end of the loop with the Next statement. The For Next loop

executes until the counter variable reaches the specified maximum value, and then control moves to the next statement outside the loop.

When the For Next loop starts, it checks that the value of the counter variable has not met the maximum value. The counter variable is a numeric value that is incremented by 1 each time the loop executes. If the variable is less than the maximum, the loop executes. If the minimum value is initially greater than the maximum value, the body of the loop never executes.

VBA provides several other statements that you can use to control the flow of a macro, such as the Do While statement, which repeats the statements as long as a condition is true. See Appendix C for additional program flow statements.

## Execute a Task a Specific Number of Times

**①** Create a new subroutine for the macro.

**Note:** See the section "Create a Macro Using the Visual Basic Editor" for more information.

**②** Declare the loop variable and any other variables needed for the subroutine.

**Note:** See the section "Declare a Variable" for more information.

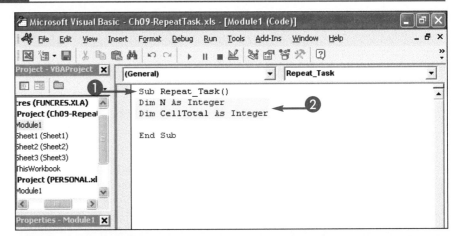

**③** Type **For N = 1 To Max**, replacing N with the variable declared for the For Next loop and Max with the maximum value of the loop.

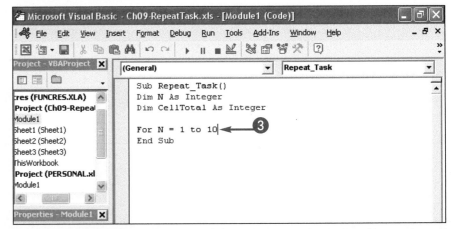

④ Type the VBA statements for the body of the loop.

**Note:** See the section "Create a Macro Using the Visual Basic Editor" for more information.

⑤ Type **Next** to indicate the end of the loop.

⑥ Type any additional code needed for your subroutine.

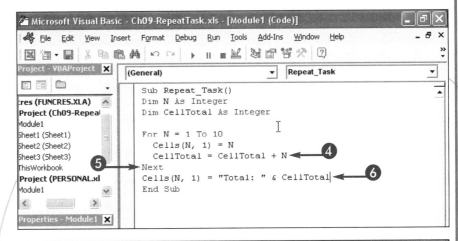

⑦ Switch to Excel and run the associated macro.

● The macro executes the contents of the For Next loop the specified number of times.

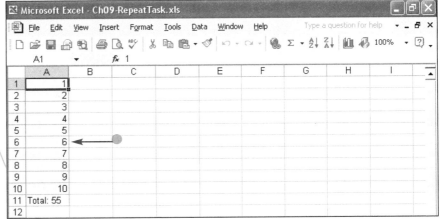

## Extra

You can specify a different value to increment the counter variable. By default, the counter variable for the For Next loop increments by one each time the loop executes. If you want to increment or decrement the counter variable by a different numeric value, you can use the Step statement and specify the increment value. If you specify a positive value, the counter variable increments by that value each time the loop cycles. If you specify a negative value, the counter variable decrements by that value each time the loop cycles. The For loop starts with an initial counter variable J of 2 and a maximum value of 20. Each time the loop cycles, the counter variable increments by 2. The TotalVal variable increments by the value of the loop. The loop executes ten times. When the initial and maximum value of the counter are equal, the loop executes a final time before it passes control to the next statement outside the loop.

**Example:**
```
For J = 2 To 20 Step 2
     TotalVal = TotalVal + J
Next
```

# Display a Message Box

You can use the `MsgBox` function to display pop-up message boxes when a VBA procedure executes. The `MsgBox` function does two things: It displays a dialog box to provide information to the user and returns a value that indicates the response from the user. You capture the user response by assigning the results of the `MsgBox` function to a variable. For example, the code `UserResponse = MsgBox("Do you want to continue?")` assigns a value between 1 and 7 indicating the user response to the `UserResponse` variable. If the user selects the OK button, the `MsgBox` function returns a constant value of `vbOK` or `1`.

The `MsgBox` function has five different arguments: `Prompt`, `Buttons`, `Title`, `Helpfile`, and `Context`. All but the first argument are optional. The `Prompt` argument indicates the value that displays in the message box. You can make this argument a text string and enclose it in quotes or use a

variable. You can combine values by using the concatenation operator (`&`), as in the example `MsgBox("Total Sum: " & TotalSum)`.

The optional `Buttons` argument enables you to specify a constant value, which displays the buttons and icons on the message box. If you do not specify a button constant, the `MsgBox` function uses the default `vbOKOnly`, which displays only the OK button.

The optional `Title` argument contains the text that displays on the title bar of the message box. If you omit this argument, Excel displays a default value of Microsoft Excel.

The final two optional arguments let you add help functions to the message box. `Helpfile` specifies the name of the help file, and `Context` specifies the context ID of the help topic to display.

## Display a Message Box

① Create a new subroutine.

② Type **Dim MsgVar As Integer**, replacing `MsgVar` with the variable to receive the `MsgBox` return value.

③ Declare other variables needed for the subroutine.

**Note:** See "Create a Macro Using the Visual Basic Editor" for more on subroutines and "Declare a Variable" for more on variables.

④ Type **MsgVar = MsgBox("Text Prompt", buttons, "Text Title")**, replacing `"Text Prompt"` with the prompt, `buttons` with the button constant, and `"Text Title"` with the title.

● You can type **+** to separate multiple button constant values.

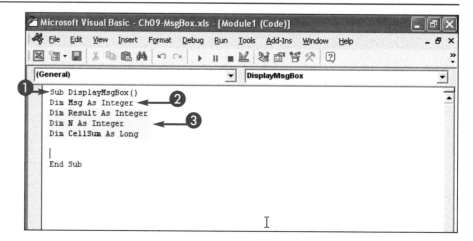

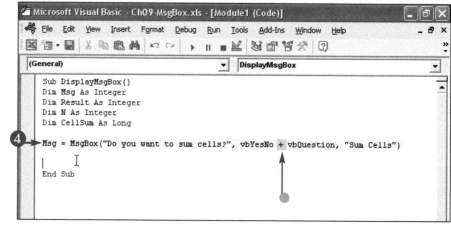

⑤ Type a conditional statement to test the value returned.

**Note:** In this example, the `If Then` statement looks to see if a value of 6 or 7 is returned.

⑥ Type additional code for the subroutine.

- ● You can type **&** to join the text string with a variable value.

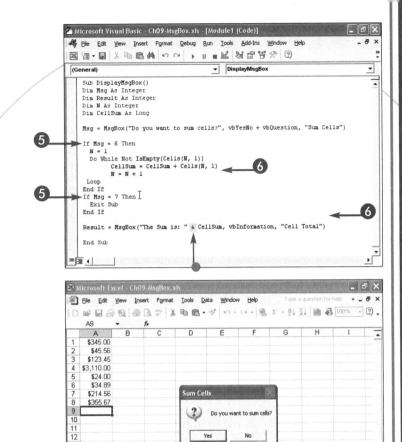

⑦ Switch to Excel and run the macro.

The message box displays and the macro processes the value of the clicked button.

---

## Extra

The `MsgBox` function returns an integer value between 1 and 7 that indicates the button selected by the user. You can determine the button clicked by the user using the value returned by looking at the integer value or using the constant value that represents the button. The following table shows the integer values returned by the `MsgBox` function and the equivalent constant value.

| MSGBOX RETURN VALUE | CONSTANT | DESCRIPTION |
| --- | --- | --- |
| 1 | vbOK | OK button clicked |
| 2 | vbCancel | Cancel button clicked |
| 3 | vbAbort | Abort button clicked |
| 4 | vbRetry | Retry button clicked |
| 5 | vbIgnore | Ignore button clicked |
| 6 | vbYes | Yes button clicked |
| 7 | vbNo | No button clicked |

If you want to display information for the user, such as results, and you do not care about a user response, you can use the `MsgBox` function without capturing the user response. The following example displays the contents of the `TotalSum` variable in a message box with the OK button. The message box closes when a user clicks OK, but Excel does not return the value of the button to your procedure. You can use the `MsgBox` function without assigning it to a variable if the only argument is the `Prompt` value.

**Example:**
```
MsgBox(TotalSum)
```

# Request User Input for a Macro

Y ou can use the `InputBox` function to prompt for specific user input during the execution of a procedure. The `InputBox` function displays a dialog box requesting specific input and returns the user response. You capture the user response by assigning the results of the `InputBox` function to a variable.

The `InputBox` has seven different arguments, but only the first is required: `Prompt`, `Title`, `Default`, `xPos`, `yPos`, `Helpfile`, and `Context`. The `Prompt` argument indicates the user prompt on the dialog box. You can make this argument either a text string enclosed in quotes or a variable. You can combine values using the concatenation operator (`&`), as in this example: `UR = InputBox("Sum: " & TSum)`.

The optional `Title` argument contains the text that appears on the title bar of the dialog box. If omitted, Excel displays

a default value of `Microsoft Excel`. The optional `Default` argument specifies the default value to display in the text box in the dialog box.

You specify the display position of the dialog box using the optional arguments `xPos` and `yPos`. If you omit them, the dialog box opens in the center of the screen. These arguments use units of measurement called *twips*. One twip equals ⅟₂₀ of a point or ⅟₁,₄₄₀ of an inch. The `xPos` argument indicates the distance from the left side of the screen to the left side of the dialog box. The `yPos` indicates the position from the top of the screen to the top of the dialog box.

You use the final two optional arguments for adding help to the dialog box. `Helpfile` specifies the name of the help file, and `Context` specifies the context ID of the help topic to display. If you specify one argument, you must specify both.

## Request User Input for a Macro

① Create a new subroutine.

② Type **Dim UserInput As Variant**, replacing `UserInput` with the variable to receive a value from the `InputBox` function.

③ Declare and initialize any other variables for the subroutine.

**Note:** See the section "Declare a Variable" for more information.

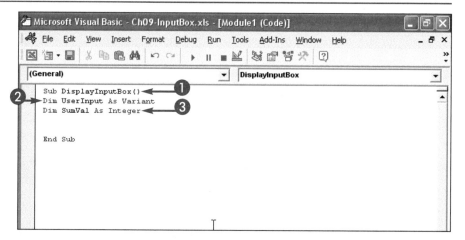

④ Type the initial VBA code.

This example uses a `Do While` loop to request values from a user until the user types **Done**.

⑤ Type **UserInput = InputBox("Text Prompt")** replacing `"TextPrompt"` with the text to display.

● You can type **&** to join the text string with a variable value.

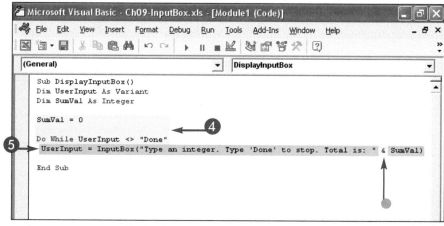

**6** Type additional code to process the value returned from the `InputBox` function.

**Note:** See Appendix C for more information about VBA functions.

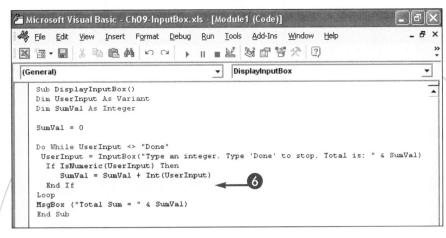

```
Microsoft Visual Basic - Ch09-InputBox.xls - [Module1 (Code)]

File   Edit   View   Insert   Format   Debug   Run   Tools   Add-Ins   Window   Help

(General)                              ▼    DisplayInputBox                    ▼

Sub DisplayInputBox()
Dim UserInput As Variant
Dim SumVal As Integer

SumVal = 0

Do While UserInput <> "Done"
 UserInput = InputBox("Type an integer. Type 'Done' to stop. Total is: " & SumVal)
  If IsNumeric(UserInput) Then
     SumVal = SumVal + Int(UserInput)        ◄─── 6
  End If
Loop
MsgBox ("Total Sum = " & SumVal)
End Sub
```

**7** Switch to Excel and run the associated macro.

The `InputBox` function requests specific input from the user.

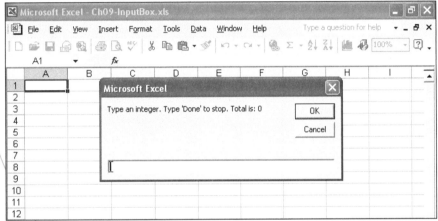

```
Microsoft Excel - Ch09-InputBox.xls

File   Edit   View   Insert   Format   Tools   Data   Window   Help       Type a question for help

A1        fx

          A       B       C       D       E       F       G       H       I
1
2      ┌─────────────────────────────────────────────────────┐
3      │ Microsoft Excel                                    X │
4      │                                                      │
5      │ Type an integer. Type 'Done' to stop. Total is: 0   │    ┌──── OK ────┐
6      │                                                      │    │            │
7      │                                                      │    │  Cancel    │
8      │ [                                                  ] │
9      └─────────────────────────────────────────────────────┘
10
11
12
```

## Extra

You can use named arguments to simplify your function calls. When you work with built-in VBA functions, you see that many of the functions have optional arguments. For example, although the `InputBox` has seven different arguments, only the first one is required. If you want to specify any additional arguments, you must specify the argument values in order, leaving a placeholder for any that you do not want to use.

**Example:**
```
UserInput = InputBox("Type a value",   , "test")
```

Instead of specifying a placeholder for each value, VBA also enables you to use named arguments with the built-in procedures. When you use a named argument, you specify the name of the argument along with the corresponding value. To specify a named argument, you type the name of the argument followed by a colon, an equals sign, and the value of that particular argument. You can specify named arguments in any order, and you do not have to specify a value for every argument.

**Example:**
```
UserInput = InputBox(prompt:="Type a value.", default:="5")
```

# Assign a Macro to a Menu

I f you frequently use specific macros to analyze your worksheet data, you may want to assign the macros to an Excel menu to make them easier to activate. You can assign a macro to any existing Excel menu. If you do not want to use existing menus, you can even create a new menu. By assigning a macro to a menu, you make the macro as accessible as any menu option. Assigning macros to menus eliminates the need to remember the shortcut key required to launch the macro.

When you add a macro to a menu, it remains on the menu for all workbooks that you open in Excel. For that matter, you should assign the macros in your Personal Macro Workbook to a menu for easy access from all workbooks. The Personal Macro Workbook stores commonly used macros for the current user and opens as a hidden file each

time that you run Excel. Because the Personal Macro Workbook is always open, any workbook can use all its macros.

To keep your macros easy to find, you may want to place them all on one custom menu. For example, you can place all of your data analysis macros on a menu named Data Analysis. You can create a new Excel menu using the Customize dialog box. Of course, whatever menu you decide to use as a home for your macro must exist in the Excel window before you can add the macro option to it.

You add options to a menu by dragging them onto the menu from the Customize dialog box. In fact, you can modify menus only when the Customize dialog box is open. You can remove menu options in a similar fashion by dragging them from the menu back to the Customize dialog box.

## Assign a Macro to a Menu

① Click Tools➪Customize.

The Customize dialog box appears.

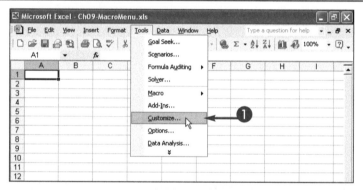

② Click the Commands tab.

③ Click Macros.

④ Click Custom Menu Item.

⑤ Drag the item to the desired menu.

The menu expands and a line indicates your position in the menu.

⑥ Release the mouse button.

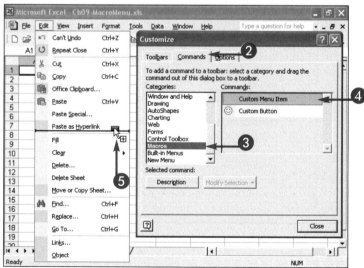

**7** Right-click the menu option.

**8** Click Name.

**9** Type the desired name for the macro menu option.

**10** Click Assign Macro.

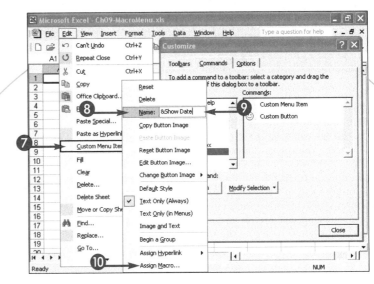

The Assign Macro dialog box appears.

**11** Click the name of the macro that you want to assign to the new menu option.

**12** Click OK.

The macro runs each time that you select the menu option.

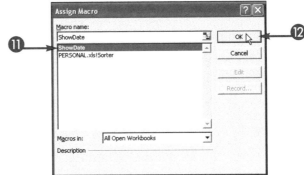

## Extra

You can keep all the macro references in one location and keep from cluttering up the existing Excel menus. To create a new menu, open the Customize dialog box. On the Commands tab, select the New Menu option as the category. A New Menu option displays as the available command. Click the New Menu option and drag it to the desired menu location. After you add the menu, you can right-click it and change the name. Now the menu is ready to receive your macros.

When you name a menu option, you can also create a shortcut key that corresponds to the menu option, which is similar to the shortcuts that you create for macros. The difference is that the menu option shortcut launches whatever command you assign to the menu option. Also, these shortcuts launch with the Alt key. To create a menu shortcut, you need to type **&** before the character in the menu item name that corresponds to the shortcut key. For example, if you want Alt + T to launch the menu option Determine Total, you place the & before the letter *T* to get "De&termine Totals," or "Determine &Totals."

# Run a Macro As a Workbook Opens

If you repeatedly perform the same tasks or execute the same macro whenever you open a workbook, you may want to have the macro execute automatically. You can create a macro that runs automatically each time a particular workbook opens. Because this type of macro executes only once as the workbook opens, it works well for launching custom menus and toolbars, opening other workbooks, determining whether specific conditions are met, or displaying welcome messages. The macro executes when the workbook opens by catching the Open event that the opening workbook triggers.

To create a macro that executes when a workbook opens, you need to create a new procedure named Workbook_Open and add it to the ThisWorkbook object code module for the workbook. In fact, all event-handling procedures that you create for monitoring workbook events must reside within the ThisWorkbook object to have Excel execute them

automatically. Although the procedure resides in the ThisWorkbook object code module, it can access other procedures within the same workbook. Therefore, you can create a Workbook_Open procedure that calls procedures located in another module.

If you have a procedure that you want to execute whenever Excel opens, you must place the procedure within the ThisWorkbook object for the Personal Macro Workbook, Personal.xls. Because the Personal Macro Workbook always loads as a hidden workbook in Excel, any procedures within this workbook appear to execute as Excel opens. Keep in mind, however, that Excel associates the Personal Macro Workbook with an individual user.

You can keep a Workbook_Open procedure from executing for a particular workbook by holding down the Shift key as the workbook opens. Because workbooks typically open rather quickly, you need to make sure that you press and hold the Shift key as soon as you select the workbook.

## Run a Macro as a Workbook Opens

① In the Project Explorer, locate the workbook to which you want to add the Workbook_Open subroutine.

② Double-click the ThisWorkbook object node under the workbook.

The code module opens for the ThisWorkbook object.

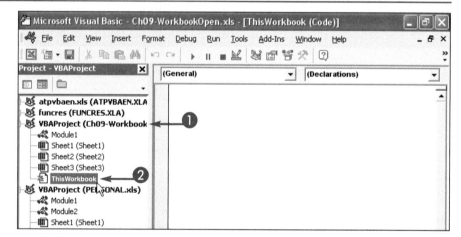

③ In the Object box, click the dropdown arrow and select the Workbook option.

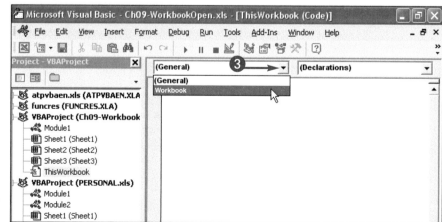

- The Visual Basic Editor creates a new `Private` subroutine named `Workbook_Open`.

④ Type the VBA code to run when the workbook opens.

⑤ Click the Save button to save the workbook including the new subroutine.

⑥ Close Excel.

⑦ Open the workbook in Excel.

- The `Workbook_Open` procedure executes the specified VBA code as the workbook opens.

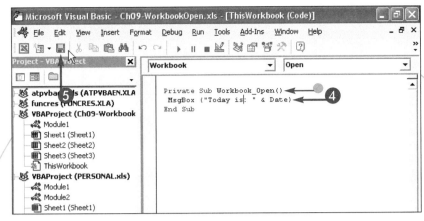

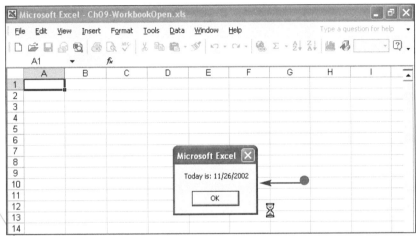

## Extra

You can use the `Open` method of the `Workbooks` collection object to specify a workbook that Excel should open whenever the current workbook opens. For example, if your workbook relies on data values within another workbook, you can open that workbook whenever the current workbook opens. For example, the following code opens a workbook called `Expenses.xls` as read-only.

**Example:**
```
Workbooks.Open Filename:="Expenses.xls", ReadOnly:=True
```

You can use the Object drop-down list box in the Code window to quickly create your `Workbook_Open` subroutine. The Object list box lists the available objects for which you can create subroutines within the current code module. For example, if you access the `ThisWorkbook` code module, the only available object is `Workbook`.

When you select the `Workbook` object from the Object list, the Visual Basic Editor automatically creates a private subroutine called `Workbook_Open`. This is because the default event for the `Workbook` object is the `Open` event. If you view the Procedure list box, you see a list of all available events for the `Workbook` object. If you select another event from the list, the Visual Basic Editor creates a new subroutine for that event.

# Using an Excel Function in a Macro

**Y**ou can add almost all of the Excel worksheet functions to your VBA code, but they provide a very limited number of built-in functions and may not cover your specific data analysis situation. However, by using the available Excel functions, you can add functionality to your macros that is not available with the VBA functions. For example, Excel provides several different financial functions that you can add to a macro to perform financial analysis.

One of the properties available for the `Application` object, the `WorksheetFunction` property is part of the Excel Object Model that VBA uses to access features of Excel. The `Application` object refers to the actual Excel program. The `WorksheetFunction` object stores all of the Excel Worksheet functions. To access one of the functions in the `WorksheetFunction` object, you use

the `WorksheetFunction` property and precede the name of the function with the statement: `Application.WorksheetFunction`. The function follows with any arguments required by the function enclosed in parentheses. For example, the code `Application.WorksheetFunction.Max(Num1, Num2, Num3, Num4)`, uses the `Max` Excel worksheet function to compare the values in four different variables to determine which variable contains the largest value.

You cannot call Excel worksheet functions that have equivalent VBA functions. For example, both VBA and Excel have functions called `Cos` that return a numeric value that represents the cosine of an angle. If you try to use the `Cos` Excel worksheet function in your macro code, you receive an error message stating "Object doesn't support this property or method." See Appendix B for a list of available Excel functions and Appendix C for available VBA functions.

## Using an Excel Function in a Macro

① Create a new subroutine for the macro.

**Note:** See the section "Create a Macro Using the Visual Basic Editor" for more information.

② Type **Dim WSVar as DataType**, replacing `WSVar` with a variable to contain the results of the function call and `Datatype` with the data type.

③ Declare any additional variables for the subroutine.

④ Initialize values of the variables.

⑤ Type **WSVar=Application. WorksheetFunction**, replacing `WSVar` with the name of the variable declared in step 2.

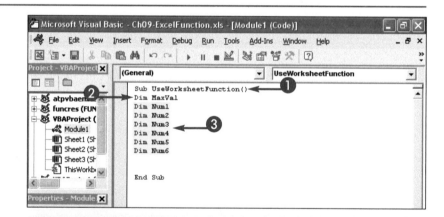

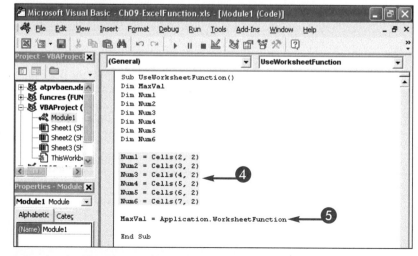

**6** Type **.FunctionName(arguments)**, replacing `FunctionName` with the Excel Function and `arguments` with the corresponding function arguments.

- As you type the argument list, Microsoft IntelliType displays a list of the required arguments for the function.

**7** Type any additional VBA code required to display the results of the Excel Function.

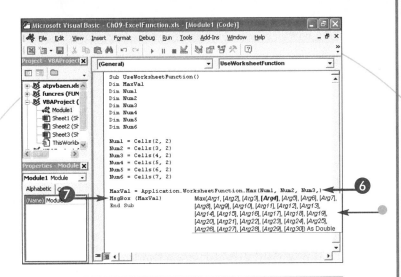

```
Sub UseWorksheetFunction()
Dim MaxVal
Dim Num1
Dim Num2
Dim Num3
Dim Num4
Dim Num5
Dim Num6

Num1 = Cells(2, 2)
Num2 = Cells(3, 2)
Num3 = Cells(4, 2)
Num4 = Cells(5, 2)
Num5 = Cells(6, 2)
Num6 = Cells(7, 2)

MaxVal = Application.WorksheetFunction.Max(Num1, Num2, Num3,)
MsgBox (MaxVal)
End Sub
```

Max(*Arg1*, [*Arg2*], [*Arg3*], [**Arg4**], [*Arg5*], [*Arg6*], [*Arg7*], [*Arg8*], [*Arg9*], [*Arg10*], [*Arg11*], [*Arg12*], [*Arg13*], [*Arg14*], [*Arg15*], [*Arg16*], [*Arg17*], [*Arg18*], [*Arg19*], [*Arg20*], [*Arg21*], [*Arg22*], [*Arg23*], [*Arg24*], [*Arg25*], [*Arg26*], [*Arg27*], [*Arg28*], [*Arg29*], [*Arg30*]) As Double

**8** Switch to Excel and run the macro.

**Note:** See the section "Run a Macro" for more information.

- The macro executes the Excel function and returns the appropriate results.

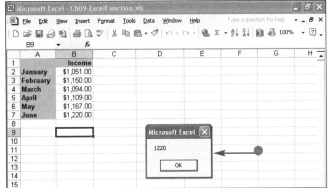

## Extra

It can be time consuming to try and determine whether or not an Excel function has a VBA equivalent. To make the process easier, you can use the Object Browser. The Object Browser in the Visual Basic Editor lists the functions that are part of the WorksheetFunction object. You can use any of the Excel functions listed for the WorksheetFunction object to create VBA macros or even other functions. See the section "Create a Custom Function" for more information.

Click View⇨Object Browser to display the Object Browser. The Object Browser provides six different object libraries that you can use to view object information. The Excel object library contains all of the objects, properties, and methods that correspond to the actual Excel program. To view the list of available Excel functions, select Excel from the library list and then type WorksheetFunction in the Search Text field. Click the Search button and the Search Results window displays the objects that match the search criteria. Click on the WorksheetFunction class to view a list of the Excel worksheet functions that you can use in the VBA code.

# An Introduction to Forms

You can use forms in Excel to capture and organize data values. Excel provides built-in data input forms, but you can also create custom forms. You can design forms in a worksheet using the available form controls combined with macros, or you can use VBA to create custom dialog boxes that display and capture information for a worksheet.

## Data Input Forms

If you want a form to capture data values for a list, you use the Data⇨Form option. When you click this option, Excel displays input fields that match the current data list. You can add new records to the list by typing values in the fields and clicking New. Because Excel creates the data entry form from the current list, you must add the initial records to the list before selecting this option.

You can also use the Data⇨Form option for locating different values in a data list. See Chapter 2 for more information on using this option.

## Custom Forms

You can design a form directly in a worksheet to capture data values. You can add different form controls to capture data; a *form control* is a graphic object that enables the user to perform an action, such as selecting a value. Common controls include check boxes, radio buttons, and list boxes. You add controls to a worksheet by using the Forms toolbar. You can assign different macros to a control to customize the worksheet based on a control selection.

For most form controls, you must define the range of cells containing the input values for the control. You can have the input values in the current worksheet or any other worksheet that you can access. You also specify the cell that receives the selection from the control.

You can control the selection in a field on a form by applying data validation rules to the cell. For example, if you want a cell to contain a value only between 10 and 100, you specify a data validation rule for the cell. If you specify a value outside the validation range, Excel displays an error message. See Chapter 3 for more information about creating a data validation rule.

## VBA Dialog Boxes

You can create a custom dialog box within the VBA Editor that opens when a particular macro executes. For example, you can create a dialog box that appears when a workbook opens by first creating the dialog box and then creating a macro called `Workbook_Open`. See Chapter 9 for information on creating a macro that executes when a workbook opens.

As with Excel form controls, you assign VBA controls to the custom dialog box. You select the different controls from the Visual Basic Editor Toolbox. After assigning the appropriate graphic image for the control, you need to create the VBA code that corresponds to the control. For example, if you add a list box to a custom dialog box, you must specify the values to display in the list box by creating a VBA procedure.

# The Forms
# Toolbar

The Forms toolbar contains the controls that you can add to a worksheet to display specific data values, perform certain actions, or capture user input. You can attach a macro to a form control that executes when the user clicks the control. See the section "Add a Form Control to a Worksheet" for more information on using controls on a worksheet.

## LABEL

Provides information about an associated control or worksheet.

## BUTTON

Runs the associated macro when clicked.

## OPTION BUTTON

Selects one of a group of options.

## GROUP BOX

Places related controls together visually on a worksheet.

## CHECK BOX

Selects or deselects an option.

## LIST BOX

Displays a list of items for selection.

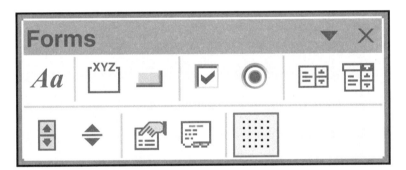

## SCROLL BAR

Increases or decreases a value when users click the arrow buttons.

## CONTROL PROPERTIES

Displays the Format Control dialog box.

## COMBO BOX

A menu that displays a list of items. The selected item appears in the text box.

## SPINNER

Scrolls up and down through a list of values.

## EDIT CODE

Displays the VBA Editor in which you can create or modify a macro for the control.

## TOGGLE GRID

Indicates whether the worksheet grid appears outlining the individual cells.

# VBA Dialog Box Basics

Every Microsoft Windows application uses dialog boxes to gather information from the user, and Excel is no exception. You can create dialog boxes in the VBA Editor to request specific information from users. For example, you frequently interact with the Open dialog box in Excel to select a file to open. You can use VBA to create dialog boxes that resemble those already in Excel. A good reference book for creating VBA forms and dialog boxes is *Excel Programming: Your Visual Blueprint for Creating Interactive Spreadsheets*, 2002.

## The Visual Basic Editor Toolbox

With the Visual Basic Editor, you can create custom dialog boxes that you can use with your Excel macros. These custom dialog boxes are referred to as *UserForms* in the Visual Basic Editor. When you create a UserForm, you design it using the various controls available in the Toolbox.

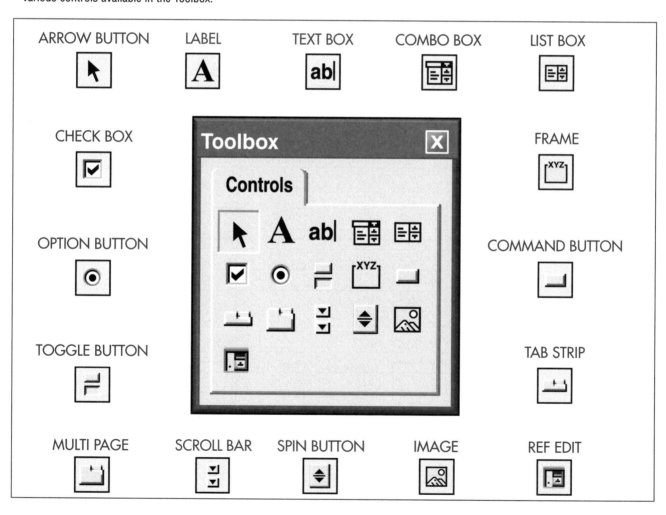

The Visual Basic Editor Toolbox appears only when you select a UserForm in the Visual Basic Editor. The Toolbox contains all the controls that you can add to your custom UserForm. See the section "Create a Custom Dialog Box" for more information about adding Toolbox controls.

---

### Arrow

Use this control to select objects in order to size or move them on a UserForm.

---

### Label

For adding text to a UserForm. The user cannot alter text labels on a UserForm; you add labels for informational purposes only.

---

### TextBox

Enables the user to input text.

---

### ComboBox

Enables a user to either click an item from the list or type an appropriate value in the text box.

---

### ListBox

Enables you to present a list of items from which a user can select an item.

---

### CheckBox

Enables the user to select or deselect options. Typically, a CheckBox control returns a value of `True` if it is selected and `False` if it is not selected.

---

### Frame

Enables you to group controls. For display purposes only.

---

### OptionButton

Enables the user to select from a list of items. You place two or more OptionButton controls in a group so that when you select one control, the other controls are deselected.

---

### CommandButton

The user clicks this to perform a specific option. When you create a CommandButton control, you specify the text that appears on the button as part of the control properties.

---

### ToggleButton

Enables you to create a button that looks either pressed and unpressed. The pressed state returns a result of `True` and the unpressed state returns a result of `False`.

---

### TabStrip

Enables you to create a multipage, or tabbed area for a section of your UserForm. You can place tab strips on each page of the UserForm.

---

### MultiPage

You use these to create tabbed dialog boxes, which let the user switch between pages of options in the dialog box. By default, the MultiPage control adds only two pages to your UserForm. You add more pages by right-clicking one of the Page tabs and selecting the New Page option.

---

### ScrollBar

Enables the user to scroll through information not originally shown on the screen or to indicate a position on a scale, such as a rating level.

---

### SpinButton

Enables the user to specify a value by clicking one of the arrow buttons to increment or decrement the value. Use either a TextBox control or a Label control to display the current value of the SpinButton control.

---

### Image

Use the Image control to add a graphic to the UserForm. Excel stores the graphic within the worksheet, so if you distribute the worksheet, the graphic is included. You can assign the graphic any of the following file formats: .bmp, .cur, .gif, .ico, .jpg, .wmf.

---

### RefEdit

Consisting of a text field and a button, this enables the user to select a range of cells from a worksheet. When the user clicks a button, the corresponding dialog box minimizes so that the user can drag the cursor across the worksheet to select the desired range of cells.

# Add a Form Control to a Worksheet

You can add different controls to a worksheet to make it easier to capture specific values in a field. This in turn allows you to capture cleaner data to analyze. For example, you can add a Spinner control to scroll up and down to select the appropriate numeric value for a cell, and you can add a list box containing the values that a user can select for a cell.

Excel provides nine different controls that you can add to a worksheet. You add the controls by selecting them from the Forms toolbar. You then specify the desired control size. Excel enables you to size each control by dragging the edges. You can also use the controls on the Forms toolbar to add controls to a Chart sheet.

When you add or select a control on a worksheet, Excel is in *design mode*. In this mode, you can modify the properties

and size of a form control, but you cannot test out its functionality. The design mode applies to the forms control that you currently have selected.

When you place a control on a worksheet, it sits on top of the worksheet. You can size it so that it appears to be located in a specific cell, but it is actually separate from the cell. Because the controls are separate from the actual worksheet cells, you can place them anywhere on the worksheet. A control can cover any portion of a cell or range of cells.

After you add controls to a worksheet, you must specify the cells containing the data values for the control. Form controls require data values that exist in a worksheet. See the section "Specify Values for a Form Control" for more information on specifying control values.

---

## Add a Form Control to a Worksheet

① Click View⇨Toolbars⇨Forms.

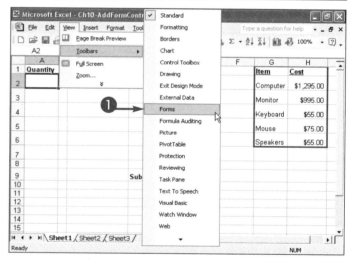

The Forms toolbar appears.

② Click the button of the form control that you want to add.

③ Drag the cursor on the worksheet to set the size of the control and release the mouse button.

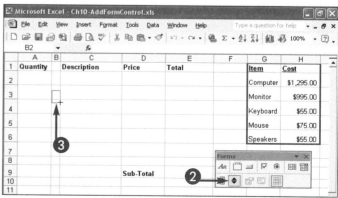

The form control appears at the specified size.

④ Drag the control to the desired location on the form.

You can repeat steps 2 to 4 to add additional controls to the worksheet, as desired.

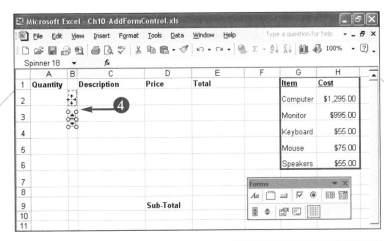

The added form controls appear in the specified locations on the worksheet.

● You can place a control in design mode to modify its properties or resize it by right-clicking it.

● To cancel design mode, click a cell of the worksheet.

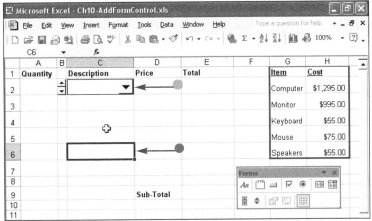

## Extra

When designing a form on a worksheet, you may not want the grid lines outlining each cell to show. To remove the grid lines from the worksheet display, click the Toggle Grid button (▦) on the Forms toolbar. You can click the button to switch between displaying and removing the grid lines. The Toggle Grid button only removes the grid lines that display when you view the worksheet in Excel. It does not affect any borders that you have applied to the worksheet.

You can remove controls from a worksheet at any time. To remove a control, right-click the control to select it and then click Cut from the menu that displays. Excel removes the selected control from the worksheet.

You can place the Forms toolbar at any location in the Excel window. If you want to dock the toolbar at the top of the window with the other toolbars, click and drag the toolbar to the desired location. You can also dock the toolbar on either side of the window or at the bottom. You can also leave the toolbar sitting undocked anywhere on your screen.

# Specify Values for a Form Control

After you add a control to a form, you must specify the values for the control. For example, if your worksheet contains a ListBox control, you specify the values to display as options for the control. With other controls, such as an option button or check box, you specify the value by indicating whether you want the option initially selected.

Some controls enable you to define a range of numeric values for the control. For example, if you use a Spinner control, you define the starting value for the control and the maximum value. Other controls expect values from a worksheet as values for the control.

If a control does not let you specify a range of numeric values, you must specify values from a worksheet range.

For example, if you use a ComboBox control, you specify values for the control by indicating the range of cells containing the values. You can have the worksheet in the current workbook or in another workbook that Excel can access when you view the worksheet.

You can also assign a linked cell for each control. If you link a cell to a control, whatever value is selected in the control becomes the value of the linked cell. By linking a cell to a control, you can quickly capture the selection and use it in a formula. The value that is in the linked cell is a numeric value representing the selection. For example, if you use a ComboBox control or ListBox control, the number that is in the linked cell indicates the position of the selected value within the list; so if you have the list Region, State, City, and you select State, the linked cell receives a value of 2.

## Specify Values for a Form Control

① Right-click the selected control.

A menu appears.

② Click Format Control.

The Format Object dialog box opens.

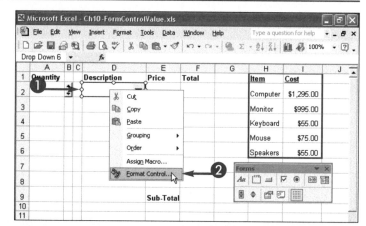

③ Click the Control tab if it is not displayed.

④ Specify the values for the control.

**Note:** See Chapter 1 for information on selecting a range of cells.

The available fields are different depending on the control type.

⑤ Specify the cell reference to link to the control.

⑥ Click OK.

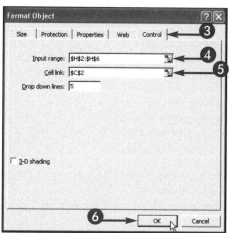

**7** Select the desired control value.

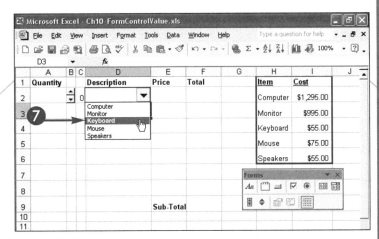

● Excel places a numeric value representing the control selection in the linked cell.

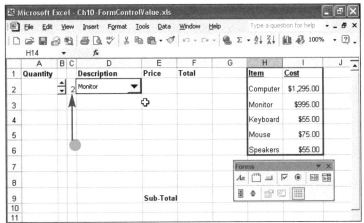

## Extra

When working with a value selected from a ListBox or ComboBox control, you typically want to use that selection to determine another cell value. For example, assume that you have the following Excel list in cells H2:I4.

**Example:**

| | |
|---|---|
| Computer | $1295 |
| Monitor | $995 |
| Keyboard | $55 |

You can use the Index function to determine the price based on the equipment selection. For example, if you select Monitor from the control, Excel places a value of 2 in the linked cell. If you want to find the cost for the selection, you type a formula similar to the following, assuming that C2 is the linked cell:

**Example:**
```
=INDEX($H$2:$I$4, C2, 2)
```

The Index function actually creates an array of the Excel list and uses the selection from the control to determine which element of the array to return. The function actually uses three different arguments:

**Example:**
```
Array, Row_num, and Column_num
```

# Customize Form Controls with Macros

You can assign macros to any of the form controls on a worksheet to perform custom functions to save you time and effort in while analyzing data. For example, if a user selects a CheckBox control, you can have Excel total specific cells.

You can create one macro for each control on a worksheet. You create a macro either by recording a series of keystrokes or by writing a VBA procedure in the Visual Basic Editor. When you select the Assign Macro menu option, Excel automatically creates a new macro with the name of the control followed by an underscore and an event name, such as _Click. Excel assigns the control name to the control when you add it to a worksheet. For example, the first OptionButton control that you add to a worksheet is named OptionButton1. If you create a macro for the

option button, Excel gives the macro the name OptionButton1_Click.

The portion of the macro name following the underscore character corresponds to an action, commonly referred to as an *event,* which occurs to the control. For example, with an OptionButton control, the user clicks the radio button to select the option, so the event is Click. If you create a macro for a ComboBox control, Excel assigns the event to the name Change because you want to execute the macro when the value of the control changes. You use the event extension of the macro name to tell Excel to monitor the control and execute the macro whenever a user clicks the control.

No matter which option you select — recording or writing VBA — Excel assigns the same name to the macro. See Chapter 9 for more information on creating macros.

## Customize Form Controls with Macros

① Right-click the selected control.

A menu appears.

② Click Assign Macro.

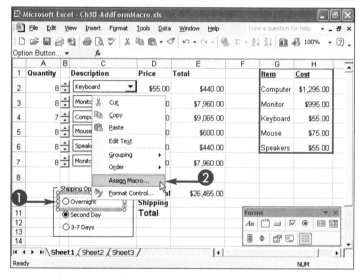

The Assign Macro dialog box opens.

● Excel assigns a default macro name for the selected control.

③ Click New to create a new macro in the Visual Basic Editor.

● You can click Record to record a macro.

**Note:** See Chapter 9 for more information on macro creation.

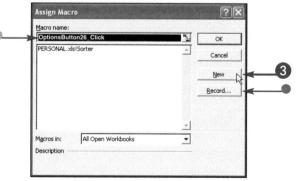

- The Visual Basic Editor creates a new macro and names it after the control.

④ Type the macro code.

⑤ Click the View Microsoft Excel button.

⑥ Click the control with the assigned macro.

- Excel executes the associated macro.

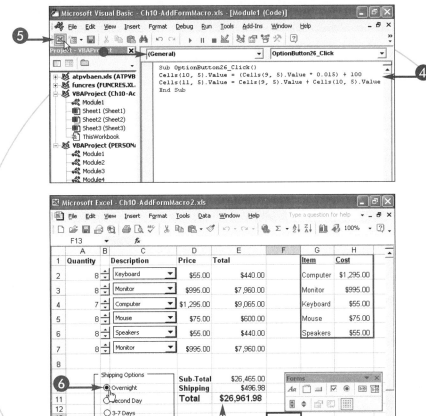

The macros that you assign to a control only execute when the corresponding event occurs for the control. For example, you may have a macro assigned to a control that computes the total amount a client must pay when a user clicks the control. If you change the values to compute the total amount after a user clicks the control, Excel does not update the total until the user clicks the control again.

You can modify a macro assigned to a control by right-clicking the control and then clicking the Assign Macro option. In the Assign Macro dialog box, select the name of the assigned macro and click Edit. The Visual Basic Editor displays the selected macro.

If you no longer want to have a macro assigned to a control, right-click the control and then click the Assign Macro option. In the Assign Macro dialog box, clear the macro name from the Macro Name field and click OK.

This removes the macro assignment from the control, but the macro still remains as part of the workbook. To remove the macro from the workbook, click Tools➪Macros➪Macro to display the Macro dialog box. Select the macro that you want to delete and click Delete.

# Create a Custom Dialog Box

You can create custom dialog boxes to use in conjunction with any of your macros. You can use this custom dialog box to simplify the data collection or data analysis process because dialog boxes add a graphical user interface, and let users click buttons to indicate a specific selection or to input an appropriate value. When you use VBA to create macros, you also gain most Visual Basic features, including the ability to create custom dialog boxes. VBA refers to these custom dialog boxes as *Forms* or *UserForms.*

You create a custom dialog box within the Visual Basic Editor with the UserForm option. The Visual Basic Editor creates a new UserForm called `UserForm1` in the Forms folder in the Project window. The Forms folder displays only if you have created UserForms for the current project.

You can change the name of a UserForm to make it easier to identify when you look at the UserForms listed in the Project window. To change the name of a UserForm, you must change the `Name` property for the UserForm within the Properties window.

After you create a UserForm, you can design it using the various Toolbox controls, which appear only when you select the UserForm window. You add controls to the UserForm by dragging them from the Toolbox to the appropriate location on the UserForm. After you add a control, you can resize it as needed. The Visual Basic Editor applies default values for each of the control properties. You can change the assigned values to the properties for the control within the Properties window. Remember that you need to select the control on the UserForm before you can set the properties.

## Create a Custom Dialog Box

① In the Projects window, select the project to which you want to add the new UserForm.

   The project name corresponds to the name of a workbook.

② Click Insert➪UserForm.

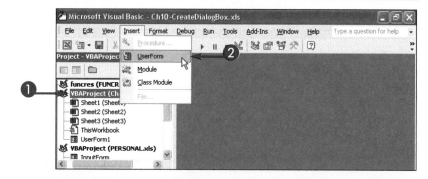

   The Visual Basic Editor creates a blank UserForm with a default name of `UserForm1`.

③ Type a new name for the UserForm in the Name field of the Properties window.

④ Click the UserForm.

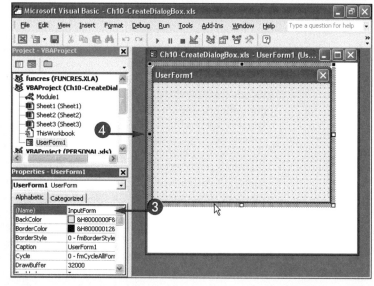

The Toolbox appears.

**⑤** Click a control in the Toolbox and drag it to the UserForm.

**⑥** In the Properties window, type a control name in the Name field.

**⑦** Continue adding controls as desired.

**⑧** Click the Run Sub/Userform button.

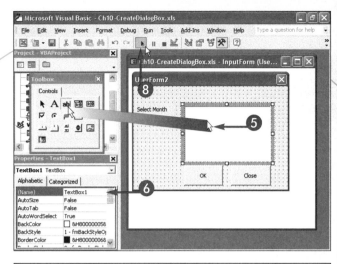

Excel displays the new dialog box.

● To return to the Visual Basic Editor, you can close the dialog box.

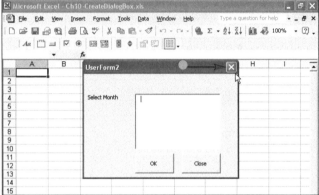

## Extra

You can specify several properties for each control that you add to a UserForm. Although each control type has it own unique properties, most properties are common to all the controls. You change the value of each property by either typing a new value or by selecting the value from the list that displays. The following table describes some of the common control properties:

| CONTROL PROPERTY | DESCRIPTION |
|---|---|
| (Name) | The name of the control. |
| BackColor | The background color of the control. |
| Caption | The text that displays on the control, such as the button text. |
| Font | The font that displays all values on the control. |
| Height | The height of the control in pixels. |
| Text | The default text value of the control. |
| TextAlign | The way that you align the text on the control. |
| Width | The width, in pixels, of the control. |

# Call a Custom Dialog Box from a Macro

You can call and display any custom dialog boxes that are part of the same project as your macro code. You use custom dialog boxes to simplify the data collection or data analysis process because dialog boxes add a graphical user interface; they let users click buttons to indicate a specific selection or to input an appropriate value. For example, you can have a dialog box open to request values from the user to perform appropriate calculations within a worksheet. See the section "Create a Custom Dialog Box" for more information on custom dialog boxes.

To display a custom dialog box, you use the Show method of the UserForm object. This method has only one optional parameter, as shown in the following code:

```
UserForm1.Show modal
```

The modal parameter determines whether the UserForm displays as a modal or modeless dialog box within Excel.

The default value of vbModal makes the dialog box modal, which means that you must either close or hide the dialog box before selecting any other options in Excel. When a modal dialog box opens, Excel passes all control to that dialog box; users can only select options in it, but not in any other dialog box. A value of vbModeless means that although the dialog box remains open until a user closes it, a user can perform other program options.

You can close a dialog box with the normal Close button, or you can close it within your macro using the Unload method. Typically, all dialog boxes contain a Close or Cancel button to allow a user to close the dialog box. You must use the Click event for these CommandButton controls to create a procedure that calls the Unload method. See the section "Capture Input from a Custom Dialog Box" for more information about specifying code to run when a user clicks a button.

## Call a Custom Dialog Box from a Macro

① Create a UserForm in the appropriate project.

**Note:** See the section "Create a Custom Dialog Box" for information on creating UserForms.

② Click Insert➪Module.

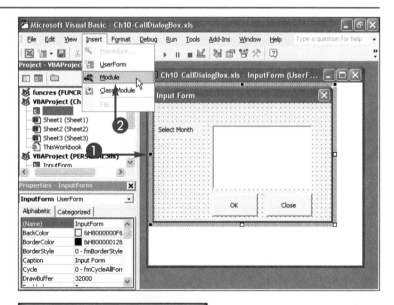

③ Type the name of the macro to create.

**Note:** See Chapter 9 for information on creating macros.

④ Press Enter.

● The Visual Basic Editor adds the End Sub statement.

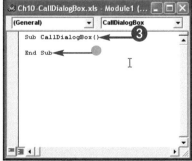

⑤ Type **UserForm1.Show vbModal**, replacing `UserForm1` with the name of the form and `vbModal` with `vbModelss` if you want to make the dialog box modeless.

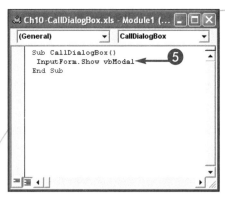

⑥ Switch to Excel and run the macro.

The specified UserForm appears as a custom dialog box.

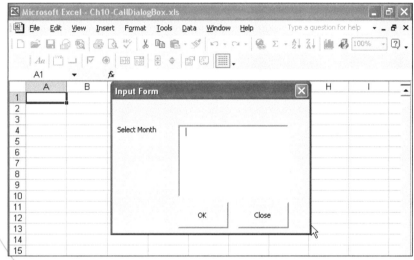

## Apply It

You can use the `Unload` statement to remove a UserForm from memory. When you call the statement, all controls on the UserForm are reset to their default values. Therefore, you cannot access the options a user specifies after the UserForm unloads from memory. To ensure that you can access the necessary values, you can either store the values in global variables or hide the UserForm until your procedure terminates. You unload a UserForm by typing the `Unload` statement followed by the name of the UserForm to unload as follows:

**Example:**
`Unload UserForm1`

You can hide a UserForm so that it is no longer visible when a macro calls it. You do so using the `Hide` method, which still enables you to access the form from your procedure. To hide a form, use the statement:

**Example:**
`UserForm1.Hide`

After you hide a form, Excel may appear to freeze as your code continues to access the UserForm. This condition clears as soon as the code that accesses the UserForm finishes processing.

# Capture Input from a Custom Dialog Box

You typically use dialog boxes in Excel to gather input from the user. You can make the input you capture from a user anything from determining which button the user pressed to what values the user typed. You can then capture the user input and return the appropriate responses by using the UserForm events. Data analysts may find this useful if they want to walk a user through a particular calculation or worksheet. For example, when the user clicks an OK CommandButton control, you use a `CommandButton_Click` subroutine to indicate what steps to perform.

Excel considers every user interaction that occurs in a dialog box as an event, such as scrolling through a list of items, selecting an OK button, or typing text in a text box. Each UserForm control has several different events that you

can capture. The most common event is `Click`, which occurs each time a user clicks a control. To generate the code that interacts with the UserForm, you must create procedures that execute when specific events occur.

Each UserForm that you create has two elements: the graphical layout window and a code window. The graphical layout window is where you add controls that appear in the dialog box. See the section "Create a Custom Dialog Box" for more information on designing custom dialog boxes. Each UserForm also has a code window that contains all UserForm-specific code and that you use to create the event procedures for each control.

By default, the Visual Basic Editor creates a `Click` event for a control when you click it. If a `Click` event already exists, the Visual Basic Editor simply displays the code window.

## Capture Input from a Custom Dialog Box

① Create a UserForm in the appropriate project.

**Note:** See the section "Create a Custom Dialog Box" for information on creating UserForms.

② In the Toolbox, click the ListBox control and drag it to the UserForm.

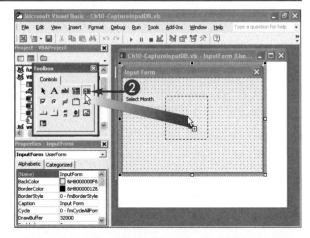

③ Click the Command button and drag it to the UserForm.

④ In the Properties window, type text for the `Caption` property value.

The text on the CommandButton changes to reflect the value of the caption property.

⑤ Double-click the CommandButton.

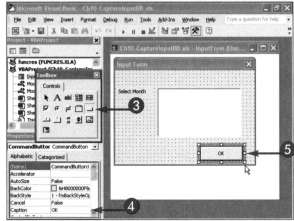

The code window for the UserForm appears.

- Excel creates a subroutine called `CommandButton1_Click()` in the code window.

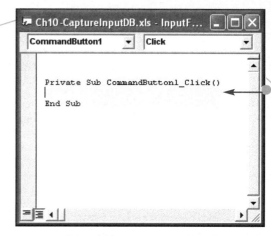

```
Private Sub CommandButton1_Click()
|
End Sub
```

**6** Type **UserSelection:=ListBox1.Value**, replacing `UserSelection` with the name of the global variable used to capture user input.

**7** Type **Unload** and follow it with the name of the UserForm.

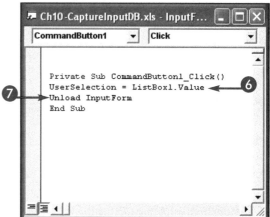

```
Private Sub CommandButton1_Click()
UserSelection = ListBox1.Value
Unload InputForm
End Sub
```

## Extra

The `Click` event occurs when the user clicks a control or a value in a control. For most controls, you can write a procedure to handle the `Click` event by placing the event name after the control name. All event-handling procedures require an underscore character between the control name and the event name.

**Example:**
```
Sub CommandButton1_Click()
```

If you need to capture the `Click` event to determine the page or tab selected with a MultiPage or TabStrip control, the procedure also includes an index parameter value that specifies the index to the page or tab.

**Example:**
```
Sub MultiPage1_Click(1)
```

With the MultiPage and TabStrip controls, you must create a separate procedure to handle the selection of each page or tab by using the corresponding index value.

Aside from an actual click of a control with the mouse, a `Click` event also occurs when you press Enter and a control is selected, when you press the accelerator key that corresponds to the control, or when you press the spacebar and a CommandButton is selected.

continued ➜

Y ou create VBA code to monitor the events of a control, such as a user clicking a button, and to determine when Excel should execute specific code. Each control has its own specific events that you can capture, and the Visual Basic Editor keeps track of those for you. You can quickly create an event procedure in the code window by selecting the appropriate control name in the Object list box and then selecting the corresponding event from the Procedure list box. When you select an event, the Visual Basic Editor creates a procedure with the name of the control followed by the event name.

All control values on a UserForm are only active as long as you have the dialog box open. If you close the dialog box prior to saving user input values, you lose the user input. To avoid any potential problems with lost data, consider

saving user responses to global variables that can pass into other procedures. For example, you typically call a UserForm from another procedure to capture user responses and then pass the values back to the main procedure.

You must declare public variables at the top of your module, before any procedure code, using the Public statement. Doing so enables you to declare variables that all procedures within a project can access.

For a procedure, you can reference specific controls on a UserForm by specifying the name of the UserForm followed by the name of the control. You can set additional properties for a control before displaying the UserForm directly within your code. You can also use the With statement to shorten the code required to set properties for an object. See Appendix C for more information about the syntax of the With statement.

---

**Capture Input from a Custom Dialog Box** *(continued)*

8 Create a new module.

**Note:** See Chapter 9 for information on creating modules to store macros.

9 Type **Public UserSelection As String**, replacing UserSelection with the name of the global variable.

10 Create a new subroutine.

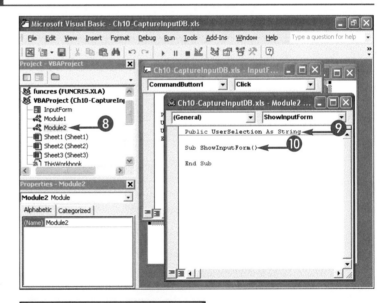

11 Type **With UserForm1.ListBox1**, replacing UserForm1 and ListBox1 with the names of the UserForm and ListBox controls, respectively.

12 Type **.AddItem "Jan"**, replacing "Jan" with the value to add to the ListBox control.

13 Repeat step 12 for each item.

14 Type **End With**.

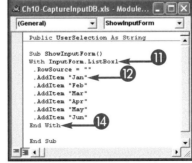

⑮ Type **UserForm1.Show**, replacing UserForm1 with the name of the UserForm.

⑯ Type additional VBA code to process the user selection value returned by the global variable.

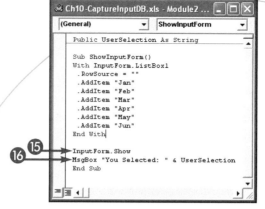

⑰ Switch to Excel and run the macro.

**Note:** See Chapter 9 to run a macro.

● The dialog box displays the list of values specified by the subroutine.

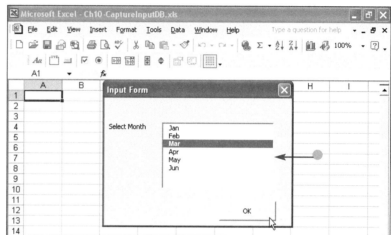

## Extra

You capture control events to determine when to execute specific code. The following list identifies the most common events that occur with the various controls placed on UserForms. Not all events are available for each control. In the code window, check the Procedure list box to see the events associated with the selected control.

| CONTROL EVENT | OCCURRENCE |
|---|---|
| BeforeDragOver | User is dragging-and-dropping data onto a control. |
| BeforeUpdate | Before data in a control is changed. |
| Change | When the Value property of the control changes. |
| Click | When user clicks the control with the mouse button. |
| DblClick | When the user double-clicks the control. |
| Enter | Before a control receives focus from the user pressing Enter. |
| KeyDown | When the user presses a key. |
| MouseDown | When the user presses the mouse button. |

# Validate Input from a Dialog Box

Validation ensures that the information that you receive for analysis is accurate and of the correct form. You must validate the values specified for controls in a dialog box before passing the values back to your procedure for two major reasons: First, you ensure that the user specifies a value for a control. If the user forgets to select a control value, you can remind him or her immediately. Second, which is probably the most important reason, you ensure that errors do not occur in your code because the wrong type of data passed to a procedure.

You can create code that checks the user input for any event that occurs on a UserForm. The easiest place to do so is prior to closing the dialog box. For example, if you have a CommandButton control, such as an OK button, that passes the values to global variables and closes the dialog box, this is an ideal place to validate your data. When you place the

validation code in that routine, you use a conditional statement, such as an `If Then` statement, to check the properties of each control. This ensures that they have the appropriate values. For example, to ensure that the user typed a string in the Name text field of the dialog box, you can add the statement `If TextBox1.Text = " " Then` to your procedure. This statement checks the `Text` property for the specified TextBox control and ensures that it contains a value. If the property is empty (nothing is in it), your VBA code can call the `MsgBox` function to display a message telling the user to input a value.

You also use the VBA validation functions to verify that a control contains the appropriate data type. For example, `If Not IsNumeric(TextBox1.Value) Then` ensures that the user typed a number in a TextBox control.

---

## Validate Input from a Dialog Box

① On the UserForm, double-click the control for which you want to validate the data values.

Typically, an OK command button is a good location for validating data values.

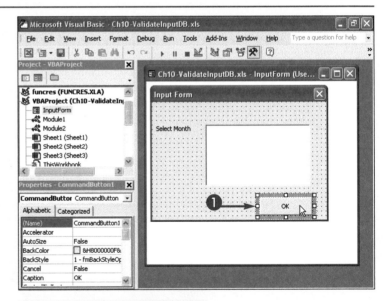

The code window opens with the cursor at the beginning of the `Click` procedure for the selected control.

**2** Type the control and property value to check.

**3** Type **MsgBox** and follow it with the text for the MsgBox.

**4** Type **Exit Sub**.

**5** Type **End If**.

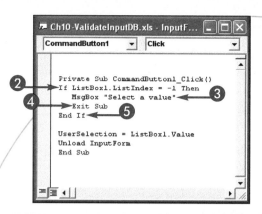

```
Private Sub CommandButton1_Click()
If ListBox1.ListIndex = -1 Then
    MsgBox "Select a value"
    Exit Sub
End If

UserSelection = ListBox1.Value
Unload InputForm
End Sub
```

**6** Switch to Excel and run the macro.

● The message box appears if a value is not selected for the control.

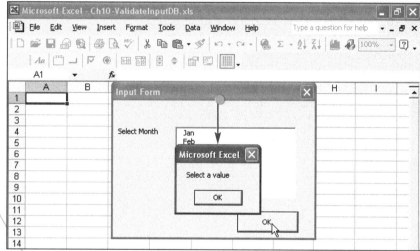

## Apply It

Instead of creating validation code that runs based on control events, you can use the UserForm events to launch code, such as capturing the QueryClose event for the UserForm. The following code ensures that a value was selected for a ListBox control prior to the closing of the dialog box.

**Example:**
```
Private Sub UserForm_QueryClose(Cancel As Integer, CloseMode As Integer)
If Not IsNumeric(TextBox1.Value) Then
      MsgBox "Must be a number"
      Cancel = 1
 End If
```

The QueryClose event has two arguments, Cancel and CloseMode. The Cancel argument accepts an integer value. If the value of the argument is anything other than zero, the QueryClose event stops, and the associated dialog box remains open. The CloseMode argument contains a constant value indicating the cause of the QueryClose event. You can change the value of this argument by typing the value 0-3 associated with the constant or using one of the four constant values. Use vbFormControlMenu to specify the user selected the Close button on the dialog box; use vbFormCode to indicate the code initiated an Unload statement; use vbAppWindows to denote that the Windows operating session is ending, and that the Windows Task Manager is closing Excel.

# Install Excel Add-ins

Y ou can use Excel to take advantage of a number of add-ins — enhancements that provide additional financial and scientific functions and options. In addition to Excel's add-ins, you can also load add-ins that other individuals create. Among the add-ins that come standard with Excel, you should consider loading:

- The Analysis ToolPak, which provides financial and scientific functions and options. For example, this add-in contains a set of functions for performing Engineering calculations, along with other financial, date and time, and mathematical functions. The Analysis ToolPak also contains the Statistical Analysis Tools described in this chapter.

- The Analysis ToolPak — VBA, which has financial, mathematical, and date and time functions. For example, you load the ACCRINT function to calculate the amount of accrued interest.

- The Conditional Sum Wizard, which lets you quickly create a formula that only calculates under situations that you specify. For more information, see the section "Using the Conditional Sum Wizard."

Excel recognizes any file with an .xla file extension as an add-in, lists them in the Add-ins dialog box, and automatically loads the add-in files to one of the following folders on your hard drive:

```
c:\Program Files\Microsoft Office\Office 10\
Addins
```

```
c:\Documents and Settings\user name\
Application Data\Microsoft\Addins
```

After loading the add-ins, Excel adds their new options to its menus. For example, if you load the Conditional Sum Wizard, Excel adds a Conditional Sum option to the Tools menu.

To free up the memory usage, you should only load the add-ins that you intend to use and unload add-ins you no longer need.

## Install Excel Add-ins

① Click Tools⇨Add-Ins.

The Add-Ins dialog box displays.

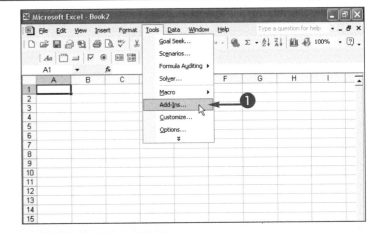

- You can click an item in the Add-Ins box to view its description.

② Click the add-ins you want to add (☐ changes to ☑ ).

**Note:** The material in this chapter mainly discusses the Conditional Sum Wizard and the analysis tools added with the AnalysisToolPak.

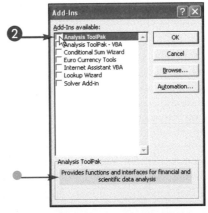

- You can repeat step 2 to load additional add-ins.
- You can click Browse to load add-ins not listed in the list box.

③ Click OK.

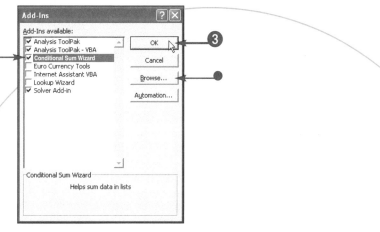

Excel loads all of the selected add-ins.

- Excel updates menus to include the selected add-ins.

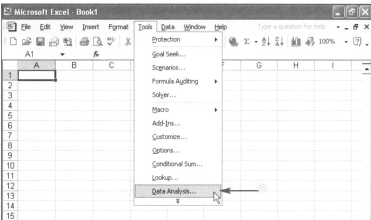

## Apply It

If you cannot find an add-in with the functionality you need to perform the desired task, you can create your own. You can save any workbook as an add-in. When you do so, Excel only uses the macros in the workbook to create the add-in file. Any other elements of the workbook are unusable as part of the add-in. Therefore, you should only consider creating add-ins from workbooks that contain macros.

If you want to share macros with other users, creating an add-in is a good way to do so. This hides the VBA code that created the macros so that users cannot view or modify it.

To save a workbook as an add-in, click File➪Save As to display the Save As dialog box. In the Save as type field, select the Microsoft Excel Add-In option. Specify the add-in name and the location where you want to save the add-in file. When you click Save, Excel creates an add-in containing the macros and custom dialog boxes created in the workbook.

If you want Excel to automatically list the add-in on the Add-Ins dialog box, save the add-in in one of the default add-in locations.

# Using the Conditional Sum Wizard

**W**hat if you want Excel to perform a calculation only if certain conditions hold true? Excel can help you build a formula that meets your needs via the Conditional Sum Wizard. For example, you can have Excel build a formula that only calculates total sales when it encounters a certain code.

To use the Conditional Sum Wizard, you must first create or open an Excel list that contains the column of values to sum. You use other columns in the list to create the criterion value for summing. For example, if you only want the amounts for Texas, you sum the amounts if the State value equals Texas.

Your list must have column headings in the first row because Excel uses them within the Conditional Sum Wizard to identify what you want to sum and what is conditional.

Before running the Conditional Sum Wizard, select at least one cell within the range for which you want a conditional sum so that the wizard can automatically select the entire range of cells. Excel selects all cells in the range until it encounters the next empty row or column. You should verify the range before continuing.

You identify the criteria that you want the summed data to meet by selecting conditions. This means you need to select a column, a comparison operator, and then the value to compare.

Excel provides the Conditional Sum Wizard as an add-in option that you can load on the Add-Ins dialog box. After you load it, you can find Conditional Sum as an option on the Tools menu. See the section "Install Excel Add-ins" for more information on loading add-in options. For more on creating conditional formulas, see Chapter 4.

## Using the Conditional Sum Wizard

① Create an Excel list or open the appropriate existing Excel document.

If desired, select a cell from the range of cells to sum so Excel automatically selects the cells for the wizard.

② Click Tools⇨Conditional Sum.

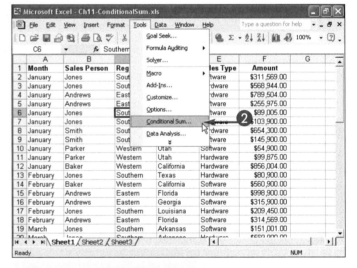

The Conditional Sum Wizard displays.

● Excels specifies the range of cells containing the list.

③ Click here to select a different range of cells.

**Note:** See Chapter 1 for more on selecting a range of cells.

④ Click Next.

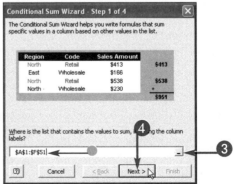

The second page of the Conditional Sum Wizard displays.

**⑤** Select the column to sum.

**⑥** Select the condition column and the conditional operator.

**⑦** Type the value for the condition or select a value from the selected column.

**⑧** Click Add Condition.

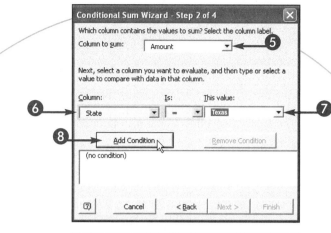

● Excel adds the specified condition to the box.

**⑨** Repeat steps 6 to 8 for each condition statement you want to create.

**⑩** Click Next.

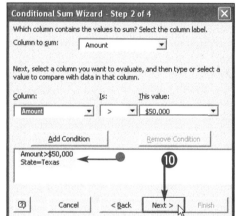

---

### Extra

When you create a conditional statement on the second page of the Conditional Sum Wizard, you need to specify the conditional operator to use. The conditional operator you select determines how Excel interprets the condition. For example, you can use a comparison operator to specify a conditional statement of:

**Example:**
Amount > $50,000.00

Only the amounts that are greater than $50,000 and match the other conditions are summed. For more on how to use comparison operators in Excel, see Appendix D.

The Conditional Sum Wizard works well for data lists where you have data records with the same values, for example, several sales amounts for the state of Texas, or multiple computer hardware sales. Using the common values in various data records, you can sum related cells quickly and paste the total amount in a cell.

If you do not have a relationship that you want to filter out within the data list, the Conditional Sum Wizard is typically not the best tool for summing columns. You should consider using the SUM function. See Chapter 4 for more information on working with the SUM function.

continued ➡

**Y**ou have the option of pasting just the formula created by the wizard into a cell in a worksheet, or you can paste the formula along with the values of each condition used to create the formula. For example, if you specified the following two conditions:

Amount > $50,000.00

State = Texas

Excel gives you the option of pasting the values $50,000.00 and Texas in different cells in your worksheet. You can use these conditional values as labels for the conditional sum on your worksheet. On the third page of the Conditional Sum Wizard, you must specify whether you want to paste the conditional values along with the formula.

Unfortunately, Excel does not allow you to select which conditional values are pasted. You can either paste all conditional values or only the conditional sum.

The final page of the wizard requests a cell reference for pasting the created formula, which you can paste into any cell. If you specified that you wanted to also paste the condition values, Excel prompts you for the cell locations for those values before the formula. The page displays separately for each value that requires a cell reference.

When you run the Conditional Sum Wizard, it creates a conditional formula using the SUM and IF functions and places it in the specified cells. You can modify the formula at any time using the Function Arguments dialog box. See Chapter 4 for more information on modifying formulas.

Once you close the Conditional Sum Wizard, you cannot use it to modify the formula. If you run the wizard again, Excel assumes you want to create a new conditional sum value.

---

**Using the Conditional Sum Wizard** *(continued)*

The third page of the Conditional Sum Wizard displays, giving you the option of pasting only the conditional formula in a cell or pasting the formula and each condition value in separate cells.

⑪ Click the desired option (○ changes to ◉).

⑫ Click Next.

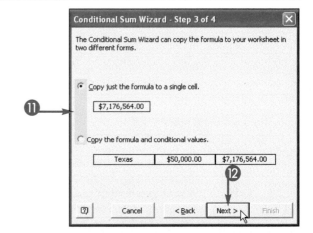

The last page of the Conditional Sum Wizard displays.

⑬ Type the cell reference for the formula.

● You can click the Collapse button to select a cell from the worksheet.

⑭ Click Finish.

**Note:** If you opted to paste the condition values, Excel displays the final page separately for each condition value.

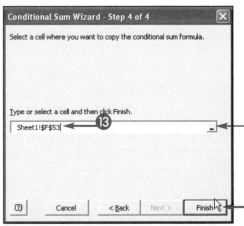

Excel pastes the formula in the specified cell.

⑮ Click the cell.

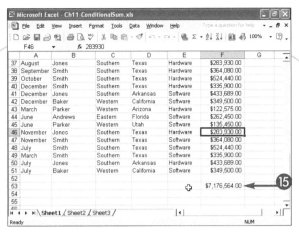

● Excel displays the formula in the Formula Bar.

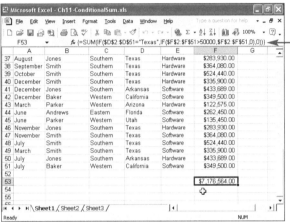

## Extra

Excel creates the conditional sum statement by combining a SUM function with a nested IF statement. You may find it a little confusing to interpret the function if you want to modify it. The nested IF statements become the Number1 argument of the SUM function. This means that the IF statements return the summed values. For example, Excel creates the following formula for a list where the conditions are to sum amounts over $50,000 and State equals Texas:

```
=SUM(IF($D$2:$D$20="Texas", IF($F$2:$F$20>50000,$F$2:$F$20,0),0))
```

This example first checks if the value of the record in column D equals "Texas." If the first condition is True, the second IF statement checks if the value in column F is greater than $50,000. If both conditions are True, Excel adds the value in column F to the sum and repeats the process for the next row in the range. If either value in the row does not match the condition, Excel adds a value of zero to the sum. See Chapter 4 for more information on creating conditional IF statements.

# Analysis of Variance for Lists of Values (ANOVA)

You can determine if there is a relationship between data sets by performing an analysis of variance, or ANOVA. The data analyst uses this tool to confirm or reject an assumption they have regarding two or more data groups. Excel has three ANOVA options from which to choose: Single-Factor ANOVA, Two-Factor With Replication, and Two-Factor Without Replication.

You perform a Single Factor ANOVA if you suspect that the quantity of an item your company sells ($\mu_1$) is directly related to the number of calls the marketing department makes ($\mu_2$). This is called the true hypothesis ($H_A$ true); the null hypothesis ($H_0$) is that the two are not related:

$$H_0: \ \mu_1 \neq \mu_2 \quad \text{and} \ H_A: \ \mu_1 = \mu_2$$

In a Two-Factor ANOVA, you may have an assumption that both the number of calls and a special promotional deal directly affect the sales of the item. You use the Two-Factor Without Replication option when you have one sample of each group of data, and the Two-Factor option when you sample each group more than once. The Single Factor tool assumes one sampling.

To perform this calculation, you must provide the range of cells containing the values you want to analyze, as well as the statistical confidence level, between 0 and 1, in the Alpha field. The Alpha field is the probability of $H_A$ being true. The default level of .05 is equivalent to a 5 percent confidence level.

Although this example shows a Single-Factor ANOVA, the steps for performing a Two-Factor ANOVA are quite similar to the steps in this section. Excel only provides the ANOVA feature as an Add-in. For more about the other Add-ins available in Excel as well as how to install them, see the section "Install Excel Add-ins."

## Analysis of Variance for Lists of Values (ANOVA)

① Select a cell in the range of data you want to analyze.

**Note:** Although this example shows a Single-Factor ANOVA, you can perform a Two-Factor ANOVA following these steps.

② Click Tools➪Data Analysis.

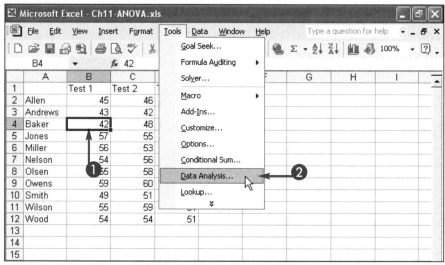

The Data Analysis dialog box opens.

③ Click Anova: Single Factor for one sampling of data for each group.

You can also select the Two-factor options for Two-way analysis.

**Note:** Although similar to the Single Factor option, the Two-Factor options have different dialog boxes.

④ Click OK.

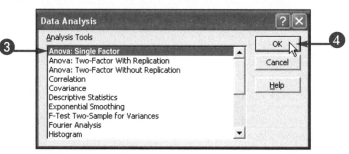

The Anova: Single Factor dialog box displays.

**5** Specify the range of cells to analyze.

**6** Click an option to specify whether your data is in columns or rows.

**7** To place the Excel-generated table in the first row of your worksheet, click Labels in first row (☐ changes to ☑ ).

**8** Specify the degree of confidence, or Alpha level (α).

**9** Specify the output location.

**10** Click OK.

Excel analyzes the data groups and creates an ANOVA report.

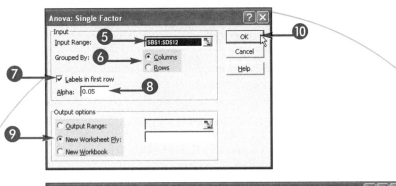

## Extra

Excel has performed your ANOVA calculations, but what do the results in the table mean? To determine whether your hypothesis is true, you look at the F statistic (F) in the table that Excel generates. A high F statistic means you should reject the null hypothesis and accept that your suspicions are true. If F statistic is close to 1, the means are truly equal, and you should reject the null hypothesis. You should also look at your P-value and your F crit value. If your F statistic value is greater than the F crit value, you can reject the null hypothesis, and if it is smaller you can not reject. If your P value is large, then you could have come by the results of the F statistic value by chance. If the P value is small, then it is unlikely that you got your F statistic by chance. The following table summarizes how to interpret your ANOVA calculations:

| F STATISTIC | F CRIT | P-VALUE | ACTION |
|---|---|---|---|
| Small | < F statistic | Large | Do not reject null hypothesis |
| Large | > F statistic | Small | Reject null hypothesis |

# Find the Correlation between Two Sets of Data

You can compare two sets of data to determine their relationship using Excel's Correlation tool. If you plot your data and observe a straight line using Excel's XY (Scatter) chart, you can statistically prove that a relationship exists by calculating the correlation and covariance. *Correlation*, a function of covariance, determines if two sets of data are dependent upon each other. To determine the *degree* they are dependent, you calculate the covariance. You can have positively or negatively correlated data sets. For example, a positive correlation is when sales of an item increase due to an increase in a specific marketing activity; a negative correlation is when sales returns increase as the age of a product with a short shelf life increases. For more on covariance, see the section "Determine the Covariance of Sets of Data." See Chapter 6 for more on Excel's charting options.

To calculate a correlation, you must provide Excel with the range of cells for both data sets as well as how you have them grouped. To make the output easier to identify, you may want to select the option that places your data labels in the first row of your worksheet.

The Correlation tool creates a table showing the degree of correlation between each group of data. The correlation coefficient is a value between -1 and 1. A coefficient value of –1 denotes a perfect negative correlation, where the values of one group increase to the same degree as the values in the other group decrease. With a coefficient value of 1, you have a perfect positive correlation, where the values of one group increase to the same degree as the values of the other group increase. If the correlation coefficient is zero, the groups of values have no relationship.

## Find the Correlation between Two Sets of Data

1 Select a cell in the range of data that you want to evaluate.

2 Click Tools⇨Data Analysis to open the Data Analysis dialog box.

3 Click Correlation.

4 Click OK.

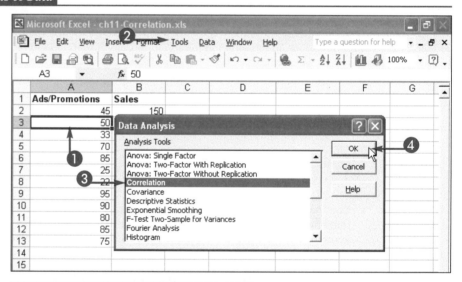

The Correlation dialog box displays.

5 Specify the range of cells to analyze.

6 Click an option to specify whether your data is in columns or rows.

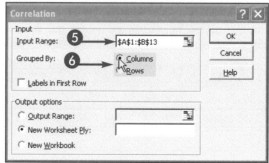

**7** To place the Excel-generated table in the first row of your worksheet, click Labels in first row (☐ changes to ☑).

**8** Specify the output location.

**9** Click OK.

● Excel analyzes the data groups and creates the correlation report.

In this example, the result is close to 1, indicating a strong positive correlation.

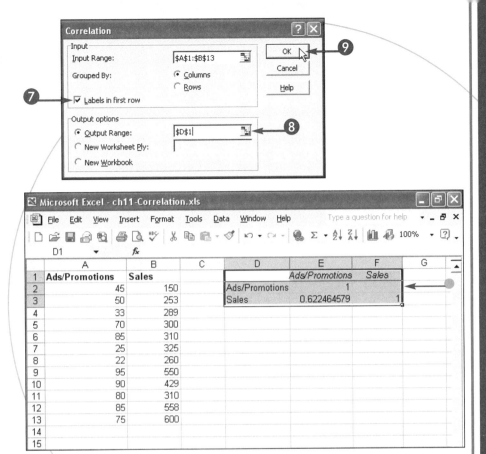

When you use the Correlation tool, Excel calculates the correlation values based upon the current sets of data. If you alter a value in a data set after computing the correlation, Excel does not update the calculated values. You need to recalculate the Correlation again to update the values.

If you want to modify the data values and have Excel automatically update the Correlation value, you must use the CORREL function to create a formula. With this function, you can examine the values in two different lists and determine the correlation. The CORREL function has two arguments:

```
=CORREL(Array1, Array2)
```

For each argument you must specify the range of cells containing the values you want to compare. The CORREL function returns a value between –1 and 1 indicating the correlation between the two sets of data values.

If you want to compare multiple sets of data values, you must create a separate CORREL formula each time you want to compare two sets.

# Determine the Covariance of Two Sets of Data

**C**ovariance calculates the average of the product of deviations of values from the means of each data set. If you plot your data and observe a straight line using Excel's XY (Scatter) chart, you can statistically prove that a relationship exists by calculating the correlation and covariance. Whereas a correlation determines if two sets of data are dependent upon each other, the *covariance* determines the *degree* to which the two sets of data are related, or *how* they vary together. Once you have both the covariance and the correlation calculations, you can use them to determine if there is, in fact, a relationship between the two data sets. See the section "Find the Correlation between Sets of Data" for more on calculating correlations, and Chapter 6 for more on plotting data.

To perform a covariance, you must provide Excel with the range of cells containing the sets of data as well as how you have the data sets grouped. You can make the output easier to identify by opting to have results and labels in the first row of your worksheet.

Excel creates a table showing the covariance value between each set of data. The covariance of a value with itself is its variance. If the covariance value is positive, the values in the data sets are increasing together. If the covariance value is negative, the values in the second data set tend to increase as the first data set decreases. If the covariance is zero, you cannot predict a correlation between the two data sets.

To learn how to load the Covariance feature as a part of the Analysis ToolPak add-in, see the section "Install Excel Add-ins."

## Determine the Covariance of Two Sets of Data

① Select a cell in the range of data.

② Click Tools⇨Data Analysis to open the Data Analysis dialog box.

③ Click Covariance.

④ Click OK.

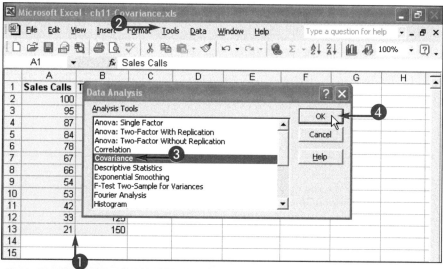

The Covariance dialog box displays.

⑤ Specify the range of cells to analyze.

⑥ Click an option to specify whether your data is in columns or rows.

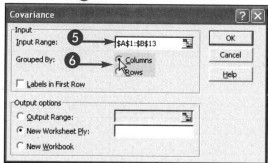

**7** To place the Excel-generated table in the first row of your worksheet, click Labels in first row (☐ changes to ☑ ).

**8** Specify the output location.

**9** Click OK.

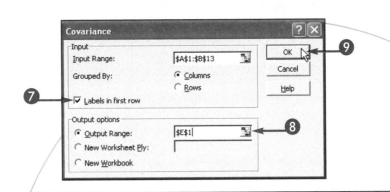

• Excel analyzes the data sets and creates the covariance report.

In this example, the covariance value is negative; the values in the second data set tend to increase as the first data set decreases.

## Apply It

If you just want to return a single covariance value for two sets of data values, you can use the COVAR function available within Excel to create a formula in the appropriate cell. When you use the COVAR function, it determines the covariance of the two sets of data by finding the average of the product of the deviations between all possible pairs of values within the sets. The function treats each set of values as separate arrays.

The COVAR function requires two arguments, as shown in the following syntax:

```
=COVAR(Array1, Array2)
```

For each argument you need to specify the range of cells containing the values you want to compare. You must specify the same number of values for both arguments, or the function returns an error. Excel ignores any cells containing text, logical values, or empty cells.

If you want to compare multiple sets of data values, you must create a separate COVAR formula each time you want to compare two sets. For example, if you want to compare sets A, B, and C, you must create three different formulas so that you compare A to B, A to C, and B to C.

# Calculate Descriptive Statistics

You can have Excel quickly calculate sixteen different statistical measurements and summarize them in a list using the Descriptive Statistics tool. For an analyst, this feature is perfect for very quickly calculating statistical information on large databases or worksheets. When you use this tool, Excel produces a table containing standard statistic calculations for each group of data values within the specified list, including the mean, standard error, median, mode, standard deviation, sample variance, kurtosis, skewness, range, minimum, maximum, sum, count, largest value, smallest value, and confidence level. For example, if you use it to compare a list containing sales amounts for different states, Excel produces a table containing the statistical values related to each state.

With the Descriptive Statistics tool, you must specify the range of cells containing the sets of data. You also must indicate whether you have your sets of data grouped in rows or columns. Each row or column must contain a different set of data. You can make the output easier to identify by opting to have results and labels in the first row of your worksheet.

You can use the last four options on the Descriptive Statistics dialog box to specify which descriptive statistics values Excel calculates. Use the Summary Statistics option to calculate all of the common descriptive statistics values. If you want to calculate the confidence level of the mean, you specify the $\alpha$-level. For example, 90% indicates a significance of 10%. The Kth Largest and Kth Smallest allow you to find specific values in the group, such as the second smallest, or third largest number. If you specify a value of 1 you receive the same values Excel gives you for the Minimum and Maximum values.

## Calculate Descriptive Statistics

① Select a cell in the range of data you want to analyze.

② Click Tools⊅Data Analysis to open the Data Analysis dialog box.

③ Click Descriptive Statistics.

④ Click OK.

The Descriptive Statistics dialog box displays.

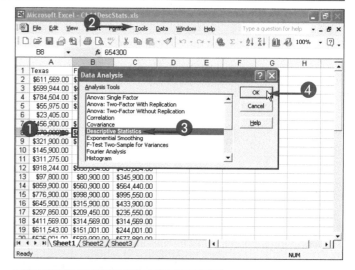

⑤ Specify the range of cells to analyze.

⑥ Specify whether data values are grouped in rows or columns.

⑦ To place the Excel-generated table in the first row of your worksheet, click Labels in first row.

⑧ Specify the output location.

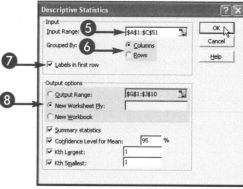

9️⃣ Click Summary statistics to produce a table with all sixteen of Excel's statistical measurements.

🔟 Click Confidence Level for Mean to show the confidence level, and type the α level.

1️⃣1️⃣ You can click Kth Largest and Kth Smallest to display specific values in each group.

1️⃣2️⃣ Click OK.

Excel analyzes the data and produces descriptive statistics for each group of values.

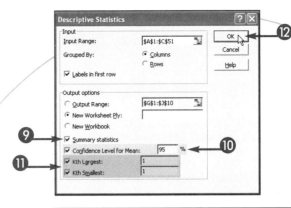

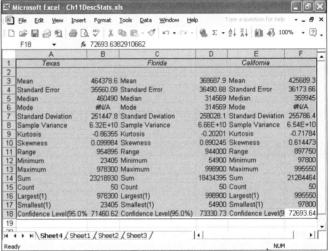

## Extra

When you use the Descriptive Statistics tool, Excel calculates several values:

| STATISTIC | DESCRIPTION |
|---|---|
| Mean | The average value, or center of the distribution, of the data group. |
| Standard Error | The square root of the sample size (n) divided into the standard deviation over the square root of the sample size (n). |
| Median | The middle value in the group of data. |
| Mode | Most common value in the group of data. |
| Standard Deviation | The dispersion of the group of data values. |
| Sample Variance | The Standard deviation squared, or the measure of the dispersion of the data. |
| Kurtosis | The direction of the curvature of the underlying distribution. |
| Skewness | The degree of symmetry in distribution around a central axis. |
| Range | Difference between the largest and smallest values. |
| Minimum/Maximum | Smallest and largest values in the group. |
| Sum | Total when all values are added for the group. |
| Count | Number of values in the group. |
| Largest(N)/Smallest(N) | The largest and smallest value in the group, where N is a specified integer. |
| Confidence Level | How much your value deviates from the mean. |

# Compare the Variances in Two Groups of Data

If you want to compare the variances between two groups of data, you can use the F-Test Two-Sample for Variances tool in Excel. *Variance* is a measurement how a group of values disperse around the group's mean value. For example, you may have two plants producing the same product, one in Indiana, and one in Texas, and both have efficiency levels of 95%, but you want to know which plant more consistently remained efficient throughout the year. When you calculate the variance of both plants' efficiency values, you may find that the Indiana plant has a lower variance than Texas, therefore more efficiently performed throughout the year.

When you use an F-test analysis, Excel compares the ratio of the variance between each data group. Excel calculates an F statistic (F) for the two sets of data, which is the ratio of the Mean Standard Square Error (MS) between the groups to the MS within the groups. If the F statistic is less than the F Critical value, you cannot reject the null hypothesis that the variances of the two groups are the same. An F statistic close to 1 indicates that two groups have equal variances.

To perform this test, you must provide Excel with the ranges of both data groups as well as an Alpha level, or the statistical confidence level you expect. The Alpha field is the probability of $H_A$ being true. You specify a value between 0 and 1 for the confidence level. The default level of .05 is equivalent to a 95-percent confidence level. To make your table easily identifiable, you can let Excel know that you have labels in the first row of your worksheet. For more on comparing two groups of data, and on how to set up statistical hypotheses ($H_A$ true and $H_0$) see the section "Analysis of Variance for Lists of Values (ANOVA)."

## Compare the Variances in Two Groups of Data

① Create two groups of data to calculate the F-Test.

② Click Tools➪Data Analysis to open the Data Analysis dialog box.

③ Click F-Test Two-Sample for Variances.

④ Click OK.

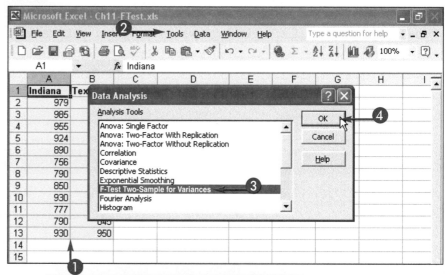

The F-Test Two-Sample for Variances dialog box displays.

⑤ Specify the first range of cells to analyze.

⑥ Specify the second range of cells to analyze.

⑦ If you have placed labels for the Excel-generated table in the first row of your worksheet, click Labels (☐ changes to ☑).

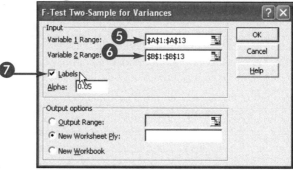

8  Type a value between 0 and 1 for the significance level (α).

9  Specify the output location.

10  Click OK.

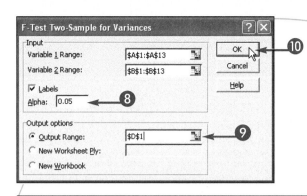

● Excel compares the variances between the two groups.

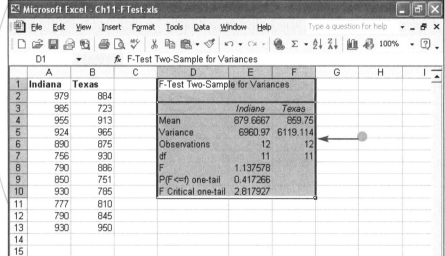

When you use the F-Test Analysis tool, Excel calculates several values, as described in the following table.

| STATISTIC | DESCRIPTION |
|---|---|
| Mean | The average value, or center of the distribution, of the data group. |
| Variance | A measurement of the spread or dispersion of the data. The average squared distance between each datum & the mean. |
| Observations | Indicates the number of values in each list. |
| df | Indicates the Degrees of Freedom, or the number of values that are free to vary after a statistic has been computed from a set of data. |
| F | The ratio of the variance of the individual groups to the entire range of values. The F statistic is the ratio of the mean square between the data sets over the mean square within the data sets. |
| P(F<=f) one-tail | A value between 0 and 1 that indicates the probability of observing a test statistic at least as extreme as the one observed. The closer the value is to one the higher the probability. |
| F Critical one-tail | The critical value of the F distribution. It is dependent on both the α level and the degrees of freedom. It is the standard against which the F statistic is compared. |

# Calculate a
# Moving Average

You can smooth out a data series that contains a lot of variability using Excel's Moving Average Tool. You might do this if you analyze a large amount of data that occasionally has peaks that do not represent the data as a whole. For example, if you collect data on the daily sales of an item, but your data occasionally includes "spikes" when you promoted the item, or placed it on sale, you might perform a moving average to calculate a more accurate average — without including the sale promotion spikes. Using a moving average, you can often spot trends in data that are not obvious in the raw data values.

You specify the number of values, or Intervals, Excel should use to calculate the moving average. If you omit an Interval value, Excel uses a default value of 3, which means that the moving average is calculated by averaging the last three values.

Unlike other tools available for Data Analysis, the Moving Average tool can only output the values to the current worksheet. You need to specify the first cell you want to use for the results. Keep in mind, if the first row contains a label, you want the data values to start in the second row.

You have the option of creating a line chart that shows the relationship between the actual values in the data set and the forecasted moving average that the Moving Average tool creates. If you select this option, Excel places the chart in the same worksheet as the moving average values.

Excel provides the Moving Average tool as part of the Analysis ToolPak add-in option that you can load on the Add-Ins dialog box. See the section "Install Excel Add-ins" for more information on loading add-in options.

## Calculate a Moving Average

1 Create the range of data to use to predict the moving average.

2 Click Tools➪Data Analysis.

The Data Analysis dialog box displays.

3 Click Moving Average.

4 Click OK.

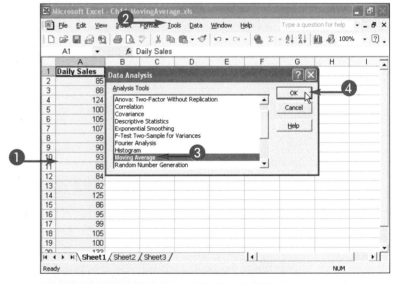

The Moving Average dialog box displays.

5 Specify the range of cells to analyze.

6 If the first row contains labels, click Labels in First Row (☐ changes to ☑ ).

7 If desired, specify an integer value for the interval.

**Note:** If omitted, Excel uses a default value of 3.

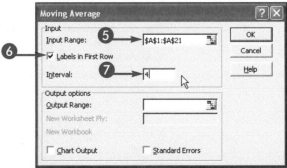

⑧ Specify the output cell reference.

⑨ Click Chart Output to chart the values.

⑩ Click Standard Errors (☐ changes to ☑ ) to create Standard Error values.

⑪ Click OK.

- Excel computes the moving average and creates a chart showing the actual and forecasted values.

- If selected, Excel computes the Standard Errors and places them in a separate column next to the moving average.

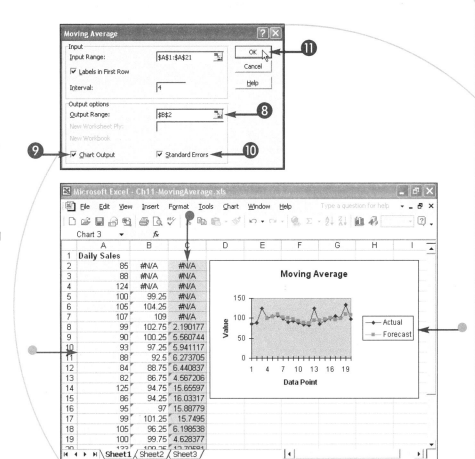

## Extra

When you use the Moving Average tool, Excel uses the AVERAGE function to determine each moving average value. The first few values in the column will contain the value #N/A. The number of cells that contain #N/A is one less than the integer value specified for the Interval value. For example, if the specified interval is 3, the first two cells in the Moving Average column contain the value #N/A because you do not have three values to average.

When you create a chart for the Moving Average, Excel automatically uses default labels for each data series, the axes, and the chart title. You can use the chart options to change the text of each label.

To change the text of the chart title and axes labels, click Chart➪Chart Options to display the Chart Options dialog box. Click the Titles tab and specify the desired labels.

To change the data series labels displayed in the legend, click Chart➪Source Data and click the Series tab. Click each series and specify the desired name. You can either type a name or specify the reference of a cell containing a label. For more about Excel charting functions, see Chapter 6.

# Determine Rank and Percentile

If you want to rank a series of values in a list, you can use the Rank and Percentile Tool. With this tool, Excel takes a specified list of numeric values and ranks them from highest to lowest by both a numeric and a percentage value. It also calculates a *percentile* for your value, which is how an individual score ranks compared to other scores. For example, you may want to rank the sales from different sale people within the organization to not only show which person had the highest sales but also determine sales person's percentile, or rank, when compared to the entire sales team. This feature is perfect for ranking the top selling item, the most efficient facility within a company, or the machine or team that produces the most product.

You can only rank one row or column of values at a time. Excel allows you to select multiple rows or columns as the input range, but only the first row or column of values within the range is analyzed. You can only have a label in the first row of a column. If the specified range contains any other text, an error message displays.

You can output the results of the Rank and Percentile tool to a specific range of cells within the current worksheet, a new worksheet, or a new workbook. If you select New Worksheet, you can specify the worksheet name or allow Excel to assign a default name.

Excel provides the Rank and Percentile tool as part of the Analysis ToolPak add-in option that you can load on the Add-Ins dialog box. See the section "Install Excel Add-ins" for more information on loading add-in options.

## Determine Rank and Percentile

① Create the range of data to analyze.

② Click Tools⇨Data Analysis.

  The Data Analysis dialog box displays.

③ Click Rank and Percentile.

④ Click OK.

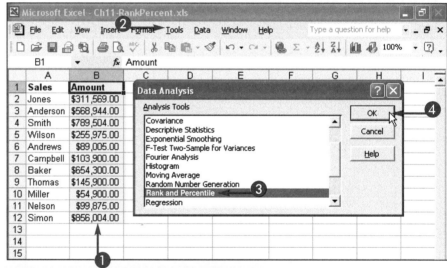

  The Rank and Percentile dialog box displays.

⑤ Specify the range of cells to analyze.

⑥ Specify whether data values are grouped in rows or columns.

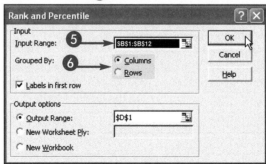

7 If the first row contains labels, click Labels in first row (☐ changes to ☑).

8 Specify the output location.

9 Click OK.

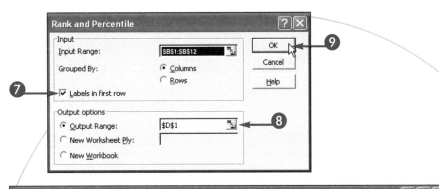

● Excel ranks the specified range of data.

Excel creates a four-column table containing ranking information for the specified values, as outlined in the following table.

| COLUMN | DESCRIPTION |
|--------|-------------|
| Point | The location of the data value within the specified input range. For example, if the value was originally the third numeric value in the input data, the Point value is 3. |
| Input | Contains the input values sorted based upon the ranking. |
| Rank | The numeric ranking of each value with 1 being the highest ranking value in the list. |
| Percent | A percentage ranking for the input values. The percentage indicates the percentage of values that are below the specified value. |

You can also use the RANK function to create a formula to rank a specific value within a data list. The RANK function returns a number that shows how the value compares with other numbers in the data list. You use the following syntax with the RANK function: =RANK(Number, Ref, [Order]). The following table provides a description of the three arguments for the RANK function.

| ARGUMENT | DESCRIPTION |
|----------|-------------|
| Number | The numeric value you want to rank. |
| Ref | The range of cells that you want to use to rank the specified value. |
| Order | A numeric value specifying the sort order for the list. If you omit the value, or the value is 0, Excel sorts the list in descending order. If the argument is any other value, Excel sorts in ascending order. The order argument is optional. |

# Excel Keyboard Shortcuts

| SHORTCUT | RESULT |
| --- | --- |
| Enter | Completes the cell entry and moves to the next cell. |
| Alt + Enter | Starts a new line within the same cell. |
| Shift + Enter | Completes the cell entry and moves up to the cell above. |
| Tab | Completes the cell entry and moves to next cell on the right. |
| Shift + Tab | Completes the cell entry and moves to the next cell on the left. |
| Esc | Cancels the cell entry and restores original cell contents. |
| Ctrl + D | Fills the active cell with the contents of the cell above it. |
| Ctrl + R | Fills the active cell with the contents of the cell to the left of it. |
| Ctrl + F3 | Displays the Define Name dialog box. |
| Ctrl + K | Displays the Insert Hyperlink dialog box. |
| F2 | Edits the active cell by placing the insertion point at the end of the cell contents. |

## Editing Shortcuts

| SHORTCUT | RESULT |
| --- | --- |
| Ctrl + C | Copies the selection. |
| Ctrl + X | Cuts the selection. |
| Ctrl +V | Pastes the selection. |
| Backspace | Deletes entire contents of a cell, or character on the left of the insertion point if you are editing the cell contents. |
| Delete | Deletes entire contents of a cell, or character on the right of the insertion point if you are editing the cell contents. |
| Ctrl + Delete | Deletes text from the insertion point to the end of the cell contents. |
| Ctrl + Z | Undoes an action. |
| Ctrl + Y | Repeats an action (Redo). |
| F4 | Repeats an action (same as Ctrl + Y). |
| Ctrl + - | Deletes the selection. |
| Ctrl + Shift + + | Inserts blank cells. |

## Formatting Shortcuts

| SHORTCUT | RESULT |
| --- | --- |
| Alt + O | Selects the Format menu on the Menu bar. |
| Alt + ' | Opens the Style dialog box. |
| Ctrl + 1 | Opens the Format Cells dialog box. |
| Ctrl + B | Applies or removes bold formatting. |
| Ctrl + I | Applies or removes italic formatting. |
| Ctrl + U | Applies or removes underlining. |
| Ctrl + S | Applies or removes strikethrough formatting. |
| Ctrl + Shift + ~ | Applies the General number format. |
| Ctrl + Shift + $ | Applies the Currency format with 2 decimal places and negative numbers in parentheses. |
| Ctrl + Shift + ^ | Applies the Exponential formatting with 2 decimal places. |
| Ctrl + Shift + # | Applies the Date format with dates formatted as dd-mm-yy. |
| Ctrl + Shift + @ | Applies the Time format with hour, minute, and AM or PM. |
| Ctrl + Shift + ! | Applies the Number format with 2 decimal places, a thousands separator, and minus sign for negative numbers. |
| Ctrl + Shift + & | Applies the outline borders. |
| Ctrl + Shift + _ | Removes the outline borders. |
| Alt + Shift + Right Arrow | Displays the Group dialog box. |
| Alt + Shift + Left Arrow | Displays the Ungroup dialog box. |
| Ctrl + 9 | Hides the selected rows. |
| Ctrl + Shift + ( | Unhides the hidden rows within the range selection. |
| Ctrl + 0 | Hides the selected columns. |
| Ctrl + Shift + ) | Unhides the hidden columns within the range selection. |

continued →

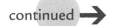

# Excel Keyboard
## Shortcuts (continued)

## Formula Shortcuts

| SHORTCUT | RESULT |
|---|---|
| Ctrl + Shift + Enter | Enters a formula as an array. |
| Ctrl + Shift + A | Inserts the argument names in parentheses for the specified function name. |
| F3 | Pastes a defined name into a formula. |
| Shift + F3 | Displays the Paste Function dialog box. |
| = | Starts a formula. |
| Alt + = | Inserts the AutoSum formula. |
| Ctrl + ; | Enters the current date. |
| Ctrl + Shift + : | Enters the current time. |
| Ctrl + Shift + " | Copies the value in the cell above the active cell into the formula bar. |
| Ctrl + ` | Alternates between displaying the value of the cell and the cell formula. |

## General Program Shortcuts

| SHORTCUT | RESULT |
|---|---|
| Ctrl + N | Creates a new workbook. |
| Ctrl + O | Displays the Open dialog box for selecting a workbook to opens. |
| Ctrl + F12 | Opens a workbook (same as Ctrl + O). |
| Ctrl + S | Saves a workbook (the Save As dialog box opens if the workbook has not been previously saved). |
| Shift + F12 | Saves a workbook (same as Ctrl + S). |
| F12 | Opens the Save As dialog box to specify the name and location of the workbook. |
| Ctrl + W | Closes the active workbook; if it is the only workbook open, it also closes Excel. |
| Alt + F4 | Closes the active workbook (same as Ctrl + W). |
| F1 | Opens Help or Office Assistant. |

## General Program Shortcuts *(continued)*

| SHORTCUT | RESULT |
| --- | --- |
| Shift + F1 | Displays the What's This? question mark. |
| F7 | Runs the spell checker. |
| F10 | Activates the Menu bar (use arrow keys to move along menu). |
| Shift + F10 | Opens a context menu containing options related to the current worksheet selection. This is the same as clicking the right mouse button. |
| F9 | Calculates all worksheets in all open workbooks. |
| Ctrl + F9 | Minimizes the workbook. |
| Ctrl + F10 | Restores or maximizes the workbook. |
| Ctrl + P | Opens the Print dialog box. |
| Ctrl + Shift + F12 | Opens the Print dialog box (same as Ctrl + P). |
| Alt + F8 | Displays the Macro dialog box. |
| Alt + F11 | Displays the Visual Basic Editor. |

## PivotTable and PivotChart Shortcuts

| SHORTCUT | RESULT |
| --- | --- |
| Up Arrow | Selects the preview field button in the list on the right. |
| Down Arrow | Selects the next field button in the list on the right. |
| Left Arrow | Selects the field button to the left. |
| Right Arrow | Selects the field button to the right. |
| Alt + R | Moves the selected field into the Row area. |
| Alt + C | Moves the selected field into the Column area. |
| Alt + P | Moves the selected field into the Page area. |
| Alt + L | Displays the PivotTable Field dialog box. |
| Alt + Down Arrow | Displays a drop-down list for the selected field. |
| Ctrl + Shift + * | Selects the entire PivotTable report. |
| Alt + Shift + Left Arrow | Groups the selected items. |
| Alt + Shift + Right Arrow | Ungroups the selected items. |

continued →

# Excel Keyboard
## Shortcuts (continued)

## Selection Shortcuts

| SHORTCUT | RESULT |
| --- | --- |
| Shift + Right Arrow | Expands the selection one cell right. |
| Shift + Left Arrow | Expands the selection one cell left. |
| Shift + Up Arrow | Expands the selection up one cell. |
| Shift + Down Arrow | Expands the selection down one cell. |
| Ctrl + Shift + * | Selects the current region, cells containing values, around the active cell. |
| Ctrl + Shift + Right Arrow | Expands the selection right to the last nonblank cell in the row. |
| Ctrl + Shift + Left Arrow | Expands the selection left to the last nonblank cell in the row. |
| Ctrl + Shift + Up Arrow | Expands the selection up to the last nonblank cell in the column. |
| Ctrl + Shift + Down Arrow | Expands the selection down to the last nonblank cell in the column. |
| Shift + Home | Expands selection to the beginning of the row. |
| Ctrl + Shift + Home | Expands selection to the beginning of the worksheet. |
| Ctrl + Shift + End | Expands selection to the end of the worksheet. |
| Ctrl + Spacebar | Selects the entire column. |
| Shift + Spacebar | Selects the entire row. |
| Ctrl + A | Selects the entire worksheet. |
| Shift + Backspace | Selects the active cell only when multiple cells are selected. |
| Shift + Page Down | Expands the selection down one screen. |
| Shift + Page Up | Expands the selection up one screen. |
| Ctrl + Shift + Spacebar | If an object is selected, selects all objects. |
| Ctrl + 6 | Alternates between hiding objects, displaying objects, and displaying object placeholders. |
| Ctrl + 7 | Shows or hides the Standard toolbar. |
| Shift + F8 | Adds another range of cells to the selection. |

**Worksheet Navigation Shortcuts**

| SHORTCUT | RESULT |
| --- | --- |
| Up Arrow | Moves the active cell up one row. |
| Down Arrow | Moves the active cell down one row. |
| Left Arrow | Moves the active cell left one column. |
| Right Arrow | Moves the active cell right one column. |
| Home | Moves to the beginning of the current row. |
| Ctrl + Home | Moves to the beginning of the worksheet (typically cell A1). |
| Ctrl + End | Moves to the last cell in the worksheet (the cell at the intersection of the last used row and column in the worksheet). |
| Page Up | Scrolls up one screen. |
| Page Down | Scrolls down one screen. |
| Alt + Page Up | Scrolls right one screen. |
| Alt + Page Down | Scrolls left one screen. |
| Ctrl + Page Up | Moves to the previous worksheet in the workbook. |
| Ctrl + Page Down | Moves to the next worksheet in the workbook. |
| Ctrl + F6 | Switches to the next open workbook. |
| Ctrl + Shift + F6 | Switches back to the previously viewed open workbook. |
| F6 | Moves between split panes of a workbook. |
| Shift + F6 | Moves back to previous pane of split workbook. |
| F5 | Opens the Go To dialog box. |
| Shift + F5 | Opens the Find and Replace dialog box. |
| Shift + F4 | Repeats the last Find command. |
| Tab | Moves between unlocked cells of a protected worksheet. |
| Ctrl + . | Moves clockwise to the next corner of the selected range of cells. |
| Ctrl + Alt + Right Arrow | Moves right to the next nonadjacent selection. |
| Ctrl + Alt + Left Arrow | Move left to the next nonadjacent selection. |

# Excel Function Quick Reference

**Legend:**

| | |
|---|---|
| `Plain courier text` = required | *Italics* = user-defined |
| [] = optional | . . . = list of items |
| \| = or | AT = Analysis ToolPak Function |

## Database Functions

| FUNCTION | DESCRIPTION |
|---|---|
| DAVERAGE(*database, field, criteria*) | Averages the values in a column that match the specified criteria. |
| DCOUNT(*database, field, criteria*) | Counts the numeric values in the column that match the specified criteria. |
| DCOUNTA(*database, field, criteria*) | Counts the values (both numeric and non-numeric) that match the specified criteria. |
| DGET(*database, field, criteria*) | Finds the value in the selected list that matches the specified criteria. |
| DMAX(*database, field, criteria*) | Finds the maximum value in the column that matches the specified criteria. |
| DMIN(*database, field, criteria*) | Finds the minimum value in the column that matches the specified criteria. |
| DPRODUCT(*database, field, criteria*) | Multiplies the values in the column that match the specified criteria and returns the product. |
| DSTDEV(*database, field, criteria*) | Estimates the standard deviation of a sample using the numbers in the column that match the specified criteria. |
| DSTDEVP(*database, field, criteria*) | Estimates the standard deviation of the entire population using the numbers in the column that match the specified criteria. |
| DSUM(*database, field, criteria*) | Totals the numbers in the column that match the specified criteria and returns the sum. |
| DVAR(*database, field, criteria*) | Estimates the variance of a sample using the numbers in the column that match the specified criteria. |
| DVARP(*database, field, criteria*) | Estimates the variance of the entire population using the numbers in the column that match the specified criteria. |

## Date and Time Functions

| FUNCTION | DESCRIPTION |
| --- | --- |
| DATE(*year, month, day*) | Creates a date by combining the specified year, month, and day values. |
| DATEVALUE(*date_value*) | Converts a date value into the serial number used by Excel to store the date. |
| DAY(*serial_number*) | Returns the day portion of a date. |
| DAYS360(*start_date, end_date*[, *method*]) | Calculates the number of days between two dates using either the U.S. (NASD) or European accounting methods. |
| EDATE(*start_date, months*) AT | Returns the date that is the specified number of months before or after a date. |
| EOMONTH(*start_date, months*) AT | Returns the last day in the month that is the specified number of months before or after the date. |
| HOUR(*serial_number*) | Returns the hour portion of a time. |
| MINUTE(*serial_number*) | Returns the minute portion of a time. |
| MONTH(*serial_number*) | Returns the month portion of a date. |
| NETWORKDAYS(*start_date, end_date*[, *holidays*]) AT | Determines the number of work days between two dates by excluding any weekend dates and any specified holidays. |
| NOW() | Returns the current date and time. |
| SECOND(*serial_number*) | Returns the second portion of a time. |
| TIME(*hour, minute, second*) | Creates a time by combining the specified hour, minute, and second values. |
| TIMEVALUE(*time_text*) | Converts a time value into the serial number used by Excel to store the time. |
| TODAY() | Returns the current date. |
| WEEKDAY(*serial_number*[, *return_type*]) | Returns a number from 1 to 7, indicating the day of the week that a date falls on. |
| WEEKNUM(*serial_number*[, *return_type*]) AT | Returns the week number representing the week when the date occurs in the year. |
| WORKDAY(*start_date, days*[, *holidays*]) AT | Finds the date that is the specified number of workdays before the date. |
| YEAR(*year, month, day*) | Returns the year portion of a date. |
| YEARFRAC(*start-date, end_date*[, *basis*]) AT | Returns a decimal value that represents the fraction of a year represented by the number of days between two dates. |

continued →

# Excel Function
## Quick Reference (continued)

### Engineering Functions

| FUNCTION | DESCRIPTION |
|---|---|
| BESSELI(*x, n*) <sup>AT</sup> | Returns the modified Bessel function In(x). |
| BESSELJ(*x, n*) <sup>AT</sup> | Returns the Bessel function Jn(x). |
| BESSELK(*x, n*) <sup>AT</sup> | Returns the modified Bessel function Kn(x). |
| BESSELY(*x, n*) <sup>AT</sup> | Returns the Bessel function Yn(x). |
| BIN2DEC(*number*) <sup>AT</sup> | Converts a binary number to a decimal number. |
| BIN2HEX(*number*[, *places*]) <sup>AT</sup> | Converts a binary number to a hexadecimal number. Unless specified, uses the minimum number of characters. |
| BIN2OCT(*number*[, *places*]) <sup>AT</sup> | Converts a binary number to an octal number. Unless specified, uses the minimum number of characters. |
| COMPLEX(*real_num, i_num*[, *suffix*]) <sup>AT</sup> | Converts real and imaginary coefficients into complex numbers. |
| CONVERT(*number, from_unit, to_unit*) <sup>AT</sup> | Converts a number from one measurement system to another, such as converting meters to feet. |
| DEC2BIN(*number*[, *places*]) <sup>AT</sup> | Converts a decimal number to a binary number. Unless specified, uses the minimum number of characters. |
| DEC2HEX(*number*[, *places*]) <sup>AT</sup> | Converts a decimal number to a hexadecimal number. Unless specified, uses the minimum number of characters. |
| DEC2OCT(*number*[, *places*]) <sup>AT</sup> | Converts a decimal number to an octal number. Unless specified, uses the minimum number of characters. |
| DELTA(*number1*[, *number2*]) <sup>AT</sup> | Determines if two numbers are equal. If the second number is omitted, it compares the first number to zero. |
| ERF(*lower_limit*[, *upper_limit*]) <sup>AT</sup> | Returns the error function integrated between the specified limits. |
| ERFC(*x*) <sup>AT</sup> | Returns the complimentary error function integrated between the specified number and infinity. |
| FACTDOUBLE(*number*)<sup>AT</sup> | Finds the double factorial of a number. |
| GESTEP(*number*[, *step*]) <sup>AT</sup> | Checks if a number is larger than the threshold value. |
| HEX2BIN(*number*[, *places*]) <sup>AT</sup> | Converts a hexadecimal number to a binary number. Unless specified, uses the minimum number of characters. |
| HEX2DEC(*number*) <sup>AT</sup> | Converts a hexadecimal number to a decimal number. |

**Engineering Functions** *(continued)*

| FUNCTION | DESCRIPTION |
|---|---|
| HEX2OCT(*number*[, *places*]) AT | Converts a hexadecimal number to an octal number. Unless specified, uses the minimum number of characters. |
| IMABS(*inumber*) AT | Returns the absolute value of a complex number. |
| IMAGINARY(*inumber*) AT | Returns the imaginary coefficient of a complex number. |
| IMARGUMENT(*inumber*) AT | Returns the theta argument for an angle measurement expressed in radians. |
| IMCONJUGATE(*inumber*) AT | Returns the complex conjugate of a complex number. |
| IMCOS(*inumber*) AT | Determines the cosine for a complex number. |
| IMDIV(*inumber1, inumber2*) AT | Finds the quotient of two complex numbers. |
| IMEXP(*inumber*) AT | Finds the exponential of a complex number. |
| IMLN(*inumber*) AT | Determines the natural logarithm of a complex number. |
| IMLOG10(*inumber*) AT | Finds the base-10 logarithm of a complex number. |
| IMLOG2(*inumber*) AT | Finds the base-2 logarithm of a complex number. |
| IMPOWER(*inumber, number*) AT | Returns the result of a complex number raised to the specified power. |
| IMPRODUCT(*inumber1, inumber2,...*) AT | Returns the product of 2 or more complex numbers. The function allows a maximum of 29 complex numbers. |
| IMREAL(*inumber*) AT | Returns the real coefficient of a complex number. |
| IMSIN(*inumber*) AT | Determines the sine for a complex number. |
| IMSQRT(*inumber*) AT | Finds the square root of a complex number. |
| IMSUB(*inumber1, inumber2*) AT | Subtracts two complex numbers. |
| IMSUM(*inumber1,[inumber2,...]*) AT | Adds the specified complex numbers. |
| OCT2BIN(*number*[, *places*]) AT | Converts an octal number to a binary number. Unless specified, uses the minimum number of characters. |
| OCT2DEC(*number*) AT | Converts an octal number to a decimal number. |
| OCT2IIEX(*number*[, *places*]) AT | Converts an octal number to a hexadecimal number. Unless specified, uses the minimum number of characters. |

continued →

## Financial Functions

| FUNCTION | DESCRIPTION |
|---|---|
| ACCRINT(*issue, first_interest, settlement, rate*) AT | Finds the total amount of interest paid by the settlement date. |
| ACCRINTM(*issue, maturity, rate*[, *par, basis*]) AT | Finds the total amount of interest paid at maturity of an investment. |
| AMORDEGRC(*cost, date_purchased, first_period, salvage, period, rate, basis*) AT | Uses the French accounting system to find the depreciation of an asset with a depreciation coefficient. |
| AMORLINC(*cost, date_purchased, first_period, salvage, period, rate, basis*) AT | Uses the French accounting system to find the depreciation of an asset. |
| COUPDAYBS(*settlement, maturity, frequency*[, *basis*]) AT | Finds the number of days between the start of the coupon period and the settlement date. |
| COUPDAYS(*settlement, maturity, frequency*[, *basis*]) AT | Finds the number of days in the coupon period and the settlement date. |
| COUPDAYSNC(*settlement, maturity, frequency*[, *basis*]) AT | Finds the number of days from the settlement date to the next coupon date. |
| COUPNCD(*settlement, maturity, frequency*[, *basis*]) AT | Finds the next coupon date after the settlement date. |
| COUPNUM(*settlement, maturity, frequency*[, *basis*]) AT | Finds the number of coupon dates between the settlement date and the maturity date. |
| COUPPCD(*settlement, maturity, frequency*[, *basis*]) AT | Finds the previous coupon date before the settlement date. |
| CUMIPMT(*rate, nper, start_period, end_period, type*) AT | Determines the cumulative interest paid on a loan between the specified dates. |
| CUMIPRINC(*rate, nper, start_period, end_period, type*) AT | Determines the cumulative principal paid on a loan between the specified dates. |
| DB(*cost, salvage, life, period*[, *month*]) | Finds the depreciation of an asset using fixed-declining depreciation. |
| DDB(*cost, salvage, life, period*[, *month*]) | Finds the depreciation of an asset using double-declining depreciation. |
| DISC(*settlement, maturity,pr, redemption*[, *basis*]) AT | Determines the discount rate for a security. |
| DOLLARDE(*fractional_dollar, fraction*) AT | Converts from a fractional to a decimal value. |

**Financial Functions** *(continued)*

| FUNCTION | DESCRIPTION |
| --- | --- |
| DOLLARFR(*decimal_dollar, fraction*) AT | Converts from a decimal value to a fractional value. |
| DURATION(*settlement, maturity, coupon, yld, frequency*[, *basis*]) AT | Finds the Macauley duration value for a security. |
| EFFECT(*nominal_rate, npery*) AT | Finds the effective annual interest rate on an investment. |
| FV(*rate, nper, pmt*[, *pv, type*]) | Finds the future value of an investment. |
| FVSCHEDULE(*principal, schedule*)AT | Finds the future value of an investment with a variable interest rate. |
| INTRATE(*settlement, maturity, investment, redemption,* [*basis*])AT | Finds the interest rate on a security. |
| IPMT(*rate, per, nper, pv*[, *fv, type*]) | Finds the interest payment on an investment for a specific period. |
| IRR(*values,* [*guess*]) | Finds the internal rate of return. |
| ISPMT(*rate, per, nper, pv*) | Finds the interest payment for a specific period. |
| MDURATION(*settlement, maturity, coupon, yld, frequency*[, *basis*]) AT | Finds the modified duration value for a security. |
| MIRR(*values, finance_rate, reinvest_rate*) | Finds the modified internal rate of return. |
| NOMINAL(*effect_rate, npery*)AT | Finds the nominal annual interest rate. |
| NPER(*rate, pmt, pv,* [*fv, type*]) | Finds the number of payments on an investment. |
| NPV(*rate, value1,* [*value2, ...*]) | Calculates the present value of an investment. |
| ODDFPRICE(*settlement, maturity, issue, first_coupon, rate, yld, redemption, frequency*[, *basis*])AT | Calculates the price of an investment with an abnormal length of the first period. |
| ODDFYIELD(*settlement, maturity, issue, first_coupon, rate, pr, redemption, frequency*[, *basis*])AT | Calculates the yield of an investment with an abnormal length of the first period. |
| ODDLPRICE(*settlement, maturity, issue, last_interest, rate, yld, redemption, frequency*[, *basis*])AT | Calculates the price of an investment with an abnormal length of the first period. |
| ODDLYIELD(*settlement, maturity, issue, last_interest, rate, pr, redemption, frequency*[, *basis*])AT | Calculates the yield of an investment with an abnormal length of the first period. |
| PMT(*rate, nper, pv*[, *fv, type*]) | Finds an investment payment. |
| PPMT(*rate, per, nper, pv*[, *fv, type*]) | Finds the amount applied to the principal for a payment period. |
| PRICE(*settlement, maturity, rate, yld, redemption, frequency*[, *basis*])AT | Calculates the price of a security with periodic interest. |

*continued*

continued →

## Financial Functions *(continued)*

| FUNCTION | DESCRIPTION |
|---|---|
| PRICEDISC(*settlement, maturity, discount, redemption*[, *basis*])AT | Calculates the price of a discounted security. |
| PRICEMAT(*settlement, maturity, issue, rate, yld*[, *basis*])AT | Calculates the price of a security with interest paid at maturity. |
| PV(*rate, nper, pmt*[, *fv, type*]) | Finds the present value of an investment. |
| RATE(*nper, pmt, pv*[, *fv, type, guess*]) | Finds the interest rate per period of an annuity. |
| RECEIVED(*settlement, maturity, investment, discount*[, *basis*])AT | Calculates the amount received at the maturity of a security. |
| SLN(*cost, salvage, life*) | Finds the straight-line depreciation of an asset. |
| SYD(*cost, salvage, life, per*) | Finds the sum-of-year's digits depreciation of an asset. |
| TBILLEQ(*settlement, maturity, discount*)AT | Finds the bond-equivalent yield for a Treasury Bill. |
| TBILLPRICE(*settlement, maturity, discount*)AT | Finds the price for a Treasury Bill. |
| TBILLYIELD(*settlement, maturity, pr*)AT | Finds the yield for a Treasury Bill. |
| VDB(*cost, salvage, life, start_period, end_period*[, *factor, no_switch*]) | Finds the depreciation of an asset over multiple periods. |
| XIRR(*values, dates*[, *guess*])AT | Calculates the rate of return for non-periodic cash flows. |
| XNPV(*rate, values, dates*)AT | Calculates the present value of non-periodic cash flows. |
| YIELD(*settlement, maturity, rate, pr, redemption, frequency*[, *basis*])AT | Calculates the yield of a security. |
| YIELDDISC(*settlement, maturity, pr, redemption*[, *basis*])AT | Calculates the yield of a discounted security. |
| YIELDMAT(*settlement, maturity, issue, rate*[, *basis*])AT | Calculates the yield of a security with interest paid at maturity. |

## Information Functions

| FUNCTION | DESCRIPTION |
|---|---|
| CELL(*info_type*[, *reference*]) | Determines formatting, location, or contents of the specified cell. |
| ERROR.TYPE(*error_val*) | Determines the error type for the selected cell. |
| INFO(*type_text*) | Finds information about the current operating system. |
| ISBLANK(*value*) | Checks for a blank cell. |
| ISERR(*value*) | Checks for any errors except #N/A. |
| ISERROR(*value*) | Checks for any errors. |
| ISEVEN(*number*) | Checks to see if a number is even. |
| ISLOGICAL(*value*) | Checks for a logical value. |
| ISNA(*value*) | Checks for a #N/A value. |
| ISNONTEXT(*value*) | Checks for any non-text value. |
| ISODD(*number*) | Checks if a number is odd. |
| ISREF(*value*) | Checks for a reference. |
| ISTEXT(*value*) | Checks for text. |
| N(*value*) | Converts a value to a number. |
| NA() | Returns an error value of #N/A. |
| TYPE(*value*) | Finds the type of the specified value. |

## Logical Functions

| FUNCTION | DESCRIPTION |
|---|---|
| AND(*logical1*[, *logical2*, ...]) | Returns a value of True if all arguments evaluate to True. |
| FALSE() | Returns a value of False. |
| IF(*logical_test*, *value_if_true*[, *value_if_false*]) | Performs conditions based on whether a condition is True or False. |
| NOT() | Reverses the value of an argument. |
| OR(*logical1*[, *logical2*, ...]) | Returns a value of True if any of the arguments evaluate to True. |
| TRUE() | Returns a value of True. |

continued ➔

## Lookup & Reference Functions

| FUNCTION | DESCRIPTION |
|---|---|
| ADDRESS(*row_num, column_num, abs_num*[, *a1, sheet_text*]) | Creates a reference to a specific cell. |
| AREAS(*reference*) | Finds the number of areas in reference. |
| CHOOSE(*index_num, value1*[, *value2,...*]) | Selects a value from a list based upon the index value. |
| COLUMN(*reference*) | Determines the column number for the reference. |
| COLUMNS(*array*) | Finds the number of columns in an array. |
| GETPIVOTDATA(*data_field, pivot_table*[, *field1, item1, field2, item2, ...*]) | Allows you to capture specific data values from a PivotTable report. |
| HLOOKUP(*lookup_value, table_array, row_index_num*[, *range_lookup*]) | Finds the value in the specified row of the matching column. |
| HYPERLINK(*link_location*[, *friendly_name*]) | Creates a shortcut to a document. |
| INDEX(*reference*[, *row_num, column_num, area_num*]) | Returns a reference to specified cells within reference. |
| INDIRECT(*ref_text*[, *a1*]) | Returns a value or a reference to a value. |
| LOOKUP(*lookup_value, array*) | Finds the specified value within an array. |
| MATCH(*lookup_value, lookup_array*[, *match_type*]) | Locates a matching value in the array. |
| OFFSET(*reference, rows, cols*[, *height, width*]) | Locates the range that is the specified number of columns and rows from the referenced range. |
| ROW(*reference*) | Determines the row number for the reference. |
| ROWS(*array*) | Finds the number of rows in an array. |
| TRANSPOSE(*array*) | Transposes the selected range from vertical to horizontal, or vice versa. |
| VLOOKUP(*lookup_value, table_array, col_index_num*[, *range_lookup*]) | Finds the value in the specified column of the matching row. |

## Math & Trig Functions

| FUNCTION | DESCRIPTION |
|---|---|
| ABS(*number*) | Finds the absolute value of a number. |
| ACOS(*number*) | Finds the arccosine of a number. |
| ACOSH(*number*) | Finds the inverse hyperbolic cosine. |
| ASIN(*number*) | Finds the arcsine of a number. |
| ASINH(*number*) | Finds the inverse hyperbolic sine. |
| ATAN(*number*) | Finds the arctangent of a number. |
| ATAN2(*x_num, y_num*) | Finds the arctangent using two coordinates of an angle. |
| ATANH(*number*) | Finds the inverse hyperbolic tangent. |
| CIELING(*number, significance*) | Rounds a number up to a specific multiple. |
| COMBIN(*number, number_chosen*) | Finds the number of unique combinations for the specified number of items. |
| COS(*number*) | Finds the cosine of an angle. |
| COSH(*number*) | Finds the hyperbolic cosine. |
| DEGREES(*angle*) | Converts a number from radians to degrees. |
| EVEN(*number*) | Rounds the number to the nearest even integer. |
| EXP(*number*) | Raises the constant to the power of the specified number. |
| FACT(*number*) | Finds the factorial of the number. |
| FLOOR(*number, significance*) | Rounds a number down to a specific multiple. |
| GCD(*number1*[, *number2, ...*])$^{AT}$ | Finds the greatest common divisor for the specified numbers. |
| INT(*number*) | Rounds a number to the nearest integer. |
| LCM(*number1*[, *number2, ...*])$^{AT}$ | Finds the least common multiple. |
| LN(*number*) | Finds the natural logarithm of the specified number. |
| LOG(*number*[, *base*]) | Finds the logarithm of a number to the specified base. |
| LOG10(*number*) | Finds the logarithm of a number to base-10. |
| MDETERM(*array*) | Finds the determinant of an array. |
| MINVERSE(*array*) | Finds the inverse of a square matrix. |
| MMULT(*array1, array2*) | Determines the product of two matrixes. |
| MOD(*number, divisor*) | Finds the remainder of the division. |
| MROUND(*number, multiple*)$^{AT}$ | Rounds a number to the specified integer multiple. |
| MULTINOMIAL(*number1*[, *number2, ...*])$^{AT}$ | Divides the sum by the product of factorials. |

*continued*

continued →

## Math & Trig Functions *(continued)*

| FUNCTION | DESCRIPTION |
|---|---|
| ODD(*number*) | Rounds the number to the nearest odd integer. |
| PI() | Returns the value of PI. |
| POWER(*number, power*) | Raises the number to the specified power. |
| PRODUCT(*number1*[, *number2*, ...]) | Multiplies the specified numbers. |
| QUOTIENT(*numerator, denominator*) | Returns the integer result of division. |
| RADIANS(*angle*) | Converts a radian measurement to degrees. |
| RAND() | Creates a random number between 0 and 1. |
| RANDBETWEEN(*bottom, top*)[AT] | Creates a random number between the specified values. |
| ROMAN(*number*[, *form*]) | Creates a roman numeral. |
| ROUND(*number, num_digits*) | Rounds a number to the specified number of digits. |
| ROUNDDOWN(*number, num_digits*) | Rounds a number down to the specified number of digits. |
| ROUNDUP(*number, num_digits*) | Rounds a number up to the specified number of digits. |
| SERIESSUM(*x, n, m, coefficients*)[AT] | Sums a power series. |
| SIGN(*number*) | Determines if a number is positive, negative, or zero. |
| SIN(*number*) | Finds the sine of an angle. |
| SINH(*number*) | Finds the hyperbolic sine. |
| SQRT(*number*) | Determines the square root of a number. |
| SQRTPI(*number*)[AT] | Determines the square root of a number multiplied by PI. |
| SUBTOTAL(*function_num, ref1*[, *ref2*,...]) | Performs a subtotal function on a portion of a list. |
| SUM(*number1*[, *number2*, ...]) | Sums the specified numbers. |
| SUMIF(*range, criteria*[, *sum_range*]) | Sums the cells in the range that match the criteria. |
| SUMPRODUCT(*array1*[, *array2, array3*, ...]) | Sums the products of the arrays. |
| SUMSQ(*number1*[, *number2*, ...]) | Sums the squares of the values. |

## Math & Trig Functions *(continued)*

| FUNCTION | DESCRIPTION |
|---|---|
| SUMX2MY2(*array_x, array_y*) | Sums the differences of the squares of two arrays. |
| SUMX2PY2(*array_x, array_y*) | Sums the squares of two arrays. |
| SUMXMY2(*array_x, array_y*) | Returns the sum of squares for the two arrays. |
| TAN(*number*) | Finds the tangent of an angle. |
| TANH(*number*) | Finds the hyperbolic tangent. |
| TRUNC(*number*[, *num_digits*]) | Truncates a number to the specified decimal digits. |

## Statistical Functions

| FUNCTION | DESCRIPTION |
|---|---|
| AVEDEV(*number1*[, *number2, ...*]) | Finds the average deviation of data points from the mean. |
| AVERAGE(*number1*[, *number2, ...*]) | Finds the average of the numbers. |
| AVERAGEA(*value1*[, *value2, ...*]) | Finds the average of numeric, logical, and text values. |
| BETADIST(*x, alpha, beta*[, *A, B*]) | Finds the distribution using the cumulative beta probability density function. |
| BETAINV(*probability, alpha, beta*[, *A, B*]) | Finds the inverse distribution using the cumulative beta probability density function. |
| BINOMDIST(*number_s, trials, probability_s, cumulative*) | Finds the probability of a number of successes in a specified number of trials. |
| CHIDIST(*x, degrees_freedom*) | Finds the chi-squared distribution. |
| CHIINV(*probability, degrees_freedom*) | Finds the inverse chi-squared distribution. |
| CHITEST(*actual_range, expected_range*) | Compares the expected range of cells to the actual range of cells. |
| CONFIDENCE(*alpha, standard_dev, size*) | Finds the confidence mean for a population mean. |
| CORREL(*array1, array2*) | Determines the correlation coefficient of two arrays. |
| COUNT(*value1*[, *value2, ...*]) | Counts the number of numeric values. |
| COUNTA(*value1*[, *value2, ...*]) | Counts the number of cells that contain values. |
| COUNTBLANK(*range*) | Counts the number of empty cells in the selected range. |
| COUNTIF(*range, criteria*) | Counts the number of cells that meet the criteria within the specified range. |
| COVAR(*array1, array2*) | Finds the covariance of two arrays. |

*continued*

continued →

## Statistical Functions *(continued)*

| FUNCTION | DESCRIPTION |
|---|---|
| CRITBINOM(*trials, probability_s, alpha*) | Finds the smallest value for the cumulative binomial distribution. |
| DEVSQ(*number1[, number2,...]*) | Sums the squares of the deviations between the specified values. |
| EXPONDIST(*x, lambda, cumulative*) | Finds the exponential distribution. |
| FDIST(*x, degrees_freedom1, degrees_freedom2*) | Finds the F probability distribution. |
| FINV(*probability, degrees_freedom1, degrees_freedom2*) | Finds the inverse of the F probability distribution. |
| FISHER(*x*) | Calculates the Fisher transformation of the specified value. |
| FISHERINV(*y*) | Calculates the inverse of the Fisher transformation of the specified value. |
| FORECAST(*x, known_y's, known_x's*) | Predicts a future value based upon the existing values. |
| FREQUENCY(*data_array, bins_array*) | Determines the number of times specific values occur within a range. |
| FTEST(*array1, array2*) | Compares two arrays and determines if the variances are equal. |
| GAMMADIST(*x, alpha, beta, cumulative*) | Finds the gamma distribution. |
| GAMMAINV(*probability, alpha, beta, cumulative*) | Finds the inverse of the gamma distribution. |
| GAMMALN(*x*) | Finds the natural logarithm of the gamma function. |
| GEOMEAN(*number1[, number2,...]*) | Determines the geometric mean of the specified values. |
| GROWTH(*known_y's[, known_x's, new_x's, const]*) | Finds the future exponential growth. |
| HARMEAN(*number1[, number2,...]*) | Determines the harmonic mean of the specified values. |
| HYPGEOMDIST(*sample_s, number_sample, population_s, number_population*) | Determines the probability of the specified number of successes based upon the population size. |
| INTERCEPT(*x, known_y's, known_x's*) | Determines the point where the line crosses the Y-axis. |
| KURT(*number1[, number2,...]*) | Determines the kurtosis of the specified values. |
| LARGE(*array, k*) | Finds the value that is the specified number within an array based upon its size. |
| LINEST(*known_y's[, known_x's, const, stats]*) | Finds the best-fitting straight line using the least squares method. |

## Statistical Functions *(continued)*

| FUNCTION | DESCRIPTION |
|---|---|
| LOGEST(*known_y's*[, *known_x's, const, stats*]) | Finds the exponential curve the fits the specified values. |
| LOGINV(*probability, mean, standard_dev*) | Finds the inverse of the lognormal cumulative distribution. |
| LOGNORMDIST(*x, mean, standard_dev*) | Finds the lognormal cumulative distribution. |
| MAX(*number1*[, *number2,...*]) | Finds the largest numeric value. |
| MAXA(*value1*[, *value2,...*]) | Finds the largest value in the list by comparing numbers, text, and logical values. |
| MEDIAN(*number1*[, *number2,...*]) | Finds the median value for a list. |
| MIN(*number1*[, *number2,...*]) | Finds the smallest numeric value. |
| MINA(*value1*[, *value2,...*]) | Finds the smallest value in the list by comparing numbers, text, and logical values. |
| MODE(*number1*[, *number2,...*]) | Finds the most frequently occurring value in a list. |
| NEGBINOMDIST(*number_f, number_s, probability_s*) | Determines the probability of the specified number of failures. |
| NORMDIST(*x, mean, standard_dev, cumulative*) | Finds the normal distribution of the specified mean and standard deviation. |
| NORMINV(*probability mean, standard_dev*) | Finds the inverse of the normal cumulative distribution using the specified mean and standard deviation values. |
| NORMSDIST(*z*) | Finds the normal distribution with a mean of 0 and a standard deviation of 1. |
| NORMSINV(*probability*) | Finds the inverse of the standard normal cumulative distribution with a mean of zero and a standard deviation of 1. |
| PEARSON(*array1, array2*) | Finds the Pearson product moment coefficient r. |
| PERCENTILE(*array, k*) | Finds the value that is the specified percentile of values in the list. |
| PERCENTRANK(*array, x*[, *significance*]) | Finds the percentage rank of a number within a list. |
| PERMUT(*number, number_chosen*) | Calculates the number of permutations created from the specified number of objects. |
| POISSON(*x, mean, cumulative*) | Calculates the Poisson distribution. |
| PROB(*x_range, prob_range, lower_limit*[, *upper_limit*]) | Determines that probability that a range of values is within the specified limits. |
| QUARTILE(*array, quart*) | Finds the quartile for a list of values. |
| RANK(*number, ref, order*) | Finds the rank of a number within a list. |
| RSQ(*known_y's, known_x's*) | Finds the square of the Pearson product moment correlation coefficient through the specified data points. |
| SKEW(*number1*[, *number2,...*]) | Finds the degree of asymmetry for a series of numbers. |

*continued*

continued →

## Statistical Functions *(continued)*

| FUNCTION | DESCRIPTION |
|---|---|
| SLOPE(*known_y's, known_x's*) | Finds the slope of a linear regression line. |
| SMALL(*array, k*) | Finds the value that is the specified number within an array based upon its size. |
| STANDARDIZE(*x, mean, standard_dev*) | Finds the value when you know the mean and the standard deviation. |
| STDEV(*number1[, number2,...]*) | Estimates the standard deviation of numeric values based upon a sample. |
| STDEVA(*value1[, value2,...]*) | Estimates the standard deviation of numeric, text, and logical values based upon a sample. |
| STDEVP(*number1[, number2,...]*) | Estimates the standard deviation of numeric values based upon the entire population. |
| STDEVPA(*value1[, value2,...]*) | Estimates the standard deviation of numeric, logical, and text values based upon the entire population. |
| STEYX(*known_y's, known_x's*) | Finds the standard error for each y-value. |
| TDIST(*x, degrees_freedom, tails*) | Finds the Student t-distribution probability for the specified value. |
| TINV(*probability, degrees_freedom, tails*) | Finds the inverse of Student t-distribution probability for the specified value. |
| TREND(*known_y's[, known_x's, new_x's, const]*) | Finds the values that match a linear trend using the method of least squares. |
| TRIMMEAN(*array, percent*) | Finds the mean of the interior of a list of numeric values. |
| TTEST(*array1, array2, tails, type*) | Determines if two samples are from the same population. |
| VAR(*number1[, number2,...]*) | Estimates the variance of numeric values based upon a sample. |
| VARA(*value1[, value2,...]*) | Estimates the variance of numeric, text, and logical values based upon a sample. |
| VARP(*number1[, number2,...]*) | Estimates the variance of numeric values based upon the entire population. |
| VARPA(*value1[, value2,...]*) | Estimates the variance of numeric, logical, and text values based upon the entire population. |
| WEIBULL(*x, alpha, beta, cumulative*) | Finds the possibilities of a Weibull distribution. |
| ZTEST(*array, x[, sigma]*) | Finds the two-tailed P-value of a Z-test. |

## Test Functions

| FUNCTION | DESCRIPTION |
|---|---|
| BAHTEXT(*number*) | Converts a number to Thai. |
| CHAR(*number*) | Returns the specified character value. |
| CLEAN(*text*) | Removes all nonprintable characters from text. |
| CODE(*text*) | Finds the character code for the first character in a text string. |
| CONCATENATE(*text1, text2, …*) | Joins the specified text strings. |
| DOLLAR(*number*[, *decimals*]) | Converts a number to a currency value. |
| EXACT(*text1, text2*) | Determines if two strings are the same. |
| FIND(*find_text, within_text*[, *start_num*]) | Locates one text string within another text string. |
| FIXED(*number*[, *decimals, no_commas*]) | Rounds a number to the specified number of decimal places. |
| LEFT(*text*[, *num_chars*]) | Returns the specified number of characters from the left side of a text string. |
| LEN(*text*) | Finds the length of a text string. |
| LOWER(*text*) | Converts a string to lowercase characters. |
| MID(*text, start_num, num_chars*) | Returns the specified number of characters from the center of the text string. |
| PROPER(*text*) | Capitalizes the first character in a string and converts the remaining characters to lowercase. |
| REPLACE(*old_text, start_num, num_chars, new_text*) | Replaces text at the specified location with the new text. |
| REPT(*text, number_times*) | Repeats a text string the specified number of times. |
| RIGHT(*text*[, *num_chars*]) | Returns the specified number of characters from the right side of a text string. |
| SEARCH(*find_text, within_text*[, *start_num*]) | Determines the starting position of one text string within another text string. |
| SUBSTITUTE(*text, old_text, new_text*[, *instance_num*]) | Replaces the specified text within a string. |
| T(*value*) | Returns the specified value. |
| TEXT(*value, format_text*) | Converts a value to the text with the specified format. |
| TRIM(*text*) | Removes all extra spacing from a text string. |
| UPPER(*text*) | Converts all letters in a string to uppercase. |
| VALUE(*text*) | Converts a text string to a number. |

# VBA and Excel Events Quick Reference

## VBA Statements Quick Reference

**Legend:**

`Plain courier text` = required     *Italics* = user-defined     | = or

[] = optional                       . . . = list of items

### File and Folder Handling

| STATEMENT | DESCRIPTION |
|---|---|
| `ChDir` *path* | Changes to the specified folder location. |
| `ChDrive` *drive* | Changes to the specified drive. |
| `Close` [*filenumber*] | Closes a file opened using the `Open` statement. |
| `FileCopy` *source, destination* | Copies a source file to the specified destination. |
| `Kill` *pathname* | Deletes files from a disk. Use wildcards * for multiple characters and ? for single characters. |
| `Lock` [#]*filenumber*[, *recordrange*] | Locks all or a portion of an open file to prevent access by other processes. |
| `MkDir` *path* | Creates a new directory or folder. |
| `Open` *pathname* `For` *mode* [`Access` *access*] [*lock*] `As` [#]*filenumber* [`Len=`*reclength*] | Opens the specified file to allow input/output operations. |
| `Print` #*filenumber*[, *outputlist*] | Writes display-formatted data sequentially to a file. |
| `Put` [#]*filenumber*, [*recnumber*,] *varname* | Writes data contained in a variable to a disk file. |
| `Reset` | Closes all files opened using the `Open` statement. |
| `RmDir` *path* | Removes the specified folder. |
| `SetAttr` *pathname, attributes* | Sets the attribute information for the specified file. |
| `Unlock` [#]*filenumber*[, *recordrange*] | Unlocks a file to allow access by other processes. |
| `Width` #*filenumber, width* | Assigns the output line width for a file opened using the `Open` statement. |
| `Write` #*filenumber*[, *outputlist*] | Writes data to a sequential text file. |

### Interaction

| STATEMENT | DESCRIPTION |
|---|---|
| `AppActivate` *title*[, *wait*] | Activates an application window. |
| `DeleteSetting` *appname, section*[, *key*] | Deletes a section or key setting from an application's entry in the Windows Registry. |
| `SaveSetting` *appname, section, key, setting* | Saves an application entry in the application's entry in the Windows Registry. |
| `SendKeys` *string*[, *wait*] | Sends one or more keystrokes to the active window keyboard buffer, as if they were typed on the keyboard. |

## Program Flow

| STATEMENT | DESCRIPTION |
|---|---|
| `[Public | Private] Declare Sub name`<br>`Lib "libname" [Alias "aliasname"] [([arglist])]` | Declares a reference to an external DLL library function. |
| `Do [{While | Until} condition]`<br>`  [statements]`<br>`Loop` | Repeats a block of statements while or until a condition is `True`. The condition is checked at the beginning of the loop. |
| `Do`<br>`  [statements]`<br>`Loop [{While | Until} condition]` | Repeats a block of statements while or until a condition is `True`. Because the condition is checked at the end of the loop, the block of statements always executes at least once. |
| `Exit Do | For | Function |`<br>`Property | Sub` | Exits the specified `Do Loop`, `For Next`, `Function`, `Sub`, or `Property` code. |
| `For Each element In group`<br>`[statements]`<br>`Next [element]` | Repeats a block of statements for each element in an array or collection. |
| `For counter = start To end [Step step]`<br>`  [statements]`<br>`Next [counter]` | Repeats a section of code the specified number of times. |
| `[Public | Private | Friend] [Static]`<br>`  Function name [(arglist)] [As type]`<br>`[statements]`<br>`[name = expression]`<br>`End Function` | Defines a procedure that returns a value. |
| `If condition Then`<br>`[statements]`<br><br>`[ElseIf condition-n Then`<br>`[elseifstatements] ...`<br><br>`[Else`<br>`[elsestatements]]`<br><br>`End If` | Conditionally executes a block of statements based upon the value of an expression. |
| `[Public | Private | Friend] [Static]`<br>`  Property Get name   [(arglist)] [As type]`<br>`[statements]`<br>`[name = expression]`<br>`End Property` | Declares the name and arguments procedure that gets the value of a property. |
| `[Public | Private | Friend] [Static]`<br>`  Property Let name ([arglist,] value)`<br>`[statements]`<br>`End Property` | Declares the name and arguments of a procedure that assigns a value to a property. |
| `[Public | Private | Friend] [Static]`<br>`  Property Set name ([arglist,] reference)`<br>`[statements]`<br>`End Property` | Declares the name and arguments of a procedure that sets a reference to an object. |

*continued*

continued →

257

## VBA Statements Quick Reference *(continued)*

### Program Flow (continued)

| STATEMENT | DESCRIPTION |
|---|---|
| Select Case *testexpression*<br>[Case *expressionlist*<br>  [*statements*]] ...<br>[Case Else<br>  [*elsestatements*]]<br>End Select | Executes one block out of a series of statement blocks depending upon the value of an expression. |
| [Private \| Public \| Friend] [Static] Sub *name* [(*arglist*)]<br>[*statements*]<br>End Sub | Declares the name, arguments, and code that form a Sub procedure. |
| While *condition*<br>  [*statements*]<br>Wend | Executes a block of statements as long as the specified condition is True. |
| With *object*<br>  [*statements*]<br>End With | Executes a block of statements on a single object or on a user-defined data type. |

### Variable Declaration

| STATEMENT | DESCRIPTION |
|---|---|
| [Public \| Private] Const *constname* [As *type*] = *expression* | Declares a constant value. |
| Dim [WithEvents] *varname*[([*subscripts*])] [As [New] *type*] | Declares variables and allocates the appropriate storage space. |
| Friend [WithEvents] *varname*[([*subscripts*])] [As [New] *type*] | Declares a procedure or variable to only have scope in the project where it is defined. |
| Option Compare {Binary \| Text \| Database} | Specifies the default comparison method to use when comparing strings. |
| Option Explicit | Forces declaration of all variable within the module. |
| Option Private | Indicates that all code within the entire module is Private. This option is used by default. You can overwrite the effects of this option by declaring a specific procedure Public. |
| Private [WithEvents] *varname*[([*subscripts*])] [As [New] *type*] | Declares variables and procedures to only have scope within the current module. |
| Public [WithEvents] *varname*[([*subscripts*])] [As [New] *type*] | Declares variables and procedures to have scope within the entire project. |

# VBA Statements Quick Reference *(continued)*

## Variable Declaration (continued)

| STATEMENT | DESCRIPTION |
|---|---|
| ReDim [Preserve] *varname*(*subscripts*) [As *type*] | Changes the dimensions of a dynamic array. |
| [Private \| Public] Type *varname*<br>*elementname* [([*subscripts*])] As *type*<br>[*elementname* [([*subscripts*])] As *type*]<br>. . .<br>End Type | Defines a custom data type. |

# VBA Function Quick Reference

## Legend:

Plain courier text = required     *Italics* = user-defined     | = or

[] = optional                    . . . = list of items

## Array Functions

| FUNCTION | DESCRIPTION | RETURNS |
|---|---|---|
| Array(*arglist*) | Creates a variant array containing the specified elements. | Variant |
| LBound(*arrayname*[, *dimension*]) | Returns the smallest subscript for the specified array. | Long |
| UBound(*arrayname*[, *dimension*]) | Returns the largest subscript for the specified array. | Long |

## Data Type Conversion Functions

| FUNCTION | DESCRIPTION | RETURNS |
|---|---|---|
| Asc(*string*) | Returns the character code of the first letter in a string. | Integer |
| CBool(*expression*) | Converts an expression to Boolean data type (True or False). | Boolean |
| CByte(*expression*) | Converts an expression to Byte data type. | Byte |
| CCur(*expression*) | Converts an expression to Currency data type. | Currency |
| CDate(*expression*) | Converts an expression to a Date data type. | Date |
| CDbl(*expression*) | Converts an expression to Double data type. | Double |
| CDec(*expression*) | Converts an expression to a decimal value. | Variant (Decimal) |
| Chr(*charactercode*) | Converts the character code to the corresponding character. Chr(9) returns a tab, Chr(34) returns quotation marks, and so on. | Variant (String) |
| CInt(*expression*) | Converts an expression to an Integer data type, rounding any fractional parts. | Integer |

*continued*

continued →

## VBA Function Quick Reference *(continued)*

### Data Type Conversion Functions (continued)

| FUNCTION | DESCRIPTION | RETURNS |
|---|---|---|
| CLng(*expression*) | Converts an expression to the Long data type. | Long |
| CSng(*expression*) | Converts an expression to the Single data type. | Single |
| CStr(*expression*) | Returns a string containing the specified expression. | String |
| CVar(*expression*) | Converts any data type to a Variant data type. All numeric values are treated as Double data types and string expressions are treated as String data types. | Variant |
| Format(*expression*[, *format*[, *firstdayofweek*[, *firstweekofyear*]]]) | Formats the expression using either predefined or user-defined formats. | Variant |
| FormatCurrency(*Expression*[, *NumDigitsAfterDecimal*[, *IncludeLeadingDigit*[, *UseParensForNegativeNumbers*[, *GroupDigits*]]]]) | Formats the expression as a currency value using the system-defined currency symbol. | Currency |
| FormatDateTime(*Date*[, *NamedFormat*]) | Formats an expression as a date and time. | Date |
| FormatNumber (*Expression*[, *NumDigitsAfterDecimal*[, *IncludeLeadingDigit*[, *UseParensForNegativeNumbers*[, *GroupDigits*]]]]) | Formats the expression as a number. | Mixed |
| FormatPercent (*Expression*[, *NumDigitsAfterDecimal*[, *IncludeLeadingDigit*[, *UseParensForNegativeNumbers*[, *GroupDigits*]]]]) | Returns the expression formatted as a percentage with a trailing % character. | String |
| Hex(*number*) | Converts a number to a hexadecimal value. Rounds numbers to nearest whole number before converting. | String |
| Oct(*number*) | Converts a number to a octal value. Rounds numbers to nearest whole number before converting. | Variant (String) |
| Str(*number*) | Converts a number to a string using the Variant data type. | Variant (String) |
| Val(*string*) | Returns the numeric portion of a string formatted as a number of the appropriate data type. | Mixed |

# VBA Function Quick Reference *(continued)*

## Date and Time Functions

| FUNCTION | DESCRIPTION | RETURNS |
|----------|-------------|---------|
| Date | Returns the current system date. | Date |
| DateAdd(*interval, number, date*) | Returns a date that is the specified interval of time from the original date. | Date |
| DateDiff(*interval, date1, date2*[, *firstdayofweek*[, *firstweekofyear*]]) | Determines the time interval between two dates. | Long |
| DatePart(*interval, date*[, *firstdayofweek*[, *firstweekofyear*]]) | Returns the specified part of a date. | Integer |
| DateSerial(*year, month, day*) | Converts the specified date to a serial number. | Date |
| DateValue(*date*) | Converts a string to a date. | Date |
| Day(*date*) | Returns a whole number between 1 and 31, representing the day of the month. | Integer |
| Hour(*time*) | Returns a whole number between 0 and 23, representing the hour of the day. | Integer |
| Minute(*time*) | Returns a whole number between 0 and 59, representing the minute of the hour. | Integer |
| Month(*date*) | Returns a whole number between 1 and 12, representing the month of the year. | Integer |
| Now | Returns the current system date and time. | Date |
| Second(*time*) | Returns a whole number between 0 and 59, representing the second of the minute. | Integer |
| Time | Returns the current system time. | Date |
| Timer | Indicates the number of seconds that have elapsed since midnight. | Single |
| TimeSerial(*hour, minute, second*) | Creates a time using the specified hour, minute, and second values. | Date |
| TimeValue(*time*) | Converts a time to the serial number used to store time. | Date |
| WeekDay(*date*[, *firstdayofweek*]) | Returns a whole number representing the first day of the week. | Integer |
| Year(*date*) | Returns a whole number representing the year portion of a date. | Integer |

*continued*

continued →

## VBA Function Quick Reference *(continued)*

### File and Folder Handling Functions

| FUNCTION | DESCRIPTION | RETURNS |
|---|---|---|
| CurDir(*drive*) | Returns the current path. | String |
| Dir[(*pathname*[, *attributes*])] | Returns the name of the file, directory, or folder that matches the specified pattern. | String |
| EOF(*filenumber*) | Returns -1 when the end of a file has been reached. | Integer |
| FileAttr(*filenumber, returntype*) | Indicates the file mode used for files opened with the Open statement. | Long |
| FileDateTime(*pathname*) | Indicates the date and time when a file was last modified. | Date |
| FileLen(*pathname*) | Indicates the length of a file in bytes. | Long |
| FreeFile(*rangenumber*) | Returns the next file number available for use by the Open statement. | Integer |
| GetAttr(*pathname*) | Returns a whole number representing the attributes of a file, directory, or folder. | Integer |
| Input (*number*, [#]*filenumber*) | Returns a string containing the indicated number of characters from the specified file. | String |
| Loc(*filenumber*) | Indicates the current read/write position in an open file. | Long |
| LOF(*filenumber*) | Returns the size in bytes of a file opened using the Open statement. | Long |
| Seek(*filenumber*) | Specifies the current read/write position with a file opened with the Open statement. | Long |

### Financial Functions

| FUNCTION | DESCRIPTION | RETURNS |
|---|---|---|
| DDB(*cost, salvage, life, period*[, *factor*]) | Specifies the depreciation value for an asset during a specific time frame. | Double |
| FV(*rate, nper, pmt*[, *pv*[, *type*]]) | Determines the future value of an annuity based on periodic fixed payments. | Double |
| IPmt(*rate, per, nper, pv*[, *fv*[, *type*]]) | Determines the interest payment on an annuity for a specific period of time. | Double |

## Financial Functions (Continued)

| FUNCTION | DESCRIPTION | RETURNS |
|---|---|---|
| IRR(*values()*[, *guess*]) | Determines the internal rate of returns for a series of cash flows. | Double |
| MIRR(*values()*, *finance_rate*, *reinvest_rate*) | Returns the modified interest rate of returns for a series of periodic cash flows. | Double |
| NPer(*rate, pmt, pv*[, *fv*[, *type*]]) | Returns the number of periods for an annuity. | Double |
| NPV(*rate, values()*) | Returns the net present value of an investment. | Double |
| Pmt(*rate, nper, pv*[, *fv*[, *type*]]) | Returns the payment amount for an annuity based on fixed payments. | Double |
| PPmt(*rate, per, nper, pv*[, *fv*[, *type*]]) | Returns the principal payment amount for an annuity. | Double |
| PV(*rate, nper, pmt*[, *fv*[, *type*]]) | Returns the present value of an annuity. | Double |
| Rate(*nper, pmt, pv*[, *fv*[, *type*[, *guess*]]]) | Returns the interest rate per period for an annuity. | Double |
| SLN(*cost, salvage, life*) | Determines the straight-line depreciation of an asset for a single period. | Double |
| SYD(*cost, salvage, life, period*) | Determines the sum-of-years' digits depreciation of an asset for a specified period. | Double |

## Information Functions

| FUNCTION | DESCRIPTION | RESULTS |
|---|---|---|
| CVErr(*error number*) | Returns a user-defined error number. | Variant |
| Error[(*errornumber*)] | Returns the error message for the specified error number. | String |
| IsArray(*varname*) | Indicates whether a variable contains an array. | Boolean |
| IsDate(*expression*) | Indicates whether an expression contains a date. | Boolean |
| IsEmpty(*expression*) | Indicates whether a variable has been initialized. | Boolean |
| IsError(*expression*) | Indicates whether an expression is an error value. | Boolean |
| IsMissing(*argname*) | Indicates whether an optional argument was passed to a procedure. | Boolean |
| IsNull(*expression*) | Indicates whether an expression contains no valid data. | Boolean |
| IsNumeric(*expression*) | Indicates whether an expression is a number. | Boolean |
| IsObject(*identifier*) | Indicates whether a variable references an object. | Boolean |
| TypeName(*varname*) | Specifies the variable type. | String |
| VarType(*varname*) | Specifies the subtype of a variable. | Integer |

*continued*

continued →

## VBA Function Quick Reference *(continued)*

### Interaction Functions

| FUNCTION | DESCRIPTION | RESULTS |
|---|---|---|
| Choose(*index, choice-1*[, *choice-2*, ...]) | Selects and returns a value from a list of arguments. | Mixed |
| DoEvents() | Yields execution so the operating system can process other events. | Integer |
| IIf(*expr, truepart, falsepart*) | Evaluates the expression and returns either the truepart or falsepart parameter value. | Mixed |
| InputBox(*prompt*[, *title*[, *default*[, *xpos*, *ypos*[, *helpfile, context*]]]]]) | Displays a dialog box prompting the user for input. | String |
| GetAllSettings(*appname, section*) | Returns a list of key settings and their values from the Windows Registry. | Variant |
| GetObject([*pathname*][, *class*]) | Returns a reference to an object provided by an ActiveX Component. | Variant |
| GetSetting(*appname, section, key*[, *default*]) | Returns a key setting value from an application's entry in the Windows registry. | Variant |
| MsgBox(*prompt*[, *buttons*[, *title*[, *helpfile, context*]]]) | Displays a message box and returns a value representing the button pressed by the user. | Integer |
| Partition(*number, start, stop, interval*) | Indicates where a number occurs within a series of ranges. | String |
| QBColor(*color*) | Returns the RGB color code for the specified color. | Long |
| Switch(*expr-1, value-1*[, *expr-2, value-2* ...]) | Evaluates a list of expressions and returns a value associated with the first True expression. | Variant |
| RGB(*red, green, blue*) | Returns a number representing the RGB color value. | Long |

### Mathematical Functions

| FUNCTION | DESCRIPTION | RESULT |
|---|---|---|
| Abs(*number*) | Returns the absolute value of a number. | Mixed |
| Atn(*number*) | Returns the arctangent of a number. | Double |
| Cos(*number*) | Returns the cosine of an angle. | Double |
| Exp(*number*) | Returns the base of the natural logarithms raised to a power. | Double |

## Mathematical Functions (continued)

| FUNCTION | DESCRIPTION | RESULT |
|---|---|---|
| Fix(*number*) | Returns the integer portion of a number. With negative values, returns the first negative value greater than or equal to the number. | Integer |
| Int(*number*) | Returns the integer portion of a number. With negative values, returns the first negative number less than or equal to the number. | Integer |
| Log(*number*) | Returns the natural logarithm of a number. | Double |
| Round(*expression*[, *numdecimalplaces*]) | Rounds a number to the specified number of decimal places. | Mixed |
| Rnd[(*number*)] | Returns a random number between 0 and 1. | Single |
| Sgn(*number*) | Returns 1 for a number greater than 0, 0 for a value of 0, and -1 for numbers less than zero. | Integer |
| Sin(*number*) | Specifies the sine of an angle. | Double |
| Sqr(*number*) | Specifies the square root of a number. | Double |
| Tan(*number*) | Specifies the tangent of an angle. | Double |

## String Manipulation Functions

| FUNCTION | DESCRIPTION | RESULTS |
|---|---|---|
| InStr([*start,* ]*string1, string2*[, *compare*]) | Specifies the position of one string within another string. | Long |
| InStrRev(*stringcheck, stringmatch*[, *start*[, *compare*]]) | Specifies the position of one string within another starting at the end of the string. | Long |
| LCase(*string*) | Converts a string to lowercase. | String |
| Left (*string, length*) | Returns the specified number of characters from the left side of a string. | String |
| Len(*string* | *varname*) | Determines the number of characters in a string. | Long |
| LTrim(*string*) | Trims spaces from the left side of a string. | String |
| Mid(*string, start*[,*length*]) | Returns the specified number of characters from the center of a string. | String |
| Right(*string, length*) | Returns the specified number of characters from the right side of a string. | String |
| RTrim(*string*) | Trims spaces from the right side of a string. | String |
| Space(*number*) | Creates a string with the specified number of spaces. | String |

*continued*

continued →

## VBA Function Quick Reference *(continued)*

### String Manipulation Functions (continued)

| FUNCTION | DESCRIPTION | RESULTS |
|---|---|---|
| Spc(*n*) | Positions output when printing to a file. | String |
| Str(*number*) | Returns a string representation of a number. | String |
| StrComp(*string1, string2*[, *compare*]) | Returns a value indicating the result of a string comparison. | Integer |
| StrConv(*string, conversion, LCID*) | Converts a string to the specified format. | String |
| String(*number, character*) | Creates a string by repeating a character the specified number of times. | String |
| Tab[(*n*)] | Positions output when printing to a file. | String |
| Trim(*string*) | Trims spaces from left and right of a string. | String |
| UCase(*string*) | Converts a string to uppercase. | String |

## Excel Events Quick Reference

### Chart Events

| EVENT | DESCRIPTION |
|---|---|
| Activate | Excel activates the chart sheet. |
| BeforeDoubleClick | Occurs before the user double-clicks the chart sheet with the mouse. |
| BeforeRightClick | Occurs before the user clicks the chart sheet with the right mouse button. |
| Calculate | Occurs after Excel plots the chart. |
| Deactivate | Excel deactivates the chart sheet. |
| DragOver | The user drags a range of cells over a chart. |
| DragPlot | The user drags and drops a range of cells onto the chart. |
| MouseDown | The user presses a mouse button over the chart. |
| MouseMove | The position of a mouse changes over a chart. |
| MouseUp | The user releases a mouse over the chart. |
| Resize | The user resizes the chart. |
| Select | The user selects a chart element. |
| SeriesChange | Occurs when the user changes the value of a chart data point. |

# Excel Events Quick Reference *(continued)*

## Application Events

| EVENT TYPE | DESCRIPTION |
|---|---|
| NewWorkbook | Occurs when Excel creates a new workbook. |
| SheetActivate | Excel activates any sheet in any workbook. |
| SheetBeforeDoubleClick | Event occurs before the user double-clicks any sheet with the mouse. |
| SheetBeforeRightClick | Event occurs before the user clicks any sheet with the right mouse button. |
| SheetCalculate | Excel calculates any worksheet. |
| SheetChange | Cells on a worksheet change either due to a user or an external link. |
| SheetFollowHyperlink | A user clicks a hyperlink on a sheet. |
| SheectPivotTableUpdate | Excel updates a sheet of a PivotTable report. |
| SheetSelectionChange | The selection changes on any worksheet. |
| WindowActivate | Excel activates a worksheet window. |
| WindowDeactivate | Excel deactivates a worksheet window. |
| WindowResize | The user resizes a worksheet window. |
| WorkbookActivate | The user activates a workbook. |
| WorkbookAddInInstall | An add-in installs a workbook. |
| WorkbookAddInUninstall | An add-in uninstalls a workbook. |
| WorkbookBeforePrint | Excel prints an open workbook. |
| WorkbookBeforeSave | Excel saves an open workbook. |
| WorkbookDeactivate | Excel deactivates a workbook. |
| WorkbookNewSheet | Excel adds a new sheet to an open workbook. |
| WorkbookOpen | Excel opens a workbook. |
| WorkbookPivotTableCloseConnection | Occurs after a PivotTable report closes the data source connection. |
| WorkbookPivotTableOpenConnection | Occurs after a PivotTable report opens the data source connection. |

*continued*

continued →

## Excel Events Quick Reference *(continued)*

### UserForm Events

| EVENT | DESCRIPTION |
|---|---|
| Activate | Excel activates the UserForm. |
| AddControl | Excel adds a run-time control to the UserForm. |
| BeforeDragOver | The user performs a drag-and-drop operation. |
| BeforeDropOrPaste | The user releases the mouse button to paste the data from the drag-and-drop operation. |
| Click | The user clicks the mouse on a UserForm object. |
| DblClick | The user double-clicks the mouse on a UserForm object. |
| Deactivate | The user deactivates the Userform. |
| Error | Excel detects a UserForm control error. |
| KeyDown | The user presses a key. |
| KeyPress | The user presses an ANSI key. An ANSI key produces a visible character. |
| KeyUp | The user releases a key. |
| MouseDown | The user presses a mouse button. |
| MouseMove | The user moves a mouse on the UserForm. |
| MouseUp | The user releases the mouse button. |
| QueryClose | Excel closes the UserForm. |
| RemoveControl | Excel removes a control from the UserForm at run time. |
| Scroll | The user repositions a Scroll box on a control. |
| Terminate | Excel terminates the UserForm. |
| Zoom | The user zooms the UserForm. |

### Worksheet Events

| EVENT | DESCRIPTION |
|---|---|
| Activate | Excel activates the worksheet. |
| BeforeDoubleClick | Occurs before the user double-clicks the worksheet with the mouse. |
| BeforeRightClick | Occurs before the user clicks the worksheet with the right mouse button. |
| Calculate | Excel calculates the worksheet. |
| Change | Occurs when a user or external link modifies cells on the worksheet. |
| Deactivate | Excel deactivates the worksheet. |
| FollowHyperlink | User selects a hyperlink on the worksheet. |
| PivotTableUpdate | Occurs after a PivotTable report is updated on the worksheet. |
| SelectionChange | Selection changes on the worksheet. |

# Excel Events Quick Reference *(continued)*

## Workbook Events

| EVENT | DESCRIPTION |
|---|---|
| Activate | Excel activates the workbook. |
| AddinInstall | An add-in installs a workbook. |
| AddinUninstall | An add-in uninstalls a workbook. |
| BeforeClose | A workbook closes |
| BeforePrint | Excel prints a portion of a workbook. |
| BeforeSave | Excel saves a workbook. |
| Deactivate | Excel deactivates a workbook. |
| NewSheet | Excel adds a new sheet to a workbook. |
| Open | Excel opens a workbook. |
| PivotTableCloseConnection | Occurs after a PivotTable report closes the data source connection. |
| PivotTableOpenConnection | Occurs after a PivotTable report opens the data source connection. |
| SheetActivate | Excel activates a sheet in the workbook. |
| SheetBeforeDoubleClick | Occurs before a user double-clicks a sheet. |
| SheetBeforeRightClick | Occurs before a user clicks a sheet with the right mouse button. |
| SheetCalculate | Excel calculates a sheet. |
| SheetDeactivate | Excel deactivates a sheet. |
| SheetFollowHyperlink | A user clicks a hyperlink on a sheet. |
| SheetPivotTableUpdate | Excel updates a sheet of a PivotTable report. |
| SheetSelectionChange | The selection changes on a workbook. |
| WindowActivate | Excel activates a workbook window. |
| WindowDeactivate | Excel deactivates a workbook window. |
| WindowResize | Excel resizes a workbook window. |

# Formula Basics in Excel

Formulas are the building blocks of data analysis in Excel. They enable you to automatically calculate and compare values within different cells so that you can interpret them. This section serves as a reference for users not familiar with Excel.

Formulas contain two basic elements: an equal sign, and an expression, which tells Excel what to do. You can use any combination of functions, cell references, named ranges, constants, and operators to create the formula statement. The only real limitation is that you cannot make your formula longer than 1,024 characters in length. If Excel cannot properly evaluate your formula, an error message displays.

## Excel Operators

*Operators* combine or compare the values that you want to analyze. Excel provides a large variety of different operators for creating formulas, most of which are the arithmetic operators. Excel also provides comparison operators, a text operator, and reference operators.

### Arithmetic Operators

You use arithmetic operators to perform numeric calculations, such as addition or subtraction. Obviously, using them on text results in an error message. Excel provides addition (+), subtraction (-), multiplication (*), division (/), percent (%), and exponential (^) operators. Placing the subtraction operator in front of a number makes it a negative number.

### Comparison Operators

You use comparison operators between two expressions to determine if they are equal (=), greater than (>), greater than or equal to (>=), less than (<), less than or equal to (<=), or not equal to (<>) each other. When you use comparison operators in a formula, Excel returns a logical value of either True or False.

### Text Operator

You can use the text operator to join or concatenate two or more strings of text together to form one string. You concatenate strings together using the Ampersand (&). Excel merges the two strings together without adding any extra spacing. If you want spaces between the strings, you must insert them yourself. For example, if you want to leave a space between the two strings, where APPLE is in cell A1, and SAUCE is in cell A2, you type:

**Example:**
```
=A1&" "&A2
```

When you use the Text operator to combine values in cells, the end result becomes a text value. This is true even if the combined values are numeric. For example, if you combine the values 14 and 92 with the Text operator, Excel creates the value 1492. Although it is a number, Excel treats 1492 as a text string because you created it using the Text operator. If you attempt to use the value in a mathematical calculation, Excel ignores the value and treats it as zero, because it is in text. In some instances, Excel may return an error message.

For example, if you use the value of a concatenated string as the denominator of a division formula, Excel returns a !DIV/0 error. This indicates that you divided by zero because Excel interprets a text string as zero.

## Reference Operators

You specify a range of cells for your formula with one of three different
operators. See Chapter 1 for more information on selecting cell ranges.
The following table describes each of the operators:

| OPERATOR | SYMBOL | PURPOSE | EXAMPLE |
|---|---|---|---|
| Range | : | Specifies a range of cells from the cell reference before the operator to the cell reference after the operator. | A1:A15 specifies all cells from A1 to A15. |
| Union | , | Combines multiple ranges in one reference. | =SUM(A1:A10, C1:C10) sums cells in A1 through A10, and C1 through C10. |
| Intersection | (space) | References the cells that are common between two ranges. | (A1:C10 B1:D10) specifies the common cells in the range A1:C10 and B1:D10. In the formula =sum(A1:C10 B1:D10), Excel sums only the values in cells B1 through C10. |

## Operator Precedence

When Excel evaluates a formula that contains operators, it uses a specific order to determine which
part of the formula it evaluates first. This is known as the *precedence order*. For example, the following
formula has a result of 19 because Excel calculates 4^2 first and then adds 16 to 3: =3+4^2. To
change the order of precedence, you can place parentheses around 3+4 so that the following formula
gives a result of 49 (7 raised to the second power): =(3+4)^2.

The following table shows the precedence order, highest to lowest, that Excel uses to evaluate
operators in formulas. If the operators in the formula all have the same order of precedence, Excel
evaluates the equation from left to right.

| PRECEDENCE | OPERATORS | SYMBOL |
|---|---|---|
| 1 | Parentheses | ( ) |
| 2 | Reference operators | : , (space) |
| 3 | Minus Sign | - (negates a number before any calculations) |
| 4 | Percent sign | % |
| 5 | Multiplication and Division | * / |
| 6 | Addition and Subtraction | + - |
| 7 | Concatenation | & |
| 8 | Comparison operators | = < > <= >= <> |

continued →

## Functions

*Functions* provide an invaluable means of analyzing data in Excel because they are pre-built formulas. Instead of writing a complex formula, you can use a function to perform a specific task, such as calculating an average, retrieving a value from a database, or performing a comparison. For example, the AVERAGE function determines the average of the numbers in a range of cells, such as: =AVERAGE(A1:A15).

You must provide the appropriate arguments for the function. *Arguments* are the values you must provide for the function to return the result. For example, if you select the FV function to determine what the future value is on an investment, you must specify values for the interest rate, number of payments, payment amount, present value, and future value, such as =FV(Rate, Npes, Pmt, PV, Type).

### Built-in Functions

You can use Excel's built-in functions to analyze your data. You can either type the function name manually into your equation, or you can insert it via the Insert Function dialog box. See Chapter 4 for more information. The Insert Function dialog box has various functions categories that are listed in the following table. See Appendix B for a complete list of the available Excel functions.

| CATEGORY | DESCRIPTION |
|---|---|
| Financial | Provides financial calculations such as the depreciation amount on an asset or the interest rate on a security. |
| Date & Time | Use these functions to compare dates, retrieve times from the system clock, or even return a portion of a date or time. |
| Math & Trig | Performs common mathematical and trigonometric calculations such as the cosine of a value or a random number calculation. |
| Statistical | Performs statistical calculations such as the variance within a list of values. |
| Lookup & Reference | Allows you to search for or reference specific values within your workbook, such as creating references to specific cells or finding the location of a value. |
| Database | Allows you to interface with values in lists or database in your workbook. |
| Text | Allow you to manipulate text values, such as changing the capitalization of a text label. |
| Logical | Perform comparisons and returns a value of True or False. For example, you use the AND function to determine if two expressions are equal, such as =AND(A1, A2). |
| Information | Returns information about your worksheet and your computer system. For example, =ISODD(A1) determines if a cell contains an odd number, and =ISBLANK(A1) checks if the cell is empty. |

### Add-in Functions

The Analysis ToolPak, an Add-in package, can greatly improve your ability to analyze data by extending Excel's built-in functions. When you load this add-in, you receive several additional functions in the Financial, Date & Time, Math & Trig, Statistical, and Information categories. Excel also adds a function category called Engineering, which provides functions such as converting decimal numbers to binary or hexadecimal, or working with complex numbers. See Chapter 11 for information on installing add-ins. See Appendix B for a list of the Engineering functions added with the Analysis ToolPak.

## Cell References

Excel uses a unique reference or address to identify every cell on a worksheet. This identification process, called the *cell reference*, allows you to quickly specify the cell or range of cells you want to use in a formula.

### Default Style

By default, Excel identifies all columns with letters and all rows with numbers, giving each cell a unique address. The cell reference forms from the column and row that intersect in the cell. For example, the top left cell of a worksheet is A1 because Column A and Row 1 intersect in that cell.

### R1C1 Reference Style

Excel also provides another cell reference style, called R1C1. With this style, Excel identifies the cell with a C, for column, followed by the column number, and an R for row, followed by the row number. The top left cell is R1C1, the second row in the first column is R2C1, and so on. If you prefer this format, you can change the setting in the Options dialog box. Although this format is available, the examples in the book use the default cell reference style.

### Absolute or Relative?

When you reference a cell in a formula, you can either use a relative or absolute cell reference. With an *absolute cell reference*, no matter where you copy and paste the formula, it always refers back to the original cell. You make a reference absolute by placing a $ before both the column and row references. For example, if you copy the formula =SUM($A$1:$A$5) in cell A6 to cell B6, the formula in cell B6 still returns the sum of cells A1 through A5.

If you want to copy a formula and have the cell reference change depending on where you paste the formula, use a *relative cell reference*. The formula keeps track of the referenced cell's location in relation to the formula cell. So if you copy the formula =SUM(A1:A5) in cell A6 to cell B6, Excel pastes the formula =SUM(B1:B5).

When you create cell references, you can use a combination of absolute and relative references. For example, you can make a column reference absolute while the row reference is relative, or vice versa. For example, the reference A$2 has a relative column reference and an absolute row reference. If you copy the cell reference to another cell, the column reference changes relative to the new cell, but the row reference remains the same.

## Formula Errors

If you create a formula that Excel cannot properly evaluate, an error message displays in the formula cell. For example, if you attempt to add two cells that contain text, the #VALUE! error message displays in the formula cell. The following table shows the formula error messages.

| ERROR | DESCRIPTION |
| --- | --- |
| ##### | Either the column is not wide enough to display the result, or an argument contains a negative date or time value. |
| #VALUE! | An argument contains the wrong type of value; for example, an attempt to add cells containing text. |
| #DIV/0 | Excel attempted to divide a number by zero. |
| #NAME? | Excel does not recognize the name of a function or range. This typically occurs when you misspell a function name. |
| #N/A | A specified cell reference is not available to the formula. |
| #REF! | A cell reference is not valid. |
| #NUM! | Formula contains invalid numeric values. This can occur when a number is specified with another character, such as a dollar sign, as the value for a formula that requires a number. |
| #NULL! | The cell ranges do not intersect. |

# What's on the CD-ROM

The CD-ROM included in this book contains many useful files and programs. Before installing any of the programs on the disc, make sure that you do not already have a newer version of the program installed on your computer. For information on installing different versions of the same program, contact the program's manufacturer. For the latest and greatest information, please refer to the ReadMe file located at the root level of the CD-ROM

## SYSTEM REQUIREMENTS

To use the contents of the CD-ROM, your computer must have the following hardware and software:

For Windows 9*x*, Windows 2000, Windows NT4 (with SP 4 or later), Windows Me, or Windows XP:

- PC with a Pentium processor running at 133 Mhz or faster.
- At least 32 MB of total RAM installed on your computer; for best performance, we recommend at least 64 MB. If running Windows XP, you should have at least 128 MB.
- Microsoft Excel 2002 or Office XP.
- Ethernet network interface card (NIC) or modem with a speed of at least 28,800 bps.
- A CD-ROM drive.

For Macintosh:

- Mac OS computer with a 68040 or faster processor running OS 7.6 or later.
- At least 32 MB of total RAM installed on your computer; for best performance, we recommend at least 64 MB.
- A network card.

## AUTHOR'S SOURCE CODE

These files contain all the sample code from the book. You can browse the files directly from the CD-ROM, or you can copy them to your hard drive and use them as the basis for your own projects. To find the files on the CD-ROM, open the D:\Samples folder.

## ACROBAT VERSION

The CD-ROM contains an e-version of this book that you can view and search using Adobe Acrobat Reader. You cannot print the pages or copy text from the Acrobat files. The CD-ROM includes an evaluation version of Adobe Acrobat Reader.

## INSTALLING AND USING THE SOFTWARE

For your convenience, the software titles appearing on the CD-ROM are listed alphabetically.

### Acrobat Reader

For Windows 95/98/NT/2000 and Linux. Freeware.

Adobe Acrobat Reader allows you to view the online version of this book. For more information on using Acrobat Reader, see the section "Using the E-Version of this Book" in this Appendix. For more information about Acrobat Reader and Adobe Systems, see www.adobe.com.

### Analyse-it

For Windows 95/98/NT/2000/XP. 30-day trial.

Analyse-it is an Excel Add-in that provides tools for analyzing statistical data. For more information about Analyse-it, see www.analyse-it.com.

### FinOptions XL

For Windows 95/98/NT/2000/XP. 30-day trial.

FinOptions XL is an Excel Add-in that provides financial functions for analyzing derivatives. For more information about FinOptions XL, see www.derivicom.com.

### 4TOPS Data Analysis

For Windows 95/98/NT/2000/XP. Shareware.

4TOPS Data Analysis is an Excel Add-in for performing data analysis of Access databases within Excel. For more information about 4TOPS Data Analysis, see www.4tops.com/dataanalysis.htm.

### Sigma XL

For Windows 95/98/NT/2000/XP. 15 Day Trial.

Sigma XL is an Excel Add-in that provides statistical problem solving. For more information about Sigma XL 1.1, see www.sigmaxl.com.

### UNISTAT

For Windows 95/98/NT/2000/XP. Demo.

UNISTAT is an Excel Add-in for working with statistical data. It provides options for data handling, analysis, and presentation quality scientific charts. For more information about UNISTAT, see www.unistat.com.

### XLSTAT Pro

For Windows 95/98/NT/2000/XP and Mac OS. Trial.

XLSTAT Pro is an Excel add-in that provides additional worksheet functions for improving data analysis capabilities and working with statistical data. For more information about XLSTAT Pro, see www.xlstat.com.

## TROUBLESHOOTING

The programs on the CD-ROM should work on computers with the minimum of system requirements. However, some programs may not work properly.

The two most likely problems for the programs not working properly include not having enough memory (RAM) for the programs you want to use, or having other programs running that affect the installation or running of a program. If you receive error messages such as `Not enough memory` or `Setup cannot continue`, try one or more of the methods below and then try using the software again:

- Turn off any anti-virus software
- Close all running programs
- In Windows, close the CD-ROM interface and run demos or installations directly from Windows Explorer
- Have your local computer store add more RAM to your computer

If you still have trouble installing the items from the CD-ROM, call the Wiley Publishing Customer Service phone number: 800-762-2974 (outside the U.S.: 317-572-3994). You can also contact Wiley Publishing Customer Service by e-mail at techsupdum@wiley.com.

# Using the E-Version of This Book

**Y**ou can view *Excel Data Analysis: Your visual blueprint for creating and analyzing data, charts, and PivotTables* on your screen using the CD-ROM included at the back of this book. The CD-ROM allows you to search the contents of each chapter of the book for a specific word or phrase. The CD-ROM also provides a convenient way of keeping the book handy while traveling.

You must install Adobe Acrobat Reader on your computer before you can view the book on the CD-ROM. The CD-ROM includes this program for your convenience. Acrobat Reader allows you to view Portable Document Format (PDF) files, which can display books and magazines on your screen exactly as they appear in printed form.

To view the content of this book using Acrobat Reader, display the contents of the CD-ROM. Double-click the eBook folder to display the contents of the folder. In the window that appears, double-click the icon for the chapter of the book you want to review.

---

## Using the E-Version of the Book

### FLIP THROUGH PAGES

1. Click one of these options to flip through the pages of a section.

   ◀ First page

   ◀ Previous page

   ▶ Next page

   ▶ Last page

### ZOOM IN

1. Click 🔍 to magnify an area of the page.

2. Click the area of the page you want to magnify.

   ● Click one of these options to display the page at 100% magnification (▢) or to fit the entire page inside the window (▢).

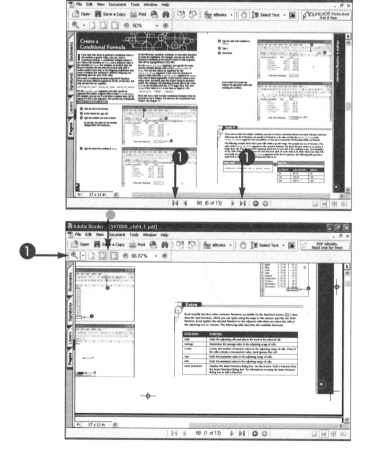

## FIND TEXT

1 Click 🔍 to search for text in the section.

● The Find dialog box appears.

2 Type the text you want to find.

3 Click Search to start the search.

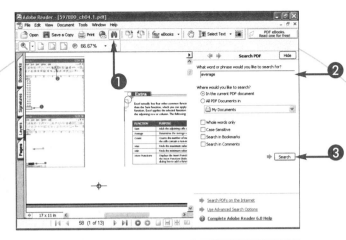

● The first instance of the text is highlighted.

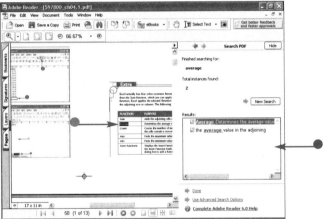

## Extra

To install Acrobat Reader, insert the CD-ROM into a drive. In the screen that appears, click Software. Click Acrobat Reader and then follow the instructions on your screen to install the program.

You can make searching the book more convenient by copying the PDF files to your computer. To do this, display the contents of the CD-ROM and then copy the Book folder from the CD-ROM to your hard drive. This allows you to easily access the contents of the book at any time.

Acrobat Reader is a popular and useful program. There are many files available on the Web that are designed to be viewed using Acrobat Reader. Look for files with the .pdf extension. For more information about Acrobat Reader, visit the www.adobe.com/products/acrobat/readermain.html Web site.

# Wiley Publishing, Inc.
# End-User License Agreement

**READ THIS.** You should carefully read these terms and conditions before opening the software packet(s) included with *Excel Data Analysis: Your visual blueprint for creating and analyzing data, charts, and PivotTables.* This is a license agreement ("Agreement") between you and Wiley Publishing, Inc. ("WPI"). By opening the accompanying software packet(s), you acknowledge that you have read and accept the following terms and conditions. If you do not agree and do not want to be bound by such terms and conditions, promptly return the Book and the unopened software packet(s) to the place you obtained them from for a full refund.

1.  **License Grant.** WPI grants to you (either an individual or entity) a nonexclusive license to use one copy of the enclosed software program(s) (collectively, the "Software") solely for your own personal or business purposes on a single computer (whether a standard computer or a workstation component of a multi-user network). The Software is in use on a computer when it is loaded into temporary memory (RAM) or installed into permanent memory (hard disc, CD-ROM, or other storage device). WPI reserves all rights not expressly granted herein.

2.  **Ownership.** WPI is the owner of all right, title, and interest, including copyright, in and to the compilation of the Software recorded on the disc(s) or CD-ROM ("Software Media"). Copyright to the individual programs recorded on the Software Media is owned by the author, or other authorized copyright owner of each program. Ownership of the Software and all proprietary rights relating thereto remain with WPI and its licensers.

3.  **Restrictions on Use and Transfer.**

    (a) You may only (i) make one copy of the Software for backup or archival purposes, or (ii) transfer the Software to a single hard disc, provided that you keep the original for backup or archival purposes. You may not (i) rent or lease the Software, (ii) copy or reproduce the Software through a LAN or other network system or through any computer subscriber system or bulletin-board system, or (iii) modify, adapt, or create derivative works based on the Software.

    (b) You may not reverse engineer, decompile, or disassemble the Software. You may transfer the Software and user documentation on a permanent basis, provided that the transferee agrees to accept the terms and conditions of this Agreement and you retain no copies. If the Software is an update or has been updated, any transfer must include the most recent update and all prior versions.

4.  **Restrictions on Use of Individual Programs.** You must follow the individual requirements and restrictions detailed for each individual program in Appendix D of this Book. These limitations are also contained in the individual license agreements recorded on the Software Media. These limitations may include a requirement that after using the program for a specified period of time, the user must pay a registration fee or discontinue use. By opening the Software packet(s), you will be agreeing to abide by the licenses and restrictions for these individual programs that are detailed in Appendix D and on the Software Media. None of the material on this Software Media or listed in this Book may ever be redistributed, in original or modified form, for commercial purposes.

5.  **Limited Warranty.**

    (a) WPI warrants that the Software and Software Media are free from defects in materials and workmanship under normal use for a period of sixty (60) days from the date of purchase of this Book. If WPI receives notification within the warranty period of defects in materials or workmanship, WPI will replace the defective Software Media.

    (b) **WPI AND THE AUTHOR OF THE BOOK DISCLAIM ALL OTHER WARRANTIES, EXPRESS OR IMPLIED, INCLUDING WITHOUT LIMITATION IMPLIED WARRANTIES OF MERCHANTABILITY AND FITNESS FOR A PARTICULAR PURPOSE, WITH RESPECT TO THE SOFTWARE, THE PROGRAMS, THE SOURCE CODE CONTAINED THEREIN, AND/OR THE TECHNIQUES DESCRIBED IN THIS BOOK. WPI DOES NOT WARRANT THAT THE FUNCTIONS CONTAINED IN THE SOFTWARE WILL MEET YOUR REQUIREMENTS OR THAT THE OPERATION OF THE SOFTWARE WILL BE ERROR FREE.**

**(c)** This limited warranty gives you specific legal rights, and you may have other rights that vary from jurisdiction to jurisdiction.

6. **Remedies.**

**(a)** WPI's entire liability and your exclusive remedy for defects in materials and workmanship shall be limited to replacement of the Software Media, which may be returned to WPI with a copy of your receipt at the following address: Software Media Fulfillment Department, Attn.: *Excel Data Analysis: Your visual blueprint for creating and analyzing data, charts, and PivotTables*, Wiley Publishing, Inc., 10475 Crosspoint Blvd., Indianapolis, IN 46256, or call 1-800-762-2974. Please allow four to six weeks for delivery. This Limited Warranty is void if failure of the Software Media has resulted from accident, abuse, or misapplication. Any replacement Software Media will be warranted for the remainder of the original warranty period or thirty (30) days, whichever is longer.

**(b)** In no event shall WPI or the author be liable for any damages whatsoever (including without limitation damages for loss of business profits, business interruption, loss of business information, or any other pecuniary loss) arising from the use of or inability to use the Book or the Software, even if WPI has been advised of the possibility of such damages.

**(c)** Because some jurisdictions do not allow the exclusion or limitation of liability for consequential or incidental damages, the above limitation or exclusion may not apply to you.

7. **U.S. Government Restricted Rights.** Use, duplication, or disclosure of the Software for or on behalf of the United States of America, its agencies and/or instrumentalities (the "U.S. Government") is subject to restrictions as stated in paragraph (c)(1)(ii) of the Rights in Technical Data and Computer Software clause of DFARS 252.227-7013, or subparagraphs (c)(1) and (2) of the Commercial Computer Software - Restricted Rights clause at FAR 52.227-19, and in similar clauses in the NASA FAR supplement, as applicable.

8. **General.** This Agreement constitutes the entire understanding of the parties and revokes and supersedes all prior agreements, oral or written, between them and may not be modified or amended except in a writing signed by both parties hereto that specifically refers to this Agreement. This Agreement shall take precedence over any other documents that may be in conflict herewith. If any one or more provisions contained in this Agreement are held by any court or tribunal to be invalid, illegal, or otherwise unenforceable, each and every other provision shall remain in full force and effect.

# INDEX

## Numbers & Symbols

##  A

# INDEX

## E

## F

# INDEX

# INDEX

# INDEX

## Q

## R

# INDEX

**Read Less–Learn More®**

# There's a Visual book for every learning level...

## Simplified®

**The place to start if you're new to computers. Full color.**

- Computers
- Mac OS
- Office
- Windows

## Teach Yourself VISUALLY™

**Get beginning to intermediate-level training in a variety of topics. Full color.**

- Computers
- Crocheting
- Digital Photography
- Dreamweaver
- Excel
- Guitar
- HTML
- Knitting
- Mac OS
- Office
- Photoshop
- Photoshop Elements
- PowerPoint
- Windows
- Word

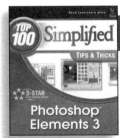

## Top 100 Simplified® Tips & Tricks

**Tips and techniques to take your skills beyond the basics. Full color.**

- Digital Photography
- eBay
- Excel
- Google
- Internet
- Mac OS
- Photoshop
- Photoshop Elements
- PowerPoint
- Windows

## Build It Yourself VISUALLY™

**Do it yourself the visual way and without breaking the bank. Full color.**

- Game PC
- Media Center PC

# ...all designed for visual learners—just like you!

## Master VISUALLY®

**Step up to intermediate-to-advanced technical knowledge.
Two-color interior.**

- 3ds max
- Creating Web Pages
- Dreamweaver and Flash
- Excel VBA Programming
- iPod and iTunes
- Mac OS
- Optimizing PC Performance
- Photoshop Elements
- QuickBooks
- Quicken
- Windows Server
- Windows

## Visual Blueprint™

**Where to go for professional-level programming instruction.
Two-color interior.**

- Excel Data Analysis
- Excel Programming
- HTML
- JavaScript
- PHP

## Visual Encyclopedia™

**Your A to Z reference of tools and techniques. Full color.**

- Dreamweaver
- Photoshop
- Windows

## For a complete listing of Visual books, go to wiley.com/go/visualtech

**Visual**
An Imprint of **⊕WILEY**
Now you know.